THE ONE YEAR®

* * *

ON THIS DAY

On
THIS DAY

* * *

DIANNE NEAL MATTHEWS

Tyndale House Publishers, Inc.
WHEATON, ILLINOIS

Visit Tyndale's exciting Web site at www.tyndale.com

TYNDALE is a registered trademark of Tyndale House Publishers, Inc.

Tyndale's quill logo is a trademark of Tyndale House Publishers, Inc.

One Year is a registered trademark of Tyndale House Publishers, Inc.

The One Year on This Day

Designed by Alyssa Force

Edited by MaryLynn Layman

Library of Congress Cataloging-in-Publication Data

Matthews, Dianne Neal.
  The one year on this day / Dianne Neal Matthews.
    p. cm.
  Includes bibliographical references and index.
  ISBN-13: 978-1-4143-0441-0 (sc : alk. paper)
  ISBN-10: 1-4143-0441-2 (sc : alk. paper)
  1. Church history. 2. Devotional calendars. I. Title.
BR153.M38 2005
270—dc22   2005016246

Printed in the United States of America

11 10 09 08 07 06 05
7 6 5 4 3 2 1

Sara Craven

Dedication

* * *

Dedicated to my parents,
Thomas and Pamelia Neal—
the first people who ever loved me,
prayed for me,
and believed in me

Introduction

* * *

Writing this book has been a learning experience in many ways. I would never have dreamed of tackling such a project, but God brought me to this point gradually and very gently. In 1986, I began taking Precept Upon Precept Bible study courses, which helped me grow in my understanding of the Bible. Around 1995, I started doing some writing for my church newsletter. In 1998, my good friend and former pastor, Rev. Dave Jankowski, encouraged me to try writing professionally and asked, "Why don't you go to a writers' seminar somewhere?"

Five months later, I received a brochure in the mail for a Write-to-Publish Conference in Wheaton, Illinois. It was there, in 1999, that I made my first contact and began writing devotionals. The next year I started writing articles for my hometown newspaper. So by the time Ken Petersen, of Tyndale House Publishers, helped me develop the idea for this book at a Write-to-Publish Conference a few years later, God had prepared me to write the first half of each day's entry as a newspaper reporter and the second half as a devotional writer.

One of the frustrations of this project was finding so much discrepancy in information. Sometimes even encyclopedias contradicted one another on basic facts and dates. I researched multiple sources whenever possible and tried to use the most authoritative ones. This problem was a reminder that only the Word of God is truly reliable and unchanging.

God also reminded me of his faithfulness during these seven months of writing. Anything that could happen to interfere with my work did happen. Then there were days when I wondered if I could *ever* come up with 365 ideas plus one for Leap Year. My prayer life got a much-needed boost, and soon I wasn't praying just for my work but for each person who would some-day read a particular day's devotional.

I appreciate my family and friends who prayed for me, especially during the last few weeks, when all sorts of things threatened to keep me from meet-ing the deadline. The burden was also lightened by the support and encour-agement I received from Mary Keeley at Tyndale. Several devotionals had input from friends, including Rob Hausam, Sherry Schildt, Dennis Taylor, and my brother Tom Neal. I also owe special thanks to MaryLynn Layman for her excellent editing skills; to the reference librarians at the Champaign (Illinois) public library who sometimes helped me track down information; and to my husband, Richard, for taking over the cooking and grocery shop-ping for a few months.

I also appreciate you for being willing to invest in my first book. There were so many days when I needed to "hear" what I was writing for my own encouragement, conviction, or inspiration. I hope these devotionals will be a blessing for you as well.

* * *

Now all glory to God, who is able,
through his mighty power at work within us, to accomplish
infinitely more than we might ask or think. Glory to him in the church
and in Christ Jesus through all generations forever and ever! Amen.
Ephesians 3:20-21

January 1

* * *

If anyone is in Christ, he is a new creation;
old things have passed away; behold, all things have become new.
2 CORINTHIANS 5:17, NKJV

N ew Year's Day is the oldest of all the holidays we celebrate. Historians believe it was first observed in ancient Babylon four thousand years ago. The celebration lasted eleven days, with different traditions observed on each day. The Babylonians considered the new year to begin in late March, at the vernal equinox, with the focus on looking ahead to new crops and new growth.

New Year's Day is a public holiday in the United States and many other countries. January 1 became generally recognized as the beginning of the year in the 1500s with the adoption of the Gregorian calendar. In the United States, the holiday is traditionally considered to be a time to take stock of one's life and to make resolutions for the coming year.

The best way for believers to celebrate each New Year's Day is to resolve to live more like the new creation that the apostle Paul says we are. Once we accept the sacrifice that Christ made on our behalf, we enter into the New Covenant and God begins a new work of creation in us. He gives us a new heart, a new self, and a new song. We're called to have new attitudes and a new lifestyle. As we grow, God brings new opportunities for service and teaches us new truths.

We also get a new future. As we read Revelation, we can take comfort in thinking about the time when God will right all wrongs, heal all hurts, and give us a new name and a new home. With the arrival of each new year, we get closer to the Ancient of Days, who promises, "Look, I am making everything new!" (Revelation 21:5).

What new thing does God want to do in your life this year?

January 2

* * *

Obscene stories, foolish talk, and coarse jokes—these are not for you.
EPHESIANS 5:4

E ach New Year's Day, Lake Superior State University releases its annual "List of Words Banished from the Queen's English for Mis-Use, Over-Use and General Uselessness." The tongue-in-cheek list was initi-ated in 1976 by then Public Relations Director Bill Rabe as a publicity stunt for the university.

Although Rabe retired in 1987, the school has copyrighted the concept and carried on the popular tradition. Throughout the year people around the world nominate hundreds of words and phrases that they feel should be purged from the English language. The new banishment list is released each January 1 and posted on the university's Web site (www.lssu.edu/banished). Recent winners include "user friendly," "you know," and "have a nice day."

Many words that were once banished from polite society have now become embedded in mainstream American language. Television networks embrace obscenities and sexual innuendos. Many song lyrics blare out bla-tantly filthy language no longer considered disgusting. Many of us have grad-ually become desensitized to language that once offended us. The results can be heard even on elementary school playgrounds, where R-rated talk is not uncommon. Coarse joking has even seeped into church gatherings.

Even in days before media influences, obscenity was a problem. Paul found it necessary to address this issue with the Colossian Christians, advis-ing them to get rid of all dirty language (Colossians 3:8). He warned the believers at Ephesus that obscene stories and coarse jokes were improper for God's holy people (Ephesians 5:4). The society around us may lower its stan-dards, but we must keep our speech purged of anything that doesn't meet God's standards. When he shares his "banished list," he doesn't give it tongue in cheek.

January 3

*** ***

[There is] one God and Father, who is over all and in all and living through all.
EPHESIANS 4:6

In January 1999, eleven European Union countries (later twelve) locked in the value of their national currencies at a permanent conversion rate to the euro. Euro bills and coins began circulating in January 2002 and by March became the sole currency of twelve of the fifteen EU member states: Austria, Belgium, Finland, France, Germany, Greece, Italy, Ireland, Luxembourg, the Netherlands, Spain, and Portugal.

The introduction of the euro was the final step in the EU's plan to establish a common currency and a single monetary authority for EU states. Advocates believe the move will strengthen Europe's standing as an economic power, increase international trade, simplify monetary transactions, and result in pricing equality throughout Europe.

Believers, too, have much in common, even though we often focus on our differences, such as social and economic distinctions. Disagreements over issues like music and worship styles can split us. Ephesians 4:4-6 is a call to remember *whom* we have in common. We have the same God ruling over us, living in us, and working through us. We share a conversion experience in our past and look forward to a common future.

In his final hours, Jesus prayed that his followers and all future believers would be one as he and the Father are one (John 17:20-21). A sense of oneness is necessary for the work and the witness of the church to be effective. We can achieve this supernatural feat only by focusing on the fact that Jesus didn't die for certain denominations or countries; he died for the world. Even where nations have different currencies to pay for purchases, all true believers have the same Savior who purchased our salvation.

January 4

* * *

We know that God causes everything to work together for the good of those who love God and are called according to his purpose for them.
ROMANS 8:28

L ouis Braille was born on this day in 1809 in Coupvray, France. At age three, he was permanently blinded by an accident with a leather-making awl in his father's saddlery. When Braille was fifteen, he began revising a method of writing that had been developed for trench warfare communication by army captain Charles Barbier. Barbier's system was rejected by the military as too complex, but Braille hoped it could be useful for blind people. Ironically, he used an awl-like stylus to make small, raised dots on paper that could be felt and interpreted. This system was not officially accepted until after Braille died in poverty in 1852. Today it is universally accepted for all written languages and for mathematics, science, and computer notation.

We seem to be surrounded by senseless tragedies like the accident that blinded Braille in his childhood. In the Old Testament, Joseph's jealous brothers sold him into slavery. He was falsely accused of attempted rape and spent years in prison. Yet he rose to become the second-most-powerful person in Egypt and saved many nations during a time of great famine. Joseph later assured his brothers, "You intended to harm me, but God intended it all for good" (Genesis 50:20).

The rebellion of Satan and the fall of man have marred the perfect world God created, opening the way for evil to infect our daily lives. But we serve a God who can bring great good out of great evil. He often uses our deepest wounds to do the most powerful work in us. As believers, we have the promise that he is working out all things—even our hurts, disappointments, and tragedies—for our good and his glory.

What painful situation has God used for good in your life?

January 5

* * *

You are worthy, O Lord our God, to receive glory and honor and power.
For you created all things.

REVELATION 4:11

eorge Washington Carver died on this day in 1943. The former slave had become a renowned scientist, internationally recognized for his agricultural research, and was honored with numerous awards. Carver spent much of his career at what is now Tuskegee University, where he focused on helping farmers improve crop production and taught more-efficient agricultural practices through conferences, demonstrations, lectures, and traveling exhibits.

Carver is especially noted for creating more than three hundred products from peanuts, such as a milk substitute, printer's ink, and soap. He also developed over seventy-five products from pecans and more than a hundred products from sweet potatoes, including flour, shoe polish, and candy. Carver's work convinced many southern farmers to grow these crops instead of cotton, providing them with new sources of income.

It's amazing to think that someone could create three hundred useful products from a peanut! It's also impossible for our finite minds to grasp the fact that God created everything we see from nothing. The book of Genesis tells us how he started from scratch and created the infinite variety in our world and beyond simply with spoken commands. Revelation gives us a glimpse of heavenly creatures praising God and declaring that he is worthy to receive honor because he created all things.

Since we are created in God's image, we have an inherent creative drive. We find fulfillment in expressing our creativity, whether it's in our job, our hobbies, the arts, or creative solutions to problems. Any creative act we perform is an act of worship for the One who placed that spark in us. Such a Creator can, and will, create something amazing out of our life.

January 6

∗ ∗ ∗

Do not be afraid, for I have ransomed you.
I have called you by name; you are mine.
ISAIAH 43:1

T oday is National Smith Day, a special day to commemorate the most common surname in English-speaking countries. This date is appropriate because it is the baptism date of one of the earliest Smiths in America, Captain John Smith, who led the group of English colonists settling in Jamestown, Virginia, in 1607.

Today there are almost two and a half million Smiths in the United States. National Smith Day salutes individuals, organizations, and businesses that bear the name *Smith* or some variation, such as *Goldsmith*, *Arrowsmith*, and *Coopersmith*.

Sometimes it's easy to feel lost in the crowd, just an ordinary face in a multitude of human beings. We may feel as if we're nothing special to anyone—including the One who created us along with billions of others. But God knows each one of us individually and so intimately that he can tell the very number of hairs on our head. To him, each person on earth is precious enough to die for, and he longs to have a close relationship with us.

Even if we're one in a crowd of people with the same name, to our Father we are unique. The Creator of the universe has chosen us and called us by name to be his adopted children. He is constantly aware of our thoughts, feelings, and needs. He always knows the details of the circumstances in our life. We may sometimes see ourselves as just another face in the crowd, but since he has called us by *our* name, we are now called by *his* name—and that's the greatest name anyone could ever have.

January 7

Each person is destined to die once and after that comes judgment.
HEBREWS 9:27

 anuary 7, 1979, saw the downfall of Pol Pot, one of the cruelest dictators in history. His brutal reign began in 1975, when he and his Communist guerilla forces (called the Khmer Rouge) overthrew the Cambodian government. As prime minister, Pol Pot removed the population of the capital city, Phnom Penh, to collective farms, where tens of thousands died from starvation, disease, and slave labor in what came to be known as "the killing fields." The Khmer Rouge also tortured and executed many more, including government officials, intellectuals, and religious leaders. In all, more than one and a half million Cambodians died under Pol Pot's rule.

When Vietnamese troops overthrew Pol Pot's government, he fled to the jungles, where he spent the remainder of his life. While international human rights activists were working to have him extradited to face charges of crimes against humanity, Pol Pot died of natural causes on April 15, 1998.

It seems so unfair when a person responsible for so much evil dies without being held accountable for his atrocities. He may have escaped human justice, but there is no escape from our ultimate Judge. God has promised to bring every deed into judgment, even the secret things (Ecclesiastes 12:14).

We will all be judged one day, believers at the judgment seat of Christ and unbelievers at God's Great White Throne Judgment described in Revelation 20. Anyone whose name is not found written in the Book of Life will be thrown into the lake of fire. No matter how much people get away with in this life, they can't escape from the Lord, who says, "I will take revenge; I will pay them back" (Deuteronomy 32:35).

January 8

* * *

Follow my example, as I follow the example of Christ.
1 CORINTHIANS 11:1, NIV

Since 2002, January has been designated National Mentoring Month by the Harvard Mentoring Project and MENTOR, an organization that works to connect kids with adult mentors. The goals of this monthlong celebration are to focus attention on the need for mentors, to raise awareness of mentoring in its various forms, and to recruit individuals and organizations to become involved, especially in programs that have a waiting list of young people.

Qualified adults can help children improve social and conversational skills, offer guidance and encouragement, and serve as role models and advocates. Studies have shown that these quality relationships can profoundly impact the future of children and teens, making the difference between success and failure for youth in lower-income urban communities. An estimated fifteen million young people are still in need of mentors.

Mentoring is a concept found throughout the Bible, from Elijah and Elisha in the Old Testament to Paul and Timothy in the New Testament. Jesus chose a group of twelve men for a close mentoring relationship—instructing, guiding, and encouraging them. He poured himself into helping these men grow, who then taught many others. The second chapter of Titus instructs the older, more spiritually mature women in the church to train the younger women, helping them grow in their relationship with God and in their family roles.

Whether or not we are in a formal mentoring relationship, someone is watching and learning from our example—good or bad. In his letters, Paul sometimes urged the recipients to follow his example. If we want to have the confidence to say the same thing, we must constantly be learning from Jesus, our perfect Role Model and Mentor.

Whose example are you following?

January 9

* * *

The way of a fool is right in his own eyes, but he who heeds counsel is wise.
PROVERBS 12:15, NKJV

On this day in 1956, the first Dear Abby column appeared in the *San Francisco Chronicle*. Pauline Phillips wrote the advice column under the pen name Abigail Van Buren, answering readers' questions about relationships, romance, health, and social issues. In 1987, Phillips's daughter, Jeanne, began writing the column with her, and the two worked together until Pauline retired in 2002. Dear Abby still appears in more than 1,200 newspapers worldwide.

Pauline's twin sister, Esther Lederer, had already begun a career as an advice columnist in 1955. She won the *Chicago Sun-Times* contest to become the second Ann Landers, after the woman who had created the column died. The column was published in more than 1,200 newspapers with ninety million daily readers until Esther's death in 2002.

We all need a little advice sometimes. The book of Proverbs has much to say about seeking counsel from others. We are urged to make plans and go to war only with good counsel and advice from others (20:18). Still, we need to be careful of the source and content of any advice we receive. It must be carefully filtered through the Bible to make sure it's not contrary to God's counsel.

Advice from trusted friends or professional counselors can be valuable and helpful if it is sound and biblically based. But we shouldn't forget God's credentials: "Common sense and success belong to me. Insight and strength are mine" (Proverbs 8:14). Isaiah even gave the name *Counselor* to Jesus hundreds of years before his birth (Isaiah 9:6). Advice columns are sometimes helpful, but before running to a newspaper column, we should go to the One who wrote the Book on wise advice.

January 10

* * *

Who created all the stars? He brings them out like an army, one after another,
calling each by its name. Because of his great power and incomparable strength,
not a single one is missing.
ISAIAH 40:26

In January 1987, a group of astronomers announced that they had been the first to witness and record the birth of a giant galaxy. The object, a protogalaxy designated as radio wave source 3C 326,1, is estimated to be twelve billion light years, or seventy-one billion trillion miles, from Earth. It is too far away for scientists to be positive, but they speculate that they watched the long-ago formation of the massive galaxy.

Scientists believe that stars form in giant clouds of gas and dust when gravity causes pockets of material inside those clouds to collapse inward. Eventually the gas heats up to the point where a thermonuclear reaction occurs, creating a star. The astronomers believe that the colors of light they observed indicate that about a billion stars were born in the gas cloud.

Thanks to the powerful and sophisticated instruments astronomers use today, we are learning more and more about our galaxy and those beyond. Sadly, some people are not interested in learning about the One responsible for these wonders. The book of Genesis records God creating the stars (1:16). Revelation tells us he will make them fall from the sky someday (6:13). God identified himself to Job as the One who guides the constellations (Job 38:32).

In relation to the vastness of space, we seem like tiny specks of dust. Yet God saw our birth as more important than the birth of a billion stars. Astronomy gives us a glimpse of the majesty and beauty of space. How much more awesome to glimpse the One who can name every star in every galaxy and yet desires to know us intimately.

January 11

* * *

There is a path before each person that seems right, but it ends in death.
PROVERBS 14:12

On this day in 1964, the surgeon general of the United States issued the first official warning that smoking is hazardous to one's health. Cigarette smoking had been growing in popularity in the United States since the beginning of the twentieth century as manufacturing advances made smoking more affordable and tobacco companies spent millions in advertising to entice buyers.

By the middle of the twentieth century a number of scientists had accumulated evidence of health threats associated with smoking, including lung cancer, heart disease, and lung disease. By the 1970s, the World Health Organization had declared tobacco smoking to be the world's single most important preventable cause of premature death. In 1971, legislation went into effect banning cigarette ads on radio and television in the United States.

People often begin smoking because it's considered cool. Years later many pay dearly for their habit by suffering from lung disease or cancer. Our culture considers many things acceptable that are contrary to God's standards. We are encouraged to "follow our heart" and do what "feels right." What we *aren't* told is what the consequences may be.

Just because something is acceptable doesn't make it wise. We may go along with what's popular and think we're okay. But human judgment is limited. We can't see the long-term consequences as God can. Every command and instruction in the Bible is there for our protection and well-being, not because God likes to lay down rules. If we don't depend on the wisdom of God's Word and the leading of his Holy Spirit to guide our choices, what we think is all right may turn out to be all wrong.

January 12

* * *

The one who plants and the one who waters work as a team with the same purpose.
Yet they will be rewarded individually, according to their own hard work.

1 CORINTHIANS 3:8, NLT-1

Henry Ford revolutionized the automobile industry when he incorporated the assembly line at his Michigan plant in January 1914. Ford's goal was to produce simple, sturdy, affordable cars. At the price of $825, the Model T was too expensive for many customers, so Ford and his executives searched for new ways to lower production costs.

One change was implementing the assembly-line method, in which conveyor belts would bring parts to the workers and each individual worker would perform a specific task, such as adding or tightening a part. Using this system reduced the assembly time of a Ford automobile from about 12½ hours to 1½ hours. The savings allowed Ford Motor Company to sell its automobiles at lower prices than ever before. Ironically, within a year Ford's plant saw a monthly employee turnover rate of 40 to 60 percent, partly due to the monotony of assembly-line work.

Christians sometimes get dissatisfied with their role in the body of Christ, feeling their part is dull or less important than that of others. When we compare our ministry with others' work, our labor may look futile if they seem to be reaping all the visible fruit. Our witness may seem ineffective, especially if others are leading more people to Christ.

Paul addressed the issue of jealousy and divisions when he wrote to the church at Corinth to assure them that the Lord had assigned each person a task. "I planted the seed, Apollos watered it, but God made it grow" (1 Corinthians 3:6, NIV). God has given each of us different gifts and specialized roles, and they are all important in fulfilling his larger purposes. Each worker is essential in the assembly of God's church.

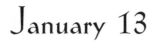

January 13

* * *

If you are a thief, stop stealing. Begin using your hands for honest work,
and then give generously to others in need.
EPHESIANS 4:28, NLT-1

H arold Rossfields Smith was convicted in 1982 of stealing $21.3 million from Wells Fargo National Bank. A former Wells Fargo branch officer who had been friends with Smith testified that the embezzlement began when Smith had him intercept a bad check that Smith had written. The scheme mushroomed into one of the largest bank embezzlements in U.S. history. Before the theft was discovered in January 1981, Harold Smith had used his ill-gotten gain to enlarge a multimillion-dollar boxing empire and to live a lavish lifestyle.

Stealing has become a common occurrence in our society, involving everything from candy bars to cars. Homeowners spend thousands of dollars on alarm systems, hoping to deter break-ins. Store owners struggle with the problem of shoplifters. Employers are plagued by the pilfering that goes on in the workplace. People seem to believe that they deserve something simply because they desire it. Honesty is not valued nearly as much as the cleverness of getting something for nothing.

Theft has been a big problem since the beginning of the human race. That's why God "laid down the law" on stealing when he gave the Ten Commandments to Moses. The eighth commandment is short and simple: "Thou shalt not steal" (Exodus 20:15, KJV). No ifs, ands, or buts. The New Testament takes this a step further. As Paul gives guidelines for living a transformed life, he instructs those who had been stealing to stop and do honest work so they would be able to share with others. Our society would truly be transformed if instead of striving to *get* something for nothing, our goal was to *give* something for nothing.

January 14

* * *

Do not be deceived, God is not mocked;
for whatever a man sows, this he will also reap.
GALATIANS 6:7, NASB

I n 2000, January was officially declared National Mailorder Gardening Month. The observance is sponsored by the Mailorder Gardening Association (MGA) to encourage people to beat their winter melancholy by browsing through gardening catalogs. The MGA promotes mail-order catalogs as time-saving planning tools and excellent sources of practical information and new ideas for the garden.

Mail-order catalogs are a popular way for gardeners to pursue their hobby. According to MGA estimates, in 2005 Americans ordered $3.07 billion worth of plants, bulbs, seeds, garden tools, and supplies. With more than twenty-four million households ordering from gardening catalogs and Web sites throughout the year, the average expenditure per household is $128.

Many gardeners use catalogs to help them plan what to grow in the spring. The Bible teaches that we all make choices about what we grow in our life. Jesus often used the themes of sowing and reaping to illustrate this principle. Proverbs assures us that the one who sows righteousness reaps a sure reward (11:18), and whoever sows wickedness reaps trouble (22:8).

Our choices don't determine all the events in our life, since we are in the hands of a sovereign God. But we do sow seeds every day that please either the Holy Spirit or the sinful nature. Galatians 5:19-26 catalogs the deeds that make the sinful nature grow and the fruits that we reap when we sow in the Spirit. All our deeds are seeds that help determine what kind of harvest we reap.

What seeds are you sowing in your life?

January 15

* * *

Don't you realize that in a race everyone runs,
but only one person gets the prize? So run to win!
1 CORINTHIANS 9:24

 his day marked the beginning of one of the most popular American sporting events. During the early 1960s, the upstart American Football League (AFL) sought to compete with the more established National Football League (NFL). On January 15, 1967, the champions of these two leagues played each other for the first time. The Green Bay Packers of the NFL beat the Kansas City Chiefs of the AFL by a score of 35 to 10. When the two leagues merged to form the modern NFL in 1970, the championship game became known as the Super Bowl.

Today, the Super Bowl is played every January between the champions of the American Football Conference (AFC) and the National Football Conference (NFC). The game is so popular with American television viewers that advertisers pay more than two million dollars for thirty seconds in the premium time slots.

Professional football players devote themselves to diligent practice and to performing their best in regular games with the dream of someday becoming Super Bowl champions. This same principle applies to the spiritual life. For example, when Jesus taught about finances, he said, "Whoever can be trusted with very little can also be trusted with much" (Luke 16:10, NIV). If we prove ourselves in the little things, God will use us for bigger purposes.

While David tended his father's sheep, he sometimes had to kill a lion or a bear. Because he had experienced these victories, David was prepared to battle Goliath and was confident that God would empower him to overcome. If we are faithful in handling our everyday challenges, perhaps God will give us the privilege, as one of his champions, of slaying a giant.

January 16

* * *

*As for me, far be it from me that I should sin against
the LORD by failing to pray for you.*
1 SAMUEL 12:23, NIV

The Persian Gulf War began the evening of January 16, 1991, when coalition forces bombed Iraqi military and industrial targets. The coalition of thirty-nine countries had been organized as a response to Iraq's invasion of the tiny nation of Kuwait on August 2, 1990. Once it had gained control of Kuwait, Iraq amassed troops on Kuwait's border with Saudi Arabia, raising fears that it would be invaded as well.

For several months, many nations pressured Iraq to withdraw from Kuwait through trade sanctions, the buildup of forces in eastern Saudi Arabia, and a United Nations resolution designed to end the conflict. Saddam Hussein ordered his forces to "fight to the death" to hold Kuwait. On January 16, a massive cruise-missile attack launched Operation Desert Storm. In little over a month, coalition military operations ceased, and on April 6 Iraq accepted the terms of a cease-fire.

Satan and his demons are constantly attacking believers, invading our thoughts, and trying to gain control of our life. During these times we need to summon our brothers and sisters in Christ to help us launch a counterattack. As the situation is bombarded with prayers for our deliverance, Satan will be forced to withdraw.

One of our greatest privileges and responsibilities as Christians is intercessory prayer. Besides praying on others' behalf, we can also call on the body of Christ in our time of need. Our enemy Satan will "fight to the death" to keep his hold on our life, but the Bible teaches that the Holy Spirit and Jesus are also continuously interceding for us (Romans 8:26-27, 34). And that's a coalition that will never fail.

January 17

* * *

God is faithful. He will not allow the temptation to be more than you can stand.
1 CORINTHIANS 10:13

On this day in 1929, a new character appeared in *The Thimble Theatre*, a ten-year-old comic strip by Elzie Segar. Popeye, a short sailor with bulging forearms, was not handsome or intelligent, but he quickly became a star. The comic strip had originally focused on Olive Oyl and her family, but when Popeye appeared on the scene, most of the old characters disappeared. When Popeye moved to television, cartoonists made nearly six hundred cartoons that are still in worldwide syndication.

The "strong to the finish" sailor man became one of the best-loved cartoon characters of all time. Popeye was long-suffering, but he eventually reached his breaking point. Then he chugged a can of spinach for strength to rescue Olive Oyl or defeat his nemesis, Bluto/Brutus. But not before uttering his well-known line, "Tha's all I can stand, 'cause I can't stands no more!"

Popeye's breaking point led him to take action against evil, and that's admirable. But sometimes we feel that way about life in general. It's bad enough when everyday irritations and annoyances pile up. Add more serious problems such as failed relationships, financial loss, health issues, and wayward children, and we want to scream, "That's all I can stand!"

James encourages us to remember the benefits of trials that test our patience and our faith. We learn endurance, which helps us mature as believers (James 1:2-4). God promises that he won't allow us to be burdened with more temptations than we can bear. He will also provide the strength we need to endure any trial, if we stay close to him. That means that in hard times when we feel like we can't stand any more, we can trust God to help us stand. Spinach is optional.

January 18

* * *

[Jesus said,] "Anyone who believes in me may come and drink! For the Scriptures declare, 'Rivers of living water will flow from his heart.'"

JOHN 7:38

D octors were baffled in July 1976 when 221 people at a Philadelphia hotel were struck with pneumonia. Thirty-four of the group died. Physicians were unable to determine the cause of the illness that displayed symptoms of fever, cough, chest pain, and difficulty breathing. They named it Legionnaires' disease because the victims had been attending an American Legion convention at the hotel.

On January 18, 1977, the mystery was solved when scientists discovered a previously unknown bacteria, which they labeled *Legionella pneumophila*. While white blood cells normally defend against infections, this bacteria is able to invade white blood cells and multiply within them. Many outbreaks are linked to the drinking water. People get the disease by inhaling water droplets or aspirating water tainted with the bacteria.

Unfortunately, the bacteria that sometimes contaminates our drinking water can be almost impossible to detect. In a similar way, our thinking can be contaminated in ways that are hard to detect. What often passes for spiritual truth today is tainted with worldliness or Satan's lies. The deception can be so subtle that a philosophy or doctrine sounds wholesome, yet if we take it in, it invades our thinking and causes us to stray from a godly worldview.

People are thirsty for God, and the world offers them a false spirituality in place of the pure, life-giving gospel. It may seem to quench their thirst at first, but it leads to spiritual disaster. Jesus invites thirsty people to come to him and drink. He offers living water, referring to the Holy Spirit given to believers after his death. We need to rely on God's Word and the guidance of his Spirit to help us drink in pure truth.

January 19

* * *

We are citizens of heaven, where the Lord Jesus Christ lives.
PHILIPPIANS 3:20

E llis Island began operating as the chief immigration reception head-quarters for the United States in January 1892. Government officials questioned arriving immigrants, and doctors examined the new arrivals. Approximately twelve million immigrants entered the country through the Ellis Island station before it closed in 1954. It is estimated that 40 percent of Americans had an ancestor arrive at Ellis Island.

In 1976, officials opened Ellis Island to tourists as part of the Statue of Liberty monument. They dedicated it as a museum in 1990 after a six-month-long renovation. The Ellis Island museum is operated by the National Park Service and contains documents and artifacts related to four centuries of American immigration.

God has a special place in his heart for immigrants. He called Abraham to leave his country and go wherever he led him. God prophesied that Abraham's descendants would be strangers in a land not their own. When Moses fled Egypt and settled in Midian, he named his firstborn son Gershom and explained the name by saying, "I have been a foreigner in a foreign land" (Exodus 2:22). God instructed his people to care and provide for strangers living among them (Exodus 23:9).

When we accept Christ, we become aliens in this world. How can we feel at home in an earthly kingdom whose values and purposes directly oppose God's Kingdom? Yet in another sense, we have found our true home because we are no longer alienated from God. The second chapter of Ephesians explains how Gentiles who were "excluded from citizenship in Israel and foreigners to the covenants of the promise" (2:12, NIV) were brought near to God. We may sometimes feel like an alien in this world, but with Christ in our heart, wherever we are is home.

January 20

* * *

My dear brothers and sisters, how can you claim that you have faith in our glorious Lord Jesus Christ if you favor some people over others?

JAMES 2:1

M artin Luther King Jr. was the most influential leader of the civil rights movement during the fifties and sixties. He used his eloquent speaking ability to articulate blacks' grievances with discrimination in the United States. King was assassinated on April 4, 1968. In 1983, Congress made the third Monday in January a federal holiday to honor King.

One of the highlights of King's career was a speech delivered on August 28, 1963, to a gathering in Washington, D.C., King said, "I have a dream that one day this nation will rise up and live out the true meaning of its creed: 'We hold these truths to be self-evident; that all men are created equal.'"

Prejudice appears to be a universal weakness in human nature, with every race and every group of people. We all struggle with a tendency to judge others by external characteristics rather than their intrinsic value as people created by God. If not skin color, we may discriminate on the basis of economic or educational status, physical attractiveness, clothing, manners, or accent.

Several Scriptures remind us that God does not show favoritism (Acts 10:34). He told Samuel that while people judge by outward appearance, the Lord looks at a person's thoughts and intentions (1 Samuel 16:7). Scripture also warns us against partiality. James says that if we show favoritism, we are committing a sin (2:9). In Galatians 3:28 we are given a beautiful picture of relationships among believers as God intended: "There is no longer Jew or Gentile, slave or free, male and female. For you are all one in Christ Jesus." One in Christ—that's a dream we should all have.

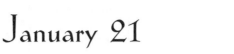

January 21

* * *

Get rid of all bitterness.
EPHESIANS 4:31

The Environmental Protection Agency has designated January as National Radon Action Month to make people aware of the danger of radon. The EPA encourages homeowners to obtain kits to test for radon in their house. Radon is a decay product of uranium and is found naturally in soil and rock, building materials, and well water. Levels of radon vary from home to home. Testing is the only way to detect dangerous levels of this colorless and odorless radioactive gas.

Specialists have identified radon as a leading cause of lung cancer in the United States, second only to cigarette smoking. There are no immediate symptoms of exposure to elevated levels. Lung cancer typically occurs five to twenty-five years after exposure. Each year in the United States, doctors attribute twenty-one thousand lung cancer deaths to accumulated radon in indoor air.

Like radon, bitterness is also often hard to detect, but is very dangerous to an individual and to a group. The book of Hebrews warns against allowing a root of bitterness to grow and cause trouble, corrupting many (12:15). When people harbor bitterness in their heart, they create a barrier with God. An entire church can be affected by one person's bitterness, resulting in broken relationships, loss of ministry, and damaged witness.

The symptoms of bitterness are not always readily apparent, but even in small amounts bitterness can cause damage. Bitterness is like a slow-acting poison that easily spreads. We must catch bitterness as soon as it begins, repent and confess it to God, and clear it out of our life. When we stay in close communion with God, he can make us aware of bitterness as soon as it begins. Then it's time for us to take action, no matter what month it is.

When have you held onto bitterness in your life?

January 22

* * *

Oh, that you would choose life, so that you and your descendants might live!
DEUTERONOMY 30:19

J anuary 22, 1973, is the anniversary of what is probably the most controversial decision ever handed down by the U.S. Supreme Court. The outcome of *Roe v. Wade* legalized abortion in all fifty states. Each year many observe the Sunday closest to January 22 as Sanctity of Human Life Sunday. Before 1973, the issue of abortion had been left up to individual state legislatures. Seventeen states had legalized abortion under certain circumstances. Thirty-three states had laws to protect life from the time of conception. The Supreme Court ruled that laws against abortion violated a woman's right to privacy.

Modern technology has shed new light on the issue of abortion. DNA evidence and photography of life in the womb have shattered the validity of the Supreme Court's statement that prior to birth there is no "personhood." Norma McCorvey, the original "Jane Roe," has become a prolife activist and in 2004 brought a direct challenge to *Roe v. Wade*.

Sadly, we get only to the fourth chapter of Genesis before we read about the first taking of innocent life, when Cain killed his brother, Abel. God's response reveals much about his heart and about the consequences of this action: "Listen! Your brother's blood cries out to me from the ground! Now you are cursed and banished from the ground, which has swallowed your brother's blood" (Genesis 4:10-11).

Since the Supreme Court made abortion legal in 1973, millions of unborn children have been aborted in the United States. These same babies who were being "knit together" by God in their mother's womb had their life cut short. If God heard the blood of Abel cry out to him from the ground, how deafening is the cry from the soil of our nation?

January 23

* * *

Faith is the assurance of things hoped for, the conviction of things not seen.
HEBREWS 11:1, NASB

The first performers to be inducted into the Rock and Roll Hall of Fame on this day in 1986 included Chuck Berry, Buddy Holly, Elvis Presley, Little Richard, and James Brown. The Rock and Roll Hall of Fame honors musicians, producers, executives, disc jockeys, and others who have played important roles in shaping rock music. Performers are eligible twenty-five years after the release of their first album.

The nonprofit Rock and Roll Hall of Fame Foundation was established in 1983 by a group of recording industry executives. Cleveland, Ohio, was selected as the site for the Hall of Fame exhibit and museum because local disc jockey Alan Freed had popularized the phrase "rock and roll" in the early 1950s. The museum documents the history of rock from its roots in other genres, including gospel, blues, and country.

God honors his own list of inductees in the eleventh chapter of Hebrews, often called the great "Hall of Faith." He gives the qualification for being selected by defining faith. All the people on the list lived with a firm conviction in the unseen reality of God and his promises. The list includes great heroes like Noah, Abraham, and Moses and lesser-known personalities such as Rahab, Barak, and Jephthah. They all demonstrated their faith by acts of obedience, sacrifice, or endurance.

Many people consider becoming a popular rock star the ultimate dream. But God urges us to have Jesus as our model and hero (Hebrews 12:2). He stands as both the reason for our faith and the perfect example of a life demonstrating confidence in the unseen God. Being acknowledged by a worldly Hall of Fame might be exciting, but how much better to be commended by the Rock when the world as we know it is rolled away.

January 24

* * *

Be sure to fear the LORD and faithfully serve him.
Think of all the wonderful things he has done for you.

1 SAMUEL 12:24

J ohn F. Kennedy was the first Roman Catholic to become president of the United States. At age 43, he was the youngest man elected to the office. Kennedy also became the youngest president to die in office when he was shot on November 22, 1963.

Kennedy successfully campaigned in the 1960 election with the promise of a "New Frontier" program. In his widely acclaimed January 1961 inaugural address, he said that Americans would "pay any price, bear any burden, meet any hardship, support any friend, oppose any foe to assure the survival and the success of liberty." Kennedy's most memorable statement urged Americans, "Ask not what your country can do for you—ask what you can do for your country."

Human beings are naturally self-serving. Even as Christians we struggle against the inclination to be consumed by our wants and needs. We tend to focus on *our* agenda, not on God's. If we're not careful, we end up treating God like Santa Claus, presenting him with our wish list and then calling it prayer. The world around us reinforces this selfish thinking.

Sometimes we forget that God was not created to serve us; rather we were made to love and serve him. God told Israel that if they did not serve him joyfully, they would serve the enemies that he would send (Deuteronomy 28:47-48). New Testament Christians are instructed to serve Christ enthusiastically (Romans 12:11). There is definitely a time and place for sharing our requests with God, but how refreshing it must be to him when we approach him in prayer asking, "What can I do for you, Lord?"

January 25

* * *

*I fear that somehow your pure and undivided devotion to Christ will be corrupted,
just as Eve was deceived by the cunning ways of the serpent.*

2 CORINTHIANS 11:3

In August 1969, Charles Manson, the charismatic leader of a southern California cult, masterminded a two-day bloody rampage in which his followers brutally murdered seven people. Manson, who thought he was Jesus Christ, believed that he received messages from the Beatles' song lyrics and the book of Revelation. In January 1971, a court found Manson guilty of the murders even though he had not killed any of the victims himself.

Manson and his followers exhibited bizarre behavior throughout the trial, with the other defendants implicating themselves but not their leader. They all received the death penalty, which was later abolished in California. Today, Manson remains in solitary confinement but retains his cult status. He receives more mail than any other U.S. inmate, much of it from devoted fans hoping to join the "family."

Deception has been a problem since the beginning of time. Satan, the great deceiver of the human race, tricked Eve in the Garden of Eden. Jesus warns that in the last days many deceivers will claim to be the Messiah (Matthew 24:4-5). Paul predicts that evil people and imposters will flourish, deceiving others and being deceived themselves (2 Timothy 3:13). During the Tribulation, the Antichrist and his false prophet will deceive the inhabitants of the earth with signs and miracles.

Even believers can be seduced by false apostles and false teaching. Although we have the Holy Spirit living in us, Satan can subtly introduce thoughts into our mind. If we submit to evil influences, we leave ourselves open to his deception. Since even Satan can disguise himself as an angel of light, we must constantly be on our guard as to whom we let master our mind.

January 26

* * *

I want you to realize what a rich and glorious inheritance he has given to his people.
EPHESIANS 1:18, NLT-1

In January 1905, Frederick Wells, a mine superintendent, noticed a large mass in a wall of the Premier mines in South Africa. At first, Wells thought he was looking at a large piece of glass embedded as a practical joke. Instead, it turned out that he had discovered the largest gem-quality diamond ever found. He later received $10,000 for finding the 3,106 karat diamond, which was named after the mine's owner, Sir Thomas Cullinan.

After the Asscher brothers in Amsterdam studied the stone for months, they cut it into three principal parts, which were further divided into nine major gems and many smaller fragments. The Cullinan I was the largest gem produced, a pear-shaped stone weighing 530.2 karats. It is now mounted in the head of the royal scepter in the British crown jewels and remains the world's largest cut diamond.

When Jesus was teaching about the Kingdom of Heaven, he used two parables about found treasure: First, he compared the Kingdom of Heaven to a treasure hidden in a field. The man who found it joyfully sold all he had to buy the field. Then, Jesus said the Kingdom of Heaven is like a merchant who searched for choice pearls. When he found one of great value, he sold all he owned in order to buy it (Matthew 13:44-46).

The man in the first illustration accidentally found his treasure, while the merchant was intentionally seeking choice pearls. But both men immediately recognized the great value of what they had found and sold all they had to possess it. What should our attitude be toward the treasure we have found in Christ? Are we willing to give up everything for the One who offers us infinite, eternal riches that make a 3,106 karat diamond seem like a piece of glass?

January 27

* * *

God, who said, "Let there be light in the darkness,"
has made this light shine in our hearts so we could know the glory of God
that is seen in the face of Jesus Christ.

2 CORINTHIANS 4:6

homas Edison invented many things, but he is best-known for the patent that was issued on this day in 1880 for an incandescent lightbulb that used a filament of carbonized thread. During the mid-1800s, numerous inventors had tried to generate light from electric energy. Several incandescent lamps were developed, but these burned out quickly because they operated on batteries. Edison's bulb improved on earlier, similar versions and paved the way to widespread use of electricity. He held a world record of 1,093 patents, singly or jointly. Almost four hundred of these related to electric light or power. Many credit Edison with laying the foundation for the technological revolution that led to our modern electric world.

In his first act of Creation, God created daylight by a simple spoken command (Genesis 1:3-5). On the fourth day of Creation, he created the sun, moon, and stars to give light to the earth (Genesis 1:14-19). Thousands of years later, Jesus called himself "the light of the world" (John 8:12). He brought spiritual enlightenment and hope to a world darkened by sin and its effects.

When we step out of the darkness of sin into the light of Christ's truth, our behavior should show that we are full of God's light (Ephesians 5:8). Someday we will live in a city that doesn't need the sun or moon, or electric bulbs. In the new Jerusalem, the glory of God will give it light and the Lamb will be its lamp (Revelation 21:23). Until that day, we are to shine our light before others so they can see the Lord, who promises to be our everlasting light (Matthew 5:14-16; Isaiah 60:19).

January 28

* * *

Take delight in the LORD, and he will give you your heart's desires.
PSALM 37:4

T he ABC television series *Fantasy Island* premiered on this day in
1977. Each week guests from all walks of life paid to come to a mysterious island somewhere in the Pacific Ocean and live out their fantasies.
They were greeted by their suave host, Mr. Roarke, played by Ricardo
Montalban, and his assistant Tattoo, played by Hervé Villechaize.

Each episode began with guests arriving by plane as Mr. Roarke
explained to Tattoo the nature of each person's fantasy and usually hinted
that the fantasy would not turn out as the person expected. Each of the two
or three story lines ended with some twist as guests learned something new
about themselves or received something unexpected. The popular series ran
for seven seasons; a remake in the late 1990s was not as successful.

Many people think that God should be more like Mr. Roarke, granting
our fantasies and wishes. Some teach that if we have enough faith and perseverance in prayer, God will grant our desires. But the promise in Psalms
includes a condition—we must first delight in him. If knowing God is our
first priority and we are finding our joy in him, then he will change our
desires. We will long for holiness more than happiness and the furtherance of
his work more than our personal success. Our desires will be in line with
God's will.

People often describe heaven like a "fantasy island"—a place filled with
whatever they think would bring them perfect happiness or something they
missed out on while on earth. That approach defines heaven from a human
standpoint, not from God's. When we arrive in heaven, we will find that
God has prepared something far superior to any fantasy that our heart could
ever desire.

January 29

* * *

This is my blood, which confirms the covenant between God and his people.
It is poured out as a sacrifice to forgive the sins of many.
MATTHEW 26:28

The American Association of Blood Banks designates January of each year as National Volunteer Blood Donor Month, encouraging people to give the gift of life by donating or pledging to donate blood. January is a slow month for blood donations due to poor weather, the aftermath of the holidays, and winter illnesses. A reduction in donations can cause blood inventory to slip to critically low levels.

Donated blood has a short shelf life, so it is imperative that the nation's blood supply be continuously replenished. Hospitals and emergency facilities need blood daily to treat accident victims, organ transplant recipients, and patients with cancer or other diseases. A single unit of donated blood may help save the lives of three different people.

Blood is an important thematic element throughout the Bible. Originally, Jewish worship involved slaughtering animals and sprinkling blood. God makes it clear that without the shedding of blood there is no forgiveness of sin (Hebrews 9:22). Then Jesus shed his own blood when he offered himself as the perfect, once and for all, sacrifice for sin.

It used to be common in sermons and hymns to hear an emphasis on the significance of blood, but today that is no longer true. It might even be said that there's a squeamishness about all the blood in the Old Testament and God's bloody final judgment of sin in Revelation 14:14-20. Yet at the same time, the news and entertainment media expose us to increasingly bloody and gory images. Christ willingly gave his blood to redeem us from sin and make us holy. It is his blood that seals our covenant relationship with God. When we were in critical condition because of sin, Jesus Christ donated his blood to save our life.

January 30

* * *

What good is it, dear brothers and sisters,
if you say you have faith but don't show it by your actions?
JAMES 2:14

The tradition of declaring New Year's resolutions dates back to the ancient Babylonians. It is thought that the most popular resolution at that time was to return borrowed farm equipment. Today we make resolutions based on something that will improve our life. We promise to break some bad habit or start a good one, such as losing weight, eating a healthier diet, or exercising. By the end of the month, however, most people have forgotten or given up on their New Year's resolutions.

Good intentions are no substitute for action. James points this out in his discussion of faith and deeds. He gives the example of a brother or sister in Christ needing food or clothes. If someone tells him or her, "Good-bye and have a good day; stay warm and eat well," but does nothing about that person's physical needs, what good is that? James asserts that in the same way, faith that doesn't show itself by good deeds is useless and dead (James 2:14-17).

With our busy life, it's all too easy to not follow through on our well-meaning intentions. We assure a friend that we will pray for a doctor's appointment, and then we forget about it until we see the friend again. We feel led to call someone or write a note but never get around to it. When we fail to act on our good intention, it doesn't count as a good deed. We create guilt for ourself and miss an opportunity to be a blessing to someone. That person misses the touch of God in his or her life. All through the year we need to resolve to express our faith through good deeds, not noble intentions.

January 31

* * *

*Now you are free from sin, your old master, and you have
become slaves to your new master, righteousness.*
ROMANS 6:18, NLT-1

he thirteenth amendment to the U.S. Constitution was proposed on this day in 1865: "Neither slavery nor involuntary servitude, except as a punishment for crime whereof the party shall have been duly convicted, shall exist within the United States, or any place subject to their jurisdiction."

President Abraham Lincoln issued his Emancipation Proclamation of 1863 to declare slaves free in the Confederate States. The thirteenth amendment completed the process of abolishing slavery in the United States when it was ratified on December 18, 1865. It represented a legal victory for the two generations of abolitionists who had worked to see slavery end in this country.

Spiritual slavery, however, is a continuing problem in the human race. Jesus said that anyone who sins is a slave to sin (John 8:34). Sin enslaved the human race until Jesus was crucified. Now we have a choice. When we identify with him, we identify with his death and resurrection. Our old self was crucified along with Christ so that we could be released from sin's hold on us.

We still have the freedom to slip back into our old bondage. Paul described his struggle with sin in Romans 7. He said that in his mind he was a slave to God's law, but in his sinful nature he was still a slave to the law of sin. The paradox is that true freedom is found through willingly becoming the slave of Christ. Peter taught, "You are a slave to whatever controls you" (2 Peter 2:19). Every day we have to answer the question, Do I want to serve my old sinful nature, or do I want to serve my new master?

February 1

* * *

Above all else, guard your heart, for it is the wellspring of life.
PROVERBS 4:23, NIV

I n 1915, a group of physicians concerned by the lack of heart disease information formed the Association for the Prevention and Relief of Heart Disease. At that time many doctors routinely considered heart patients doomed and prescribed complete bed rest. Interest spread in wanting more information about heart disease, and similar groups soon formed in other cities. Recognizing the need for a national organization to share resources and research findings, six cardiologists founded the American Heart Association (AHA) in 1924.

Today, the AHA is a national network of local divisions involved in research, education, community programs, and fund-raising. The organization's goal is to provide credible information about cardiovascular diseases, our nation's No. 1 killer. Since 1963, Congress has required the president to proclaim February as American Heart Month to focus on raising funds and distributing current information about these health risks.

The word *heart* in its biblical sense does not refer to the seat of emotion as in our current English usage; rather it denotes the center of personality, understanding, and decision making. All our words, attitudes, and actions flow out of our heart. The condition of our heart affects what we take in as well. Jesus warns that when the heart becomes hardened, we have difficulty seeing and hearing the truth (Matthew 13:15).

The book of Proverbs advises us to set a strict guard over our heart to jealously protect it more than any other treasure. We do this by constantly keeping our mind trained on God's truth. If we don't make a deliberate choice to let God reign over our heart every day, then it will be ruled by the world or our human nature. That's a health risk none of us can afford to take.

February 2

* * *

*God has not given us a spirit of fear and timidity, but of power,
love, and self-discipline.*

2 TIMOTHY 1:7

A ccording to tradition, February 2 is the date that the groundhog, or
woodchuck, wakes up from winter hibernation and comes out of its
burrow. The legend says that if the sun shines that day, the groundhog will be
scared by its own shadow, return to its burrow, and winter will last another six
weeks. If the day is cloudy and the groundhog doesn't see its shadow, it will
stay outside and spring will come soon.

For several hundred years, European farmers had similar traditions
involving badgers, bears, and other animals. Early German settlers brought
their custom to Pennsylvania. Plentiful in the eastern and midwestern states,
the groundhog became the animal linked with our Groundhog Day custom in
America. Since 1887, "Punxsutawney Phil" has been the official weather
prophet in well-attended Groundhog Day celebrations in Punxsutawney,
Pennsylvania.

We've all experienced the desire to hide from circumstances that threaten
us, just like the traditional groundhog. Some Bible scholars assume that Paul's
allusion to timidity or cowardice refers to a problem that Timothy had. Others
interpret it as a general encouragement to Paul's young protégé as Timothy
spread the gospel in hostile environments. In either case, the verse reminds us
that the Holy Spirit does not bring fear but instills in us the ability to control
ourselves beyond our natural capabilities.

Fear is a problem with everyone to some degree. God told Isaiah that the
Lord is the only one we are to fear (Isaiah 8:13). Fear will be replaced by faith
if we concentrate on pleasing the One who holds our destiny in his hands.
Then we can say with David, "I prayed to the LORD, and he answered me. He
freed me from all my fears" (Psalm 34:4). There's no need to be frightened by
scary shadows around us as long as the Son is shining.

**How do your fears keep you from
being all God wants you to be?**

34

February 3

* * *

[Jesus said,] "Sin will be rampant everywhere,
and the love of many will grow cold."
MATTHEW 24:12

The coldest recorded temperature in North America occurred on this day in 1947 at the Snag Airport in Yukon, Canada. Workers for the Weather Service of Canada filed a notch into the glass casing of their thermometer because the indicator had fallen below the lowest number, eighty degrees below zero. They sent the thermometer to Toronto, where officials determined that the temperature at Snag had been minus 81.4 degrees Fahrenheit.

Weathermen who were stationed at the Snag airstrip remember throwing water into the air and watching it freeze into pellets before it hit the ground and listening to local sounds magnified by the severe temperature inversion. It is believed that there were colder spots that day, such as in remote villages to the north that lacked an official thermometer.

When the disciples asked Jesus about signs of the end of the age, he predicted persecution, betrayal, and deception by false prophets and apostles. As wickedness increases, those who are not true believers will fall away and their love will grow cold. Since love is not primarily an emotion but an active commitment to God and others, those who are spiritually dead will not demonstrate this kind of love.

Jesus' message to the church at Ephesus in Revelation 2 commends these Christians for their deeds, hard work, proper handling of false teachers, and endurance of hardships. Then Jesus points out the fatal flaw in their behavior—a lack of love. He warns that they will cease to exist as a church unless they repent and return to the works they did at first. Letting our love for God and others cool off is serious business. Regardless of the outside temperature, our internal love thermometer should always register "hot."

February 4

* * *

Don't lord it over the people assigned to your care,
but lead them by your own good example.
1 PETER 5:3

During the Revolutionary War, General George Washington led an inexperienced, poorly equipped army of civilian soldiers to victory over one of the world's great powers. After the war, a colonel suggested that the army set up a monarchy with Washington as king. The general received the idea "with abhorrence" and ordered his officer to banish such thoughts from his mind. Hoping for a quiet retirement, Washington surrendered his military commission.

By 1786, it was obvious that the new government needed to be strengthened to prevent anarchy. The drafters of the Constitution created the office of president with Washington in mind; however, Washington wrote that if he accepted the appointment, it would be "with more diffidence and reluctance than I ever experienced before in my life." On this day in 1789, the sixty-nine voting electors unanimously elected Washington the first president of the reorganized government. He also served a second term but refused a third.

Washington demonstrated a humility that is often lacking among leaders. Peter wrote that church leaders should not serve because they have to or because they are greedy for money. They should not lord their power over others but be eager to serve those God has entrusted to them and willingly serve as examples (1 Peter 5:2-3).

We all serve in some leadership role, whether in a church, work, social, or family setting. As always, Jesus serves as our role model. He told his disciples that whoever wants to be great must become a servant: "For even the Son of Man came not to be served, but to serve" (Mark 10:45). Some described Washington as "first in the hearts of his countrymen." We can only have the respect that Washington earned if we lead with the same attitude as the only One who has the right to be Lord over us all.

February 5

* * *

You shelter them in your presence, far from accusing tongues.
PSALM 31:20

S enator Joseph McCarthy gained national attention in February 1950 by announcing that Communists had infiltrated the State Department. Even after an investigating committee cleared the State Department, McCarthy repeated the charges on radio and television. When challenged to produce his evidence, he refused.

In 1953, McCarthy became chairman of the Senate permanent investigations committee. For two years, McCarthy pursued those he classified as Communists and subversives through publicized hearings based on the use of unidentified informers. In 1954, the Senate acted on a motion of censure against McCarthy, and his influence in the Senate steadily diminished. His actions led to the term *McCarthyism* to denote assaults marked by sensationalist tactics and unsubstantiated accusations.

When God gave his law to the Israelites, he made provisions for the problem of false accusations. A person could be convicted of a crime only on the testimony of two or three witnesses. If a man maliciously accused another of a crime, the two stood before the priests and judges. If a thorough investigation proved that the witness had given false testimony, he was to be punished according to what he intended to do to his brother (Deuteronomy 19:15-19).

Revelation 12:9-10 calls Satan the accuser of all believers. He accuses us before God day and night, but God knows the truth about us. If the accusation is false, he dismisses it, and if it's true, he forgives it when we repent. Satan also accuses us in our thoughts. He knows he can do a lot of damage by reminding us of past sins or by implanting false guilt over imagined failures. By honest self-examination and repentance of real sins, we can censure Satan's accusations and diminish his influence on our mind.

February 6

* * *

Pay all your debts, except the debt of love for others. You can never finish paying that! If you love your neighbor, you will fulfill all the requirements of God's law.
Romans 13:8, NLT-1

The first week in February is designated as National Pay Your Bills Week and the third week as Pay Your Bills Week. Perhaps we need two weeks because we have so many bills to pay. Besides paying for living expenses, the average American household averages 2.3 credit cards for purchases. As of 2002, there were 1,452 million cards in circulation and $1,638 billion in credit-card spending. For 2005, the Nilson Report projects $2,022 billion in credit-card spending and $922 billion in outstanding credit card debt. According to the Federal Reserve, over 40 percent of American families spend more than they earn. Almost one out of every one hundred households will file for bankruptcy.

God does not want his people to be struggling with debt. In the early days of Israel, God instructed that all debts be cancelled every seven years, without requiring further payment (Deuteronomy 15:1-2). This foreshadowed God's payment of the biggest debt of all by having Jesus die on the cross. Our penalty for sin was paid in full.

Once our debt of sin is settled, that leads to another debt—a permanent one. When we experience the love of God through Jesus Christ, it should flow through us to everyone we meet. We have a lifelong obligation to share his love with others by having their best interests at heart. As New Covenant believers, that is how we fulfill the law. That's one bill we can joyfully make payment on every single day.

How are you making payments on your debt of love for others?

February 7

***

Woe to those who call evil good, and good evil.
ISAIAH 5:20, NKJV

D onatien-Alphonse-François de Sade, better known as the Marquis de Sade, was born in Paris in 1740 and began to show signs of mental illness in his twenties. His life was marked by violent scandals over his sexual conduct, acts of cruelty, and feuds with enemies. His behavior and writings led to his imprisonment most of the time between 1768 and 1803. Soldiers arrested Sade in February 1777 and sent him to the Fortress of Vincennes, where he spent a number of years before being transferred to the Bastille. In 1803, officials placed him in an asylum, where he died in 1814.

Although Sade wrote many short stories, essays, plays, and novels, many were not published until the mid-1900s because of their pornographic and blasphemous nature. Sade attempted to demonstrate that criminal acts and sexual abnormalities are a natural part of human behavior. In recent years, many have come to view him as a brilliant writer who defied moral conventions and who deserves a prominent place in French literature.

God gave Isaiah a list of Israel's sins that would bring judgment or "woe." The Israelites had rebelled against God's authority and decided to make up their own morality, even reversing God's standards. They called evil good, and vice versa. God warned that a failure to carefully distinguish between right and wrong leads to confusion and ends in destruction.

This same arrogant attitude is prevalent in our society today. Anyone who dares to suggest absolutes of right and wrong is branded an extremist. We are reaping the fruit of replacing God's standards with moral relativism. People not only tolerate evil but sometimes elevate it as good. What woe is in store for a nation that admires the man whose name inspired the word *sadism* to denote the enjoyment of cruelty. Doesn't that seem like a no-brainer?

February 8

* * *

Come before him, singing with joy.

PSALM 100:2

O n this day in 1933 in New York City, Western Union offered the first singing telegram. George Oslin, a public relations director, receives credit for originating the idea. In the 1930s, the post–World War I genera-tion associated telegrams with news of injury or death on the battlefield. Oslin wanted to show that telegrams could be fun.

The singing-telegram business made millions for Western Union until the widespread installation of telephones in the 1960s. In the early 1970s, Western Union closed many of its telegraph offices and in 1974 suspended its singing-telegram service. Small private services soon emerged and kept the singing telegram alive. Today, singing telegram businesses exist in many U.S. cities, and rural areas have access to online or telephone versions.

The Bible is filled with singing from beginning to end. God told Job that the morning stars sang for joy at creation (Job 38:7). Both David and Heze-kiah appointed some of the priests to sing joyful songs, accompanied by instruments (1 Chronicles 15:16, NIV; 2 Chronicles 31:2, NIV). In John's vision of heaven, he heard every creature in heaven, on earth, under the earth, and in the sea singing to God and to the Lamb (Revelation 5:13).

Our voices may be less than heavenly, but God still expects us to "make a joyful noise" to him. We are encouraged to sing psalms, hymns, and spiritual songs with gratitude to him (Colossians 3:16). Paul explains that part of being filled with the Spirit is "making music to the Lord" in our heart (Ephe-sians 5:19). Thankfully, just as God looks at the condition of our heart rather than our outward appearance, he is more interested in our attitude than the quality of our voice. We have no excuse for not delivering singing telegrams to him every day.

February 9

* * *

[Jesus said,] "Beware of false prophets who come disguised as harmless sheep, but are really wolves that will tear you apart."

MATTHEW 7:15, NLT-1

Americans popularized professional wrestling in the early twentieth century as wrestlers toured the country, taking on opponents from the audience. These "volunteers" had usually been approached beforehand and knew they were supposed to lose the match. In the 1930s, promoters began booking matches in arenas. With the growth of television, broadcasters chose professional wrestling as a popular programming option.

In today's professional wrestling, showmanship often takes center stage rather than skill. Matches often pair up a "hero" and a "villain" in outlandish costumes and give the impression of extreme violence. In February 1989, the World Wrestling Federation went to court to persuade the New Jersey State Senate that their "sport" is not dangerous and therefore does not need regulation. Officials testified that pro wrestling is a staged activity for the purpose of entertainment rather than genuine athletic competition.

Just as pro wrestling may be entertainment disguised as a sport, Jesus warned about false prophets disguised as Christians. In their letters, Paul and Peter urged readers to be on the lookout for false teachers and false apostles who infiltrate the church. These deceivers seem harmless but inflict serious damage by introducing subtle errors in doctrine, leading people away from the truth.

Jesus explained that not all who look religious are really godly. They may refer to him as Lord, but that doesn't mean they have a relationship with him. On Judgment Day, many people will argue that they prophesied, cast out demons, and performed many miracles—all in Jesus' name. But he will say, "I never knew you" (Matthew 7:21-23). Even true believers can be self-deceived and not realize that their good works are being done for show, not from love and obedience. We need to continually examine our motives to make sure that our Kingdom activity is genuine, not staged.

February 10

*** * ***

*Wash your hands, you sinners; purify your hearts, for your loyalty is divided
between God and the world.*

JAMES 4:8

S ir Joseph Lister, a physician known for enacting new methods of
sterilization, died on this day in 1912. Lister entered the medical
profession at a time when even trivial operations were usually followed by
infections, and death occurred in up to one-half of all surgeries. After reading
about Louis Pasteur's germ theory of disease in 1865, Lister realized that the
best way to prevent infections must be to kill the microbes before they
reached the open wound.

Lister instituted strict antiseptic procedures such as having doctors wash
their hands before operations and cleaning instruments and dressings. As a
result, the postoperative mortality rate was drastically reduced. Queen Victo-
ria honored Lister's work in introducing antiseptic surgery by elevating him
to the House of Lords. In honor of Joseph Lister's antiseptic work, the Pfizer
company named their mouthwash, Listerine, after him.

God gave specific rules about cleansing to the Israelites involving preparation for worship and participation in Passover. Aaron and his sons were to
wash in a bronze washbasin before going into the Tabernacle to minister, or
they would die. There were purification rituals associated with childbirth and
with leprosy and other diseases. All these regulations pointed to God's holiness and foreshadowed the new, better cleansing that Christ would introduce
through his death.

Before we draw near to God, James 4:7-10 recommends that we wash our
hands and purify our heart. We can't approach a holy God with hands contaminated by sin and hearts divided between God and the world. Although
Jesus' sacrifice removed the stain of our sin, we still need a daily cleansing.
Our hands get dirty from living in a fallen world. In 1 John 1:9, John tells
how to prevent spiritual infection: "If we confess our sins to him, he is faithful and just to forgive us our sins and to cleanse us from all wickedness."

February 11

* * *

Give honor to marriage, and remain faithful to one another in marriage.
HEBREWS 13:4

I n 1981, couples in Baton Rouge, Louisiana, urged the mayor, governor, and bishop to proclaim Valentine's Day as "We Believe in Marriage Day." The event proved successful, and the national leadership of Worldwide Marriage Encounter adopted the idea. The following year, forty-three governors proclaimed the day, and celebrations spread to U.S. military bases in several foreign countries. The name was changed to World Marriage Day in 1983 and designated as the second Sunday in February.

Each year the celebrations grow to include more countries and faith expressions. World Marriage Day honors husband and wife as head of the family, the basic unit of society. The permanent theme is "Love One Another," emphasizing that loving each other is a simple but challenging daily decision. The symbol is a husband and wife as two candlelike figures (reminding us that married love calls us to help enlighten the world), joined by a heart.

God performed the first marriage ceremony when he created Eve and presented her to Adam. God designed them to become united as one. The Old Testament metaphorically refers to Israel as God's wife. The New Testament often uses marriage to illustrate the relationship between Christ and his church. It's obvious that marriage is precious to God, a sacred covenant not to be broken.

Today the institution of marriage is under attack as never before. Divorce rates are growing, and extramarital affairs have become excusable in many people's eyes. Gay and lesbian groups are pushing for legalization of same-sex unions. Marriage has become a mockery of what God intended it to be. Since the husband and wife are the basic building block of society, it's everyone's job to respect marriage and fight for its preservation.

February 12

* * *

"I will restore you to health and I will heal you of your wounds,"
declares the LORD.
JEREMIAH 30:17, NASB

I n February 1929, Sir Alexander Fleming, a Scottish physician, observed that a plate culture of staphylococcus bacteria had been contaminated by a blue-green mold and that colonies of the bacteria adjacent to the mold were being dissolved. He then grew the mold in a pure culture and found that it produced a substance capable of killing a number of disease-causing bacteria. Fleming's discovery—penicillin—in time became one of the most widely used antibiotic agents.

Fleming published the results of his investigation, noting that penicillin might have therapeutic value if it could be produced in quantity. Widespread use of the antibiotic began in the 1940s when researchers were able to isolate its active ingredient and develop a powdery form of the medicine. Penicillin became readily available during World War II, when it rapidly wiped out the biggest wartime killer—infected wounds.

In addition to physical healing, we all need spiritual healing sometimes, as well. Even though Jesus provided the ultimate healing when he delivered us from the penalty of our sin, we can still become contaminated from living in a fallen world. Sometimes we suffer from battle wounds received in spiritual warfare.

God has the miraculous cure for what ails our soul. David refers to God's medicine in Psalm 107:20: "He sent out his word and healed them." God's spoken and written Word has the power to ease pain, bind up brokenness, and kill infections caused by sin. No matter what type of wounds we are suffering from, the answer is "mold"—letting God's Word mold us into the image of Christ.

What kind of healing do you need from God?

February 13

* * *

A truly wise person uses few words.

PROVERBS 17:27

O n this day in 1981, the *New York Times* published what was thought to be the longest sentence ever printed in a newspaper. The 1,286-word sentence quoted a high school student when asked what he had been learning at school. One observer remarked that it seemed that half the words were "you know" and "uh."

According to past editions of *Guinness World Records*, the longest sentence in English literature was one from *Ulysses* by James Joyce and contains 4,391 words. The publication of *The Rotters Club* in 2001 surpassed the Joyce record with a sentence of 13,955 words. Author Jonathan Coe says he was inspired by a Czech novel that consists of one long sentence. Bohumil Hrabal's novel sentence, *Dancing Lessons for the Advanced in Age*, is 128 pages long.

The book of Proverbs has much to say about our words. It warns against talking too much: "Too much talk leads to sin. Be sensible and keep your mouth shut" (Proverbs 10:19). Talking without restraint can lead to misunderstandings, arguments, or the unintentional sharing of information meant to be confidential. Unfortunately, not many of us are in the habit of thinking before we speak. Our mouths seem to operate much faster than our brains.

We need to watch the quality, as well as the quantity, of our words. The gift of language is too precious to waste on useless, empty words that have no purpose. Our goal should be to say the right thing at the right time in the right way. If we spend our words wisely, then we will come close to the beautiful word picture in Proverbs 25:11: "A word aptly spoken is like apples of gold in settings of silver" (NIV).

February 14

* * *

[Jesus said,] "I am giving you a new commandment: Love each other."
JOHN 13:34

Valentine's Day is one of the most widely celebrated unofficial holidays. There are several different explanations for the holiday, which was declared a celebration of martyrs in A.D. 496 by Saint Pope Gelasius I. Some authorities believe the celebration was designed to divert Christians from the pagan observance of Lupercalia, an ancient Roman festival. Other experts link the custom of exchanging valentines with the old English belief that birds chose their mates on that day.

The early church had two saints named Valentine. In one story the Roman Emperor Claudius II forbade young men to marry, thinking that single men made better soldiers. A priest named Valentine disobeyed and secretly married young couples. Another version asserts that Valentine was an early Christian who made friends with children. When the Romans imprisoned him, the children threw loving notes through his cell window.

Jesus condensed the Ten Commandments into two: Love God with all your heart, soul, mind, and strength, and love others as yourself (Mark 12:30-31). He said the love we have for one another will prove to the world that we are his followers (John 13:35). Once we experience God's lavish, unconditional love, the only reasonable response is to share that love with others.

Jesus also gave a command that appears illogical and impossible: We are to love our enemies and do good to those who hate us (Luke 6:27). Our natural tendency is to love only those who love us, which Jesus said is no credit to us. The selfless love he described can be expressed only with supernatural help from God's Spirit, but it offers the world an undeniable witness of God's transforming love and power. Maybe we should use February 14 to reach out to those who *don't* come to mind when we think of valentines.

February 15

* * *

It is wrong to show favoritism when passing judgment.
PROVERBS 24:23

C ontroversy arose in February 2002 at the Winter Olympics in Salt Lake City. French skating judge Marie-Reine Le Gougne claimed that French Ice Sports Federation president Didier Gailhaguet had pressured her to vote in favor of the Russian pair in the free-skate ice-dancing competition even though she felt the Canadians had presented a better program. In a controversial decision, the International Skating Union decided to award a second gold medal to the Canadian pair.

Several French judges came forward to claim that Gailhaguet had similarly pressured them in the past. Le Gougne, however, later recanted and said she had accused Gailhaguet after feeling physically and psychologically threatened by other judges and skating officials. After a two-day hearing by the ISU council, the council banned Le Gougne and Gailhaguet from all ISU activities for three years and barred them from participating in the 2006 Winter Olympics.

Unlike human judges, God does not show favoritism when he passes judgment, the apostle Paul explains in the second chapter of Romans. The Jews could not rely on their special status as his chosen people and the recipients of the Law. God will judge Jews and Gentiles alike for their sin. His judgment will be based on their actual behavior, not their knowledge of the Law.

God also does not play favorites among his children, although it may appear that way to us at times. Favoritism is not part of God's character. He desires the same thing for every person—a close relationship with him and a vibrant ministry in the church and in the world. Every believer has been given spiritual gifts and the power of the Holy Spirit to accomplish great things for God's Kingdom. We live our lives before a judge who wants us all to "get the gold."

February 16

* * *

Please, LORD, rescue me! Come quickly, LORD, and help me.
PSALM 40:13

G reat Britain implemented an emergency telephone system in 1937—the first country to do so. The first 911 call in the United States was not placed until February 16, 1968. After months of hearings and correspondence between the White House and a commission studying law enforcement, the concept of a single emergency number finally reached the Federal Communications Commission (FCC).

In January 1968, AT&T announced that 911 had been designated as the universal emergency number and that the plan would be implemented shortly. Bob Gallagher, president of the independent Alabama Telephone Company, decided to beat AT&T to the punch. His plant manager identified the perfect site and worked with technicians to set up a 911 system. The first call was placed at 2:00 p.m. by Alabama Speaker of the House Rankin Fite from the Haleyville City Hall to U.S. Representative Tom Bevill at the police station.

Some people think the Bible says, "The Lord helps those who help themselves." What the Bible actually teaches is that God helps those who know they *can't* help themselves. He is always ready to come to the aid of his children when we call out to him. David, who was called a man after God's own heart, often expressed his dependency on God by freely and unashamedly crying out for help from him.

When we don't know what number to call in an emergency, we can dial 911 and the appropriate help will be sent. In a similar way, Romans 8:26-27 says that the Holy Spirit helps us in times of distress. Sometimes we don't know what to pray for, or even how to pray. At those times, the Spirit relays our needs with groanings that words can't express, always in line with God's will. Even when we don't know what *number* to call, we know *whom* to call.

February 17

* * *

Be happy with those who are happy, and weep with those who weep.
ROMANS 12:15

T*he Secret Storm*, a popular soap opera that ran from February 1954 to February 1974, achieved notoriety for possibly the worst casting decision in soap opera history. When Christina Crawford became ill, her adoptive mother, Joan Crawford, filled in for her, even though Joan was thirty years older than the character on the show.

Soap operas, daily serial melodramas, originated on daytime radio and got their name from the first sponsors, soap manufacturers. Many consider them one of America's original art forms. In the 1950s, soaps moved to television, and during the late seventies, they began to influence nighttime television as weekly shows with soap-opera-like plots gained popularity.

Some people ridicule soap operas because viewers get so caught up in the emotional, dramatic plot lines. Instead, believers need to be involved in one another's lives. The body of Christ is meant to function like a human body. If one part suffers, all the other parts do, too. When someone is honored, every-one else is glad (1 Corinthians 12:26). Paul said that we obey the law of Christ when we share one another's problems and troubles (Galatians 6:2). We can't do that if we keep our "storms" secret.

If we stay in a close relationship with the Lord and with fellow believers, we will be able to handle the *Dark Shadows* that are bound to come during the *Days of Our Lives As the World Turns*. Even when we feel as though we are on the *Edge of Night*, we can keep our eyes on our *Guiding Light* until we arrive at *Another World* and our Father opens his arms and says, "Welcome home, *All My Children*."

How are you sharing the joys and sorrows of other believers?

February 18

* * *

Jesus told his disciples, "Now gather the leftovers, so that nothing is wasted."
JOHN 6:12

John Bunyan published one of the most popular books in the English language in February 1678. In *The Pilgrim's Progress*—an allegory with people and places symbolizing vices and virtues—the hero, Christian, sets out from the City of Destruction to go to the Celestial City. Along the way he meets characters who try to harm him, such as the Giant Despair, and others who help him, such as Faithful.

Bunyan was a tinker in England. Though he had little education, he became a lay preacher. In 1660, he was arrested for disobeying the royal edicts banning nonconformist preaching. Bunyan spent the next twelve years in prison, studying the Bible and writing many religious works. Upon his release, he became pastor of his nonconformist church. Bunyan was briefly jailed again in 1675, when he wrote his most celebrated work.

David wrote some of the psalms while he was in a prison of sorts, hiding in hills and caves from King Saul, who wanted to kill him. Joseph was falsely accused and spent many years in prison. He used the time to minister to others and grow. By the time he was released, Joseph was prepared to rule Egypt as second in command.

God does not waste anything—not food, not experiences, not suffering. When we seem to be stuck in a prison, we can know that God has something in mind. He may use our situation to help us minister to others. We may need the time to grow in our faith and obedience. The book describing our life may not be a best seller, but we can expect something good and useful to come out of every situation we face. All our times are in God's hands until we finally reach the Celestial City.

February 19

* * *

For we know that when this earthly tent we live in is taken down (that is, when we die and leave this earthly body), we will have a house in heaven, an eternal body made for us by God himself and not by human hands.

2 CORINTHIANS 5:1

I n February 1984, a twelve-year-old boy named David touched his mother for the first time. Born with a rare disorder called severe combined immune deficiency that made even the mildest infection danger-ous, David had spent his entire life at a children's hospital, living inside a sterile environment, a plastic "bubble."

In September 1983, doctors attempted to replace David's bone marrow with healthy cells from his sister. The transplant appeared successful at first, but David later developed fever and diarrhea. After recovering from these symptoms, he was allowed out of the bubble, but David died two weeks later.

All of us are like David, in a way. We live with a barrier that separates us from our heavenly Father. We see glimpses of him all around us. We read the Book he has written for us. We sense his presence in our life. But no matter how close we feel to God at times, there is still a barrier between us. We can't physically touch him. There is something in the way.

That barrier is our body, which Paul calls our earthly tent in 2 Corinthi-ans 5:1-8. We live in a corrupt, decaying body that prevents our complete communion with God. When we get to leave this "bubble," or shell, we will slip into our heavenly body and be released from the sin-infected environ-ment where we have been trapped. Just as David's mother longed to be able to hold her little boy close, our Father is longing for the day when he can wrap his arms around us with nothing in the way.

February 20

* * *

Trust in the LORD with all your heart; do not depend on your own understanding.
PROVERBS 3:5

The city of Los Angeles, California, experienced its most deadly industrial accident on this day in 1947 as the result of errors in a chemical mixing process. The explosion at the O'Connor Electro-Plating Company tore apart a four-block area and opened a crater twenty-two feet wide and six feet deep. The blast destroyed or damaged 116 buildings and shattered windows across a one-square-mile area. Seventeen people were killed and 150 injured.

The problem began when the plant manager, Robert J. O'Connor, hired a chief chemist, Robert M. Magee, who lacked the proper credentials. Though Magee had presented himself as qualified for the job, he actually was a former dairy foreman who only dreamed of being a chemist. He had not even earned a high school diploma.

Sometimes things in our life seem to blow up in our face. It may be because we have based our decisions on a faulty formula. No matter how perceptive we think we are, we may not see the situation clearly. And just because others have impressive credentials does not mean they have sound judgment. Relying on human wisdom alone is a surefire path to destruction.

The only way to prevent errors in our thinking and lifestyle is to follow God's directions. The second chapter of Proverbs outlines the benefits of God's wisdom, which leads to knowledge and understanding. Wisdom brings us joy, keeps us safe, and shows us how to choose the right course of action in every situation. Knowing God's Word and obeying it is the only fail-safe formula for a successful life.

Are you basing your decisions on God's truth or human wisdom?

February 21

* * *

We all hear these people speaking in our own languages
about the wonderful things God has done!

ACTS 2:11

In 1999, the General Conference of the United Nations Educational, Scientific, and Cultural Organization (UNESCO) unanimously voted to observe each February 21 as International Mother Language Day for the purpose of promoting a fuller awareness of the linguistic and cultural traditions throughout the world. Recognizing that languages are the most effective instruments of preserving and developing our heritage, UNESCO set its goal to promote recognition and practice of the world's mother tongues, especially minority ones.

It's been estimated that half of the world's six to seven thousand languages are in danger of extinction. UNESCO member states promote multilingualism through educational and cultural programs to protect the world's oral heritage. UNESCO's program called "Initiative B@bel" is designed to redefine universal access to all languages in cyberspace.

Our great variety of languages is the result of sin and arrogance when our ancestors conspired to build a monument to their greatness. God came down and gave them many languages so they would scatter and fill the earth as he had instructed. In John's vision of heaven, John saw a vast crowd of people from every nation, tribe, and language praising God and the Lamb. We don't know what language they were using. Maybe it was an original, perfect language that was lost at the tower of Babel.

When God gave the Holy Spirit to the disciples, Jews from many different nations were in Jerusalem. They all heard the disciples preaching in the Jews' native language. Today groups like Wycliffe Bible Translators are working tirelessly to see that the same thing happens with the printed Word. It is important to preserve native tongues, but the best use of a mother language is to let people read their Father's words.

February 22

* * *

The righteous will flourish like a palm tree, they will grow like a cedar of Lebanon.
PSALM 92:12, NIV

February 22, 1918, is the birthday of the tallest man in history for whom there is irrefutable evidence. Robert Pershing Wadlow was born in Alton, Illinois, to parents of average height. He weighed eight pounds, eight ounces at birth and maintained a normal weight until age two, when he began to grow at an astonishing rate. At age twelve, doctors found that he had an overactive pituitary gland.

Wadlow enjoyed good health except for problems associated with his size 37AA feet. At age twenty-two he received a brace to strengthen his ankles, but it was poorly fitted and a septic blister formed on an ankle. Because of limited sensation in his feet, the blister went unnoticed until a fatal infection had set in. Wadlow died in his sleep on July 5, 1940. He had reached a height of 8 feet, 11.1 inches.

Every day we grow, older if not taller. The most important growth happens on the inside. New believers are urged to continually feed on "pure spiritual milk" so they can grow and develop spiritually (1 Peter 2:2). Maintaining correct doctrine in a spirit of love causes the body as a whole to grow up into Christ, who is the head (Ephesians 4:15).

The Christian life is not static. Paul was thankful for the Thessalonians because their faith was growing more and more, and all the members' love for one another was increasing. God's children should be continuously growing in the knowledge of their Savior (2 Peter 3:18). There is visible evidence of this internal growth as our behavior and attitudes mature into Christ's likeness. We may not earn a place in any record book, but when God calls us home, we will be walking tall.

February 23

* * *

You have raised a banner for those who fear you—
a rallying point in the face of attack.
PSALM 60:4

O n this day in 1945, the Marines captured Mount Suribachi, the highest point on the island of Iwo Jima and an important defense position. It was one of the costliest battles of the Pacific campaign of World War II and was fought in February and March 1945. Approximately 6,800 United States personnel, including about 6,000 Marines, lost their lives in capturing the eight square miles of Iwo Jima. Experts estimated Japanese losses at more than 21,000. The island played an important part in the war because its two airstrips provided landing sites for damaged B-29s and allowed fighter planes to cover the bombers during their raids on Japanese cities.

Associated Press photographer Joe Rosenthal captured the best-known picture of the war when he caught the image of a group of soldiers raising the American flag. The familiar photograph earned Rosenthal a Pulitzer Prize and is the basis for the U.S. Marine Corps War Memorial in Washington, D.C.

In a similar way, God has raised a banner over believers. His banner serves several purposes: It unites those who belong to him. It serves as a sign to our enemies to show where we stand. It energizes and empowers us for battle, even while signifying the final victory through his strength, protection, and aid.

Sometimes life gets confusing, and we get careless. We may run to a different banner without realizing it. Our allegiance shifts to the world, or self, or even the enemy of our soul. If we continually experience defeat, it may be because the wrong standard is over us. Isaiah 11:10 identifies God's banner of salvation as "the heir to David's throne," Jesus Christ. In the midst of life's battles, we need to make sure we choose his banner to rally under.

February 24

* * *

For everything there is a season, a time for every activity under heaven.
ECCLESIASTES 3:1

Mardi Gras (French for "Fat Tuesday") marks the final day before Lent, a forty-day period of self-denial. The date for Mardi Gras varies from year to year, always falling between February 3 and March 9. The holiday is also called Shrove Tuesday or carnival and usually refers to the much longer period of celebrations leading up to Mardi Gras. It is seen as the last opportunity for revelry and indulgence in food and drink before Lent.

Modern carnival traditions date back to the Middle Ages in Europe as part of the ritual calendar of the Roman Catholic Church. The city of New Orleans hosts the most well-known celebration in the United States. Spectacular parades begin twelve days before Mardi Gras featuring colorful floats, pageants, elaborate costumes, masked balls, and dancing in the streets. The holiday draws more than three million people and generates about a billion dollars for the city.

Solomon wrote that there is a time for everything, "a time to cry and a time to laugh. A time to grieve and a time to dance" (Ecclesiastes 3:4). God planned festivals and regular times of celebration for Israel. Jesus performed his first miracle at a wedding reception and often attended dinner parties. The Bible also teaches that there are appropriate times for fasting and periods of self-denial for the purpose of prayer (concerning spiritual warfare and growth).

What the Bible does not promote is extremes. We are frequently warned against gluttony, drunkenness, and sensuality. On the other hand, Paul explains that religious prohibitions and human traditions are only superficial and have no power to restrain our sinful urges (Colossians 2:23). Our challenge is to live a well-balanced life, as Jesus did, combining self-denial and social interaction, always for God's glory. Then whether we are feasting or fasting, every day will be a celebration.

In what areas of your life do you need to be more balanced?

February 25

* * *

*Each one must do just as he has purposed in his heart, not grudgingly or under
compulsion, for God loves a cheerful giver.*

2 Corinthians 9:7, NASB

In its early history, our nation relied mainly on tariffs on imported goods to provide government funding. The costs of the Civil War prompted the first income tax in 1861. This tax was repealed in 1872, but the concept didn't disappear. In 1894, as part of a tariff bill, Congress enacted a two-percent tax on incomes over four thousand dollars. The Supreme Court declared the tax unconstitutional.

In 1909, Congress again attached a provision for an income tax to a tariff bill. Opponents hoped to kill the idea for good by proposing a constitutional amendment enacting such a tax. They were surprised when state after state ratified the bill; the sixteenth amendment took effect on February 25, 1913. At that time, because of generous exemptions and deductions, less than one percent of the population paid income taxes, at the rate of one percent of net income.

God's guidelines for funding his work differ significantly from the government's. In the Old Testament, the Israelites were required to give a tenth, along with all the prescribed offerings and sacrifices. The New Testament introduces a new giving plan. Everyone is to prayerfully decide what to give back to God. The attitude is more important than the amount. He wants us to give freely, not reluctantly or because we feel forced to give.

Paul advises us to remember, however, that anyone who sows sparingly will reap sparingly (2 Corinthians 9:6). Since God owns everything and has ultimate control over our finances, we can never give too much to him. He will always provide for our needs. As long as we give to God with a sincere and willing heart, our budget will never be taxed—except by the sixteenth amendment.

February 26

* * *

Can anything ever separate us from Christ's love?
ROMANS 8:35

The Grand Canyon National Park was established in February 1919 and receives about four million visitors a year. This park, in northern Arizona, contains the world-famous Grand Canyon, which was carved out by the Colorado River. The great chasm is 277 miles long, about 5,000 feet deep, and up to 18 miles wide. The entire canyon is extremely beautiful and contains towering buttes, spectacular mesas, and deep valleys. .

The northern rim of the canyon is on average 1,200 feet higher than the southern rim. Such extreme variations in elevation from the canyon depths to the northern rim create four distinct zones of climate and plant life. The southern rim is sparsely covered with juniper and piñon trees, while dense forests of pine, fir, spruce, and aspen grow on the colder northern rim.

The vastness of the Grand Canyon is nothing compared to the gulf between God and humans caused by Adam and Eve's disobedience. In that instant, sin opened up an infinite chasm separating God and the people he created and loves. We became alienated from God because his holy nature cannot be in the presence of sin. All the Old Testament sacrifices and all our good works are not able to close the gap.

Such an infinite chasm could be bridged only by the infinite love of God. He provided his Son's death on a cross to reach across the gulf carved out by our sin and to bring us close to him. Once we accept his gift of salvation, he holds us in his unyielding grip that can never be loosened by anything—not death nor life, not angels nor demons, not fears for today nor worries about tomorrow, not even the powers of hell (Romans 8:38). In his grip is a grand place to be.

February 27

* * *

The LORD comforts his people.
ISAIAH 49:13, NIV

T he teddy bear was introduced to America in February 1903. The toy got its name from an editorial cartoon in the *Washington Post*. President Theodore (Teddy) Roosevelt was helping settle a border dispute between Mississippi and Louisiana. While on a bear hunt, he found a wounded cub and ordered its mercy killing. The cartoon, called "Drawing the Line in Mississippi," incorporated both the state-line dispute and the bear hunt.

Although there is disagreement over who was first, one popular story says that Morris Michtom made the first official toy called the teddy bear. His wife, Rose, made toy bears for their candy and novelty store in Brooklyn, so Michtom sent one to Roosevelt, who granted permission to use the teddy-bear name. Michtom and a company called Butler Brothers began to mass-produce the toy, which soon became a universal symbol of comfort and reassurance.

Isaiah recognized that our greatest source of comfort is God. When we are hurt, worried, or frightened, we naturally want a family member or friend to reassure us. But God offers powerful comfort no human can ever match. Sometimes he leads us to a Scripture that speaks directly to our situation. Sometimes he soothes our spirit with a renewed sense of his presence and provision. Or he may send practical help through circumstances or other believers.

Paul explained to the church at Corinth that God comforts us in all our troubles and sorrows so we can comfort others (2 Corinthians 1:4). God's comfort is meant to be passed on when others need it. The more we suffer for Christ, the more God will pour out his comfort through Jesus Christ (2 Corinthians 1:5). Then later it will be our turn to share that encouragement with others and help them endure as they go through similar trials.

How have you experienced God's comfort in times of trouble?

February 28

* * *

You do not belong to yourself, for God bought you with a high price.
So you must honor God with your body.
1 CORINTHIANS 6:19-20

Since 1987, the National Eating Disorders Association (NEDA) has designated the last week of February as National Eating Disorders Awareness Week. NEDA is a nonprofit organization working to prevent eating disorders by increasing public awareness of the problem and by promoting healthy eating habits and a healthy body image.

An estimated five to ten million people in the United States, mostly women, suffer from eating disorders, which include anorexia nervosa, bulimia nervosa, and binge eating. Eating disorders are associated with serious physical health consequences including heart disease and heart failure, kidney failure, gastric rupture, peptic ulcer, gall bladder disease, diabetes, and premature death. Psychological problems include depression, substance abuse, and suicide.

It seems impossible to escape the influence of our society's unhealthy obsession with body size and weight. In our Barbie world, even preschool girls sometimes worry about being too heavy. Girls and women with eating disorders often have a false image of themselves. When they look in the mirror, they see a fat person rather than an unnaturally thin person who is damaging her health.

God created us in his own image (Genesis 1:26-27). Our body has been marred by sin like everything else on earth, but it is still precious to him. Not only did God create us, he bought us back with a high price—the death of Jesus Christ. Our body does not really belong to us. Although our earthly body is temporary, we honor God by taking good care of it. To see our true image, we need to look in the mirror of God's Word, not the mirror on the wall.

February 29

* * *

People who accept discipline are on the pathway to life,
but those who ignore correction will go astray.

PROVERBS 10:17

Under the Julian calendar instituted in 46 B.C., every fourth year was a leap year, based on the belief that Earth orbited the sun every 365.25 days. Since the earth's actual orbital period is 365.24219 days, the calendar eventually got out of sync with the seasons. The Gregorian calendar, adopted in 1582, made just one small correction: A leap day is added to the calendar once every four years except for century years not exactly divisible by 400.

A "common year," any year that is not a leap year, is made up of fifty-two weeks and one day. Because of the extra day, a given date of the year will fall on the next day of the week the following year. But a leap year is fifty-two weeks plus two days. So a date during a leap year will skip ahead two days of the week instead of one. It "leaps" over a day of the week.

Sometimes we need to correct more than our calendar. We may begin to make little compromises or fail to notice subtle lies woven in with truth. Minor mistakes can add up and result in huge errors in our thinking, our behavior, and our doctrine. Before we know it, we're out of sync with God's Holy Spirit and with others.

One of the purposes of the Word is correction (2 Timothy 3:16). God doesn't mince words on this topic. The book of Proverbs says that anyone who hates correction is stupid (Proverbs 12:1, NIV), but whoever heeds correction is honored (Proverbs 13:18, NIV). Whether we need a small adjustment or a complete overhaul, God offers it in the pure truth found in his Word. We choose what we do with that correction—we can be stupid or be honored.

March 1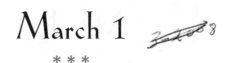

* * *

[Jesus said,] "As you sent me into the world, I am sending them into the world."
JOHN 17:18

In 1960, Senator John F. Kennedy challenged students at the University of Michigan to serve their country and the cause of peace by living and working in developing countries. As a result, the Peace Corps was established on this day in 1961. The Corps has sent out 178,000 volunteers to 138 countries. Volunteers have served in the areas of health, water sanitation, forestry, education, agriculture, environment, and business development.

As of April 2005, the Peace Corps had 7,733 volunteers and trainees in 72 countries. The organization has responded to the issues of the times by educating communities about the HIV/AIDS threat and helping schools develop computer skills. The Peace Corps strives to meet new challenges with innovation, creativity, determination, and compassion.

God has a plan to make the world a better place, too. His plan is to leave believers here to minister to hurting people so they can see his love, while we keep ourselves distinct from the world's sin and value system. Just before Jesus died, he prayed for his disciples and for everyone who would ever believe in him (John 17:14-20). He said that we are not part of this world any more than he is. Yet Jesus asked God not to take us out of the world, but to keep us safe from Satan while we are here doing his work.

It's hard to belong to a heavenly kingdom while living in an earthly one. Sometimes we wish we didn't have to get involved in the world around us with all its problems and messes. But if believers isolate themselves behind church walls, a multitude of unsaved people will miss seeing Christ. Our challenge is to be a blessing to the world without being corrupted by it. Jesus called us "the salt of the earth" (Matthew 5:13). To be effective salt, we have to be sprinkled over our earth.

March 2

* * *

[Jesus said,] "Keep on knocking, and the door will be opened."
LUKE 11:9

S chools across the country participate each year in the National Education Association's "Read Across America" campaign to honor the March 2 birthday of the best-selling children's author in the world. Born in Massachusetts in 1904, Theodor Seuss Geisel studied English literature and then worked as a cartoonist until 1937, when he wrote and illustrated his first children's book under the pen name Dr. Seuss.

Twenty-seven publishers rejected *And to Think That I Saw It on Mulberry Street* before it was printed. Before his death in 1991, Geisel, writing as Dr. Seuss, created about forty books filled with made-up creatures, simple rhymed text, and nonsense words, including the first-grade reader *The Cat in the Hat.* In 1984, Geisel received a special Pulitzer Prize citation for his lifetime contribution to the education and enjoyment of American children and their parents.

Theodor Geisel knew about persistence. Jesus taught that persistence is vital in prayer by sharing a parable about a man who wanted to borrow bread from a friend (Luke 11:5-10). The friend wouldn't get out of bed until the man pestered him by continuing to knock at his door. Unlike the friend in the story, God is a loving Father who delights in supplying our needs.

Sometimes, though, God doesn't answer our requests immediately. But he knows best, and his timetable is different from ours. Sometimes he delays answering to help us learn to depend more fully on him. When it seems as though our prayer is not answered, we need to examine our motives and make sure that our request is in line with God's will. Then we can keep on asking until the blessing is granted.

Are you persistent in prayer even when you feel like giving up?

March 3

* * *

*The man without the Spirit does not accept the things that come from
the Spirit of God, for they are foolishness to him, and he cannot understand them,
because they are spiritually discerned.*

1 CORINTHIANS 2:14, NIV

Born near Springfield, Massachusetts, in 1866, Anne Sullivan suffered a childhood illness that left her nearly blind, but surgeries in 1881 and 1887 restored most of her vision. In March 1887, Sullivan traveled to Alabama to serve as governess to six-year-old Helen Keller, who was blind, deaf, and mute from an illness she had contracted at the age of nineteen months.

With touch as her only means of communication, Keller had become an ill-tempered, undisciplined child. Within a month, Sullivan taught Keller that things had names by spelling out words on Keller's hands. Keller's rapid progress after this breakthrough and her gifted intelligence gained national attention. Sullivan accompanied Keller as she attended school, graduated from college, and began lecturing worldwide.

Until Anne Sullivan taught her to communicate, Keller could not make sense of the world around her by relying only on the sense of touch. In 1 Corinthians 2:10-16, the apostle Paul explains that unbelievers are the same way. If people don't have God's Spirit in them, they lack spiritual discernment and the spiritual world doesn't make sense to them. They find believers and spiritual truths beyond their comprehension.

Once we receive God's Spirit, a new world opens up to us. We understand the Bible as if reading it for the first time. Songs and spiritual truths take on new meaning. We need to remember, though, what it was like when we were spiritually blind, deaf, and mute. We should be sensitive to the fact that when we share the gospel with unbelievers, it will seem foolish to them until the Holy Spirit breaks through and communicates the truth to them.

March 4

* * *

*Then Jesus explained: "My nourishment comes from doing the will of God,
who sent me, and from finishing his work."*

JOHN 4:34

The American Dietetic Association (ADA) sponsored National Nutrition Week in March 1973. Because of the increased public interest in the subject of nutrition, in 1980 the ADA expanded National Nutrition Week to a month-long observance. National Nutrition Month is an information and education campaign with activities designed to focus attention on the importance of making wise food choices and developing sensible eating and exercise habits.

The campaign also promotes the ADA as a valuable source for current, scientifically based information on food and nutrition issues. The ADA is the world's largest organization of food and nutrition professionals; the goal of the organization is to promote optimal nutrition and well-being for all people.

God provided the Israelites with the perfect food, the optimal nutrition, to sustain them while they wandered in the desert for forty years. Each evening God rained down manna from heaven, which the Israelites gathered and made into cakes (Exodus 16). Jesus later identified himself as the "true bread that came down from heaven" that gives eternal life to anyone who eats it (John 6:58).

Once when his disciples were urging him to eat, Jesus told them that he had food they didn't know anything about. He explained that his nourishment came from doing God's will and finishing his work (John 4:32-34).

Every day we make choices about our physical food *and* our spiritual food. If we feed on a steady diet of junk food, the result is physical weakness and poor health. If we fill our life with empty activities and our mind with worldly ideas and values, we will grow spiritually weak. Drawing nourishment from Jesus and doing his will is the authentic recipe for optimal health and well-being.

How are you nourishing your spirit?

March 5

* * *

Where can I go from Your Spirit? Or where can I flee from Your presence?
PSALM 139:7, NKJV

I n March 1930, astronomers at Lowell Observatory in Arizona announced the discovery of a ninth planet in our solar system, which they named Pluto. In 1915, American astronomer Percival Lowell had predicted the location of an unknown planet. After his death, astronomers continued his work with more powerful telescopes and confirmed the existence of the distant planet. At 2.7 billion miles from Earth, Pluto appears as a dim speck of light in even our most powerful telescopes.

Pluto is the most distant planet from the sun, almost forty times farther away from the sun than is Earth. During the day, Pluto receives only 1/1500th the intensity of sunlight that Earth receives. It is one of the coldest places in our solar system. Pluto takes nearly 249 years to make one trip around the sun, its long, looping orbit taking it above and below the paths of the other planets.

God's Spirit fills not just the heavens and the earth, but all the solar systems, including the coldest, darkest, most distant planets. David described God's omnipresence beautifully in Psalm 139. David found comfort that there was no place where he could escape from God's presence. If David went up to heaven or down to the place of the dead, God was there (v. 8). If he could "ride the wings of the morning" or live by the farthest oceans, even there God would guide and support him (vv. 9-10).

Sometimes we go through cold, dark places in life and feel we are far away from God. We may not sense his presence or see him working in our life, but that doesn't mean he isn't there. There are no circumstances that can take us out of the reach of God's comforting, nurturing hands—even when our life takes a long, looping orbit.

March 6

* * *

Do not conform any longer to the pattern of this world,
but be transformed by the renewing of your mind.
ROMANS 12:2, NIV

In 1943, rubber shortages during World War II led to the invention of Silly Putty, a classic American toy. When the government searched for something plentiful to use in developing a synthetic rubber, researchers began working with silicone. An inventor at General Electric added a little boric acid to silicone oil, and a gooey, bouncy substance resulted. It didn't work as a substitute for rubber, but after the war a manufacturer marketed it to the public as a toy called Silly Putty in March 1950.

Apollo 8 astronauts used Silly Putty to stabilize their tools in the zero gravity environment of space, storing it in sterling silver eggs. The toy still sells well today, with manufacturer Binney & Smith producing twenty thousand eggs of Silly Putty a day. The substance can be stretched, shaped into any form, rolled into a ball and bounced, or pressed on pictures and newsprint to make impressions.

The apostle Paul warns believers against conforming to this world (Romans 12:2). The verse gives the idea of being pressed into a pattern or mold. Our culture tries to shape us according to current ideas, attitudes, and lifestyles. Even though we have the Holy Spirit in us, we can end up looking and living like carbon copies of everyone around us.

God calls us to be nonconformists, but not just on the outside. By actively pursuing prayer, Bible study, service, and fellowship with other believers, we will be renewed on the inside. Then we will be able to discern and obey God's will, and our life will be transformed day by day. We can't afford to be passive. If we don't let God transform our thinking, then we'll be like putty in the world's hands—and that's worse than silly.

What or whom are you allowing to shape your attitudes and lifestyle?

March 7

* * *

Humble yourselves before God. Resist the devil, and he will flee from you.
JAMES 4:7

When Adolf Hitler became chancellor of Germany in January 1933, he was determined to overturn the military and territorial provisions of the Treaty of Versailles. He also began to create a German empire in Europe. Germany had engaged in secret rearmament before the Nazi Party seized power and then began expansion afterward. Hitler reestablished military conscription in March 1935, in open violation of the treaty.

In the Treaty of Locarno, Germany had agreed to honor the inviolability of its borders with France and Belgium and the demilitarization of the Rhineland. However, on March 7, 1936, Hitler violated this agreement when German armed forces crossed into the Rhineland. France and Great Britain condemned Hitler's actions but did not intervene. Someone observed that even Hitler was amazed that he met no resistance.

Believers are urged several times in the New Testament to resist the devil. The more we give in to his temptations, the more he will pursue us. James gave the key to successfully resisting Satan: We have to first humble ourselves before God. Satan works hard to obstruct our humility and submission to God. When we submit to God, we have power to recognize and resist Satan's influence.

God is not the only one who has his eye on us. The apostle Peter warned that the devil prowls around like a lion, looking for someone to devour (1 Peter 5:8). We must constantly guard against attacks from him. We have God's promise of strength and his provision of armor to stand against the devil. There is no excuse for letting Satan and his army invade the borders of our soul.

March 8

*** * ***

Our old sinful selves were crucified with Christ so that
sin might lose its power in our lives.
ROMANS 6:6

J ohn Dillinger committed his first armed robbery in 1924. After his release from prison in 1933, Dillinger and his gang committed a string of crimes over a period of thirteen months, robbing banks and holding up police stations to free captured gang members. J. Edgar Hoover labeled Dillinger "public enemy number one."

Dillinger's notoriety increased in March 1934, when he broke out of a heavily guarded jail in Crown Point, Indiana, where he was awaiting trial for murder. Dillinger used a mock gun carved out of wood to take two of his keepers hostage. He then locked up the warden and slipped past the turnkey and one of the national guardsmen who had been stationed there to prevent his escape. Dillinger made off through a side door and drove away in the sheriff's car—accomplishing his daring escape with a fake weapon.

In contrast, since believers have died with Christ, sin no longer has to control us. Our sinful nature was put to death with him, so our physical body need no longer be ruled by corrupt, evil desires and tendencies. Yet even though its power is broken, the old nature still struggles to get the upper hand. In relation to our soul, our sinful nature is our "personal enemy number one."

To remain free from sin's power, we need to have the attitude that we are dead to sin. Every day we have to choose to not let sin control the way we live and dedicate ourselves to doing what glorifies God (Romans 6:11-14). Sin may cause us trouble, but it can never take us hostage again unless we let it. When our old, sinful nature tries to overpower us, we need to remember that it has only what power we give it—and any weapon it has is no more dangerous than a fake gun.

When have you allowed sin to overpower you?

March 9

* * *

Set up road signs; put up guideposts. Mark well the path by which you came.

JEREMIAH 31:21

B efore the 1920s, the U.S. government had little involvement in interstate roads. Boosters selected a route over existing roads, chose a colorful name, and formed an association to promote the trail and collect dues from towns and businesses along the way. By the mid-1920s, trail associations had named over 250 routes, including the Dixie Overland Highway (Savannah to San Diego) and the Yellowstone Trail (Boston to Seattle).

As the number of trails increased, they caused increasing problems. Many times, the trail associations routed trails through dues-paying cities instead of creating the shortest route for motorists. And many trails overlapped, causing confusion. In 1917, Wisconsin was the first state to adopt a uniform road-numbering system. In March 1925, the American Association of State Highway Officials began plans for a numbered highway system for the entire country.

When the Israelites entered the Promised Land, God showed them what road to follow. It was numbered one through ten. Moses had relayed the Ten Commandments and then urged the Israelites to stay on the path that God had commanded so they would live long and prosperous lives (Deuteronomy 5:33). Israel rebelled, but God promised to teach the Israelites how to live if they returned to him. Whether they turned to the right or left, they would hear a voice saying, "This is the way you should go" (Isaiah 30:21).

David often asked God to lead him in the right path and show him which way to turn (Psalm 5:8). He knew that he couldn't discern God's path of truth on his own. God's Word gives us clear-cut directions for what path in life to take. His Holy Spirit guides us and helps us stay on the right road. We may make mistakes that lead to temporary detours, but we have no excuse for getting lost.

March 10

* * *

I plead with you to be of one mind, united in thought and purpose.
1 Corinthians 1:10, NLT-1

I n astronomy a syzygy occurs when three celestial bodies within a solar system are situated along a straight or nearly straight line. The word *syzygy* is Greek for "yoked together." People generally use the term in the context of the sun, the Earth, and either the moon or a planet. Solar and lunar eclipses are dramatic results of syzygy. Often people use the word to describe interesting configurations of planets. On this day in 1982, a syzygy occurred when all nine planets aligned on the same side of the sun.

Yoking together a diverse group of people with different backgrounds, personalities, and opinions makes for some interesting configurations, and sometimes divisions, in the church. When Paul listed the results of following the desires of the sinful nature, he included divisions along with idolatry and sexual immorality (Galatians 5:20). He pleaded with the believers at Corinth to stop arguing and to strive for harmony. Divisions and disagreements hamper the church's ministry and hurt its witness to the world.

In one of his final prayers, Jesus prayed for unity among believers (John 17:21). The prayer applies to believers within a local church and to relationships between churches. Jesus didn't mean that we should tolerate false teaching or heretical doctrine. But we should not let personal opinions or petty disagreements drive a wedge between us and interfere with our working toward the common goal of showing Christ to the world. When we focus on our commitment to the saving power and lordship of Jesus Christ, then all members of the body will be aligned.

March 11

* * *

The orchards and fields of my people will yield bumper crops.
EZEKIEL 34:27

In honor of John Chapman, who died in March 1845, we know March 11 as "Johnny Appleseed Day." Although "Johnny Appleseed" is known primarily as a folk hero in novels, stories, and poems, Chapman was a dedicated nurseryman. He helped pave the way for nineteenth-century pioneers by planting a series of apple nurseries from the Allegheny Mountains to Ohio and beyond. Chapman eventually owned about 1,200 acres of orchards.

Several distinctive characteristics led to the "Johnny Appleseed" legend of a primitive man: Johnny's love for the wilderness, his affinity with animals, his knowledge of medicinal herbs, his devotion to the Bible, his harmony with the Indians, and his eccentric appearance. On his westward travels, Chapman sold or gave away thousands of seedlings to pioneers. Acres of productive orchards soon became a memorial to the real man and his dedication.

Jesus commented about fruit trees when he was teaching a crowd on a mountainside. He said that a good tree doesn't produce bad fruit, and a bad tree doesn't produce good fruit. The way we identify a tree or a person is by the kind of fruit produced (Matthew 7:18-20). We can judge the character of people by inspecting their fruit, or their deeds.

Jesus said that his true disciples produce much lasting fruit that brings glory to the Father (John 15). How can we produce this lasting fruit? We died to the power of the law and sin when we died with Christ on the cross. Now that we are no longer controlled by our old sinful nature, we are able to produce good fruit—or genuine good deeds—for God (Romans 7:4). With his help we can have a bumper crop year-round.

March 12

* * *

*I am certain that God, who began the good work within you, will continue his work
until it is finally finished on the day when Christ Jesus returns.*

PHILIPPIANS 1:6

N ational Procrastination Week begins on the first Monday in March
and ends on Sunday. Of course, it's celebrated the following week.
The celebration furthers the cause of putting things off and promotes procrastination as a favorable aspect of life. National Procrastination Week has been
observed for approximately forty years.

In 1956, someone in Philadelphia, Pennsylvania, thought it would be
funny for an organization called the Procrastinators Club to postpone its first
meeting. An actual meeting became necessary because an announcement by
the Bellevue-Stratford Hotel caught the attention of the press. The Procrastinators Club of America has 14,500 members worldwide. There are members
in every country in Europe, as well as in Japan, Australia, Israel, New Zealand, and other countries.

Most of us are always in a rush, trying to accomplish more and more. On
the other hand, a lethargic approach to life leads to procrastination, which
results in missed opportunities. If we commit each day to God and let him
help arrange our schedule, we will accomplish what is truly important and
not be pressured by unfinished and half-finished projects.

How wonderful that God never procrastinates the way we do. Our life is
a grand project he has planned down to the last detail—to help us grow up
into the image of Christ and to use us to bring honor and glory to his name.
Because of God's faithfulness, we can be confident that he will complete the
work he started in us. Nothing in heaven or on earth can sidetrack him from
his plans. He will finish right on time.

March 13

✳ ✳ ✳

The whole law can be summed up in this one command:
"Love your neighbor as yourself."
GALATIANS 5:14

O n March 13, 1964, in Queens, New York, as twenty-eight-year-old Catherine ("Kitty") Genovese arrived home from work at approximately 3:20 a.m., a man attacked her in the parking lot of her apartment building. People in the nearby buildings turned some lights on, but the only response to her screams came from one man who shouted at her attacker. The attacker left but returned twice to beat and stab her, following her trail of blood into her building.

A neighbor finally called the police at 3:50 a.m. The police arrived within two minutes to find Genovese dead. Her neighbor admitted that he had phoned the police only after much thought and a phone call to a friend. "I didn't want to get involved," he said. Police discovered that thirty-seven other neighbors had witnessed at least part of the half-hour stalking and stabbing. The case led social psychologists to research what became known as the "bystander effect."

On more than one occasion, Jesus reminded people to "love your neighbor as yourself." When someone asked Jesus, "Who is my neighbor?" he answered by telling a story about a man who was robbed and left half dead. A priest and then a Levite passed by the wounded man without stopping to help. Finally, a Samaritan bandaged the beaten man's wounds and took him to an inn, where the Samaritan paid the innkeeper to care for the wounded man. Jesus explained that the one who got involved, the Samaritan, was a neighbor to the man (Luke 10:29-37).

Jesus said loving our neighbor is equal in importance to the command to love God with all our heart, mind, soul, and strength (Mark 12:31). Loving our neighbor as ourself means more than helping when he or she is being attacked. It means caring for that person's best interests and being a source of good in his or her life. To do that, we *have* to get involved.

Has God placed someone in your life who needs a Good Samaritan?

March 14

* * *

The Holy Spirit produces this kind of fruit in our lives: love, joy, peace,
patience, kindness, goodness, faithfulness, gentleness, and self-control.
There is no law against these things!
GALATIANS 5:22-23

I n 1949, a reporter wanted to write a story about the "toughest guys" being sought by the Federal Bureau of Investigation. The FBI provided the names of ten wanted criminals, and the article was a hit. On this day in 1950, the agency debuted its "Ten Most Wanted Fugitives" list, posting it in public buildings. Today the Internet makes it possible to circulate the list all over the world in seconds.

In order to be on the list, a suspect must be considered extremely dangerous. The second criterion is whether or not publicity will likely assist in the apprehension of the fugitive. In the early days, the list mostly included burglars, bank robbers, and car thieves. Today, terrorists, serial murderers, organized crime figures, and international drug dealers dominate the list.

In contrast, Paul presents a "Nine Most Wanted" list of the kinds of fruit the Spirit produces (Galatians 5:22-23). After listing the evil acts that result from giving in to the desires of our sinful nature, he lists the fruit that comes from letting the Holy Spirit control our life. These nine characteristics should be cultivated and sought by every believer: love, joy, peace, patience, kindness, goodness, faithfulness, gentleness, and self-control.

People frantically chase love and joy but seldom catch them. Many value material success over faithfulness and kindness. Many people define goodness by worldly standards and lack peace. Our society often misinterprets gentleness and patience as being wimpy and weak-willed. For many people self-indulgence has replaced self-control. Yet a life demonstrating these nine traits of a renewed spirit gives a picture of Christ that can't be ignored. And that's what is most wanted in our world today.

March 15

* * *

*Even my best friend, the one I trusted completely, the one who shared my food,
has turned against me.*

PSALM 41:9

I n the ancient Roman calendar, each of the twelve months had an
"ides," the day intended to mark the full moon. The ides fell on the
fifteenth day in March, May, July, and October. In the other months, the ides
fell on the thirteenth. Since the solar calendar months and lunar months had
different lengths, the term lost its original purpose of marking the full moon.
We associate "ides" with March because of Roman emperor Julius Caesar's
assassination on this day.

In 44 B.C., Julius Caesar refused a crown, but he offended the republicans,
who opposed a monarchy, when he set up a statue of himself. As Caesar
entered the senate chamber on the Ides of March, sixty senators surrounded
him and attacked him with daggers. At first Caesar tried to defend himself,
but when he saw his friend Marcus Brutus with a knife, he gave up.

Scripture describes many examples of betrayal. David knew the pain of
betrayal. When Saul became jealous of David's popularity, he tried to kill
David. Later, when David was king, his son Absalom rebelled and tried to
destroy him and take over the kingdom. One of Jesus' disciples betrayed him.
Another disciple denied knowing Jesus, and most of the others deserted him
when soldiers arrested him.

Few things are more painful than having someone you love and trust
turn against you. But sometimes when we feel hurt by friends' words, the
friends are trying to help us in love. They may see some problem or sin in our
life that we're not aware of. In these cases, "wounds from a sincere friend are
better than many kisses from an enemy" (Proverbs 27:6). The words may be
painful at first, but they can turn out to be healing. Just because we feel a stab
of pain doesn't mean we are being stabbed in the back.

March 16

* * *

How you have fallen from heaven, O star of the morning, son of the dawn!
Isaiah 14:12, NASB

I n 1941, the Glenn Miller Orchestra performed the song "Chatta-nooga Choo Choo" in the movie *Sun Valley Serenade*. The record sold more than a million copies in less than three months. As a publicity stunt, RCA Victor took a master copy of the song and sprayed it with gold lacquer. The music company surprised Miller with the "gold record" award during a live radio broadcast.

Ten years later, the Recording Industry Association of America (RIAA) borrowed the idea of the Gold Record award and trademarked it. The bench-mark for a Gold Record is the sale of five hundred thousand copies of a single song or an album—a definite mark of success. The RIAA awarded the first Gold Record single to Perry Como in March 1958 for his recording of "Catch a Falling Star."

In Isaiah 14:12, the prophet uses the image of a falling star to represent failure rather than success. The verse refers to the downfall of the king of Babylon and Satan, who were both brought low by the same sin—pride. Nei-ther of them was satisfied with his lofty position. Both wanted to climb to the highest heavens and be like God (Isaiah 14:13-14). Neither of them fell alone. Babylon was destroyed along with its king. When Satan fell, one third of the angels joined him in his rebellion (Revelation 12:4).

We are all susceptible to pride. It starts out as a subtle self-centeredness. Pride doesn't seem as bad as sins such as adultery or murder. But if left unchecked, our focus shifts more and more off God and onto self, which is a form of idolatry. Proverbs 16:18 warns, "Pride goes before destruction, and haughtiness before a fall." Perhaps we should remind ourselves of that each day in a song: "If we think a star is our calling, pretty soon we'll be falling."

March 17

3-18-08
4-13-2010

* * *

May the grace of the Lord Jesus Christ, the love of God,
and the fellowship of the Holy Spirit be with you all.

2 CORINTHIANS 13:14

S aint Patrick's Day celebrates Ireland's patron saint and one of the most successful missionaries in history. Born in Britain near the end of the fourth century, sixteen-year-old Patrick was carried off as a slave by Irish raiders. Patrick served as a herdsman in Ireland for six years before escaping and returning home. After a dream called him to return to Ireland to preach the gospel, he spent years in study and preparation before traveling back to Ireland.

For thirty years Patrick converted the Irish people tribe by tribe, planting hundreds of churches before his death in approximately A.D. 460. Many people believe that Patrick's use of the shamrock to explain the Trinity led to its becoming the traditional symbol of Ireland.

Some want to dismiss the concept of the Trinity, yet the threefold nature of God is seen throughout the Bible. Genesis 1:1-2 shows that God and the Spirit were present at creation. John 1:1-3 reveals that Jesus also participated. When Jesus was baptized, the Holy Spirit took the form of a dove, while God the Father spoke from heaven (Matthew 3:16-17).

All three persons of the Trinity secured our salvation. The Father showed his love and mercy by giving us new life through the Spirit obtained by the Son's sacrifice (Titus 3:4-6). Our finite brains struggle to understand a God who is Three and One at the same time; now we only know things incompletely (1 Corinthians 13:9). Later we will understand completely (1 Corinthians 13:12); then knowledge of the Trinity will be as plain as the leaves on a shamrock.

March 18

* * *

You happily put up with whatever anyone tells you, even if they preach a different Jesus than the one we preach, or a different kind of Spirit than the one you received, or a different kind of gospel than the one you believed.

2 CORINTHIANS 11:4

O n this day in 1986, the United States Treasury Department announced plans to weave a clear, polyester thread into bills to thwart counterfeiters. Today, other measures being used to stop the illegal duplication of currency include holograms and a makeover of the portraits on each bill.

Counterfeiting is one of the oldest crimes in America. In the early days of our nation, banks designed and printed their own currency. Officials had difficulty distinguishing the thousands of counterfeits from the thousands of genuine banknotes. They hoped that the counterfeiting problem would be solved with the adoption of a national currency in 1863. However, it quickly became necessary for the government to take enforcement measures.

Counterfeiting is also a serious problem in the spiritual realm. Paul expressed shock that the Galatian Christians were turning away from God to follow a different teaching that only pretended to be the Good News. He called for a curse on anyone who preached a different gospel than the one they had accepted (Galatians 1:6-9).

The message that saves us from sin and serves as the basis for our faith is incredible but simple: Christ died for our sins, was buried, and rose from the dead (1 Corinthians 15:3-4). Although our methods for sharing the gospel change, there is no new and improved version. Today the gospel is watered down, added to, tweaked, and twisted—sometimes blatantly, sometimes subtly. We will be able to detect error only if we immerse ourselves in the pure truth of God's Word. That immersion will give us the training to be able to spot counterfeits and help take them out of circulation.

March 19

* * *

Then the dust will return to the earth, and the spirit will return to God who gave it.

ECCLESIASTES 12:7

The return of the swallows on March 19 to San Juan Capistrano, California, has been recorded since 1776. Located sixty miles southeast of Los Angeles, the city grew up around a mission founded there in the eighteenth century and named after St. John of Capistrano, a crusader. Although an earthquake ruined the mission church in 1812, the chapel is still in use daily.

The swallows return to the ruins of the church from their wintering grounds on March 19, although human pressures have reduced their numbers and make the date of their return less reliable. Tradition says they depart from California on October 23, the date of the death of St. John of Capistrano. Every March, people look for the swallows' return as a sign of spring.

God desired the spiritual return of the Israelites even when they turned their back on him and worshipped other gods. He urged them to respond to his discipline, repent of their sins, and return to him. Even after God scattered them among other countries, he promised to bring them back to Jerusalem if they would return to him and obey his laws (Nehemiah 1:9).

In the New Testament, Jesus tells a parable about a son who rebelled against his father's authority (Luke 15:11-32). The son realized his foolishness and sin after he ran out of money. When he returned home, he hoped to be received simply as a servant. Instead, his father welcomed him with joy and restored him to his position in the family. Sometimes believers wander away from God, either through rebellion or failure to nurture their faith. But if we are his children, there is nothing that can keep us from returning to our Father, if we come in repentance. We don't even have to wait until spring.

In what ways do you need to return to your Father?

March 20

* * *

Many women do noble things, but you surpass them all.
PROVERBS 31:29, NIV

I n March 1974, Wonder Woman first appeared on television in an ABC movie. Viewers gave the show a lukewarm response, but ABC later developed a series more faithful to the original comic books. *The New Original Wonder Woman* was a hit that ran on ABC for one season in 1975, before airing on CBS for two more seasons.

William Moulton Marston, creator of the systolic blood pressure test and a champion of women's causes, originated the Wonder Woman character. While employed as an educational consultant for Detective Comics (now known as DC Comics), Marston wondered why the line did not include a female superhero. The head of DC Comics was intrigued and told Marston to create a female comic-book hero—a "wonder woman."

The book of Proverbs has a lot to say about women, much of it in unflattering comments about a nagging wife or a seductive adulteress. But the last chapter seems to go to the other extreme with a picture of a superhuman wife and mother (31:10-31). This woman possesses every desirable character trait. She works from before dawn until late at night as both homemaker and businesswoman. She meets all her husband's and children's needs and also reaches out to the poor and needy.

It's not very likely that the Proverbs 31 "wonder woman" was one single woman. But she gives us a picture of the ideal we can all strive for—using all our gifts and talents to serve our family and our community, being a wise steward of our assets, and making choices that grow our integrity and character. Verse 30 shows that the worth of a woman is not in charm or beauty as our culture thinks, but in fearing the Lord. That will make a wonder out of any woman—or man.

March 21

* * *

Whether you eat or drink, or whatever you do, do it all for the glory of God.
1 CORINTHIANS 10:31

J ohann Sebastian Bach was born on this day in 1685 into a German family that produced at least fifty-three prominent musicians over seven generations. Johann gained public admiration as an organist, but his musical compositions received little notice until the mid-nineteenth century. Though skilled in a wide range of musical forms, many consider Bach to be the greatest genius of baroque music.

Bach believed that he could serve God through his music, whether he was employed as a church organist or appointed as director of chamber music at the court of Prince Leopold. Bach often wrote *I.N.J.*, for the Latin words meaning "In the Name of Jesus," on the manuscripts of even his secular compositions.

We often think of our life as being divided into sacred and secular compartments. We may have special clothes and activities reserved for Sundays. We may even have a special "holy" personality that disappears when Monday morning comes. If we're busy with a full-time job and a family, we may feel guilty that we have no time for ministry.

If Christ is living in us, we have no need to separate the sacred and the secular. Even everyday aspects of our life can reflect his holiness. When we carpool kids on Monday morning, we are serving him as much as when we lead worship music on Sunday. The lawyer's or truck driver's career is no less sacred than the minister's or missionary's vocation, if each person has committed his or her work to the Lord. If our goal is to glorify God, then every activity of every day, whether we're cleaning a bathroom or writing a cantata, should be signed *I.N.J.*

March 22

* * *

I have discarded everything else, counting it all as garbage,
so that I could gain Christ.

PHILIPPIANS 3:8

T rash disposal became a crisis on Long Island in the 1980s when officials discovered that landfills were contaminating the area's ground-
water. Businessman Lowell Harrelson suggested transferring Long Island's
trash to southern landfills. So on March 22, 1987, the barge *Mobro* left New
York Harbor carrying 3,186 tons of garbage from the town of Islip.

A number of states—along with Mexico, Belize, and Cuba—barred the
Mobro from docking. The loaded barge became a symbol to groups concerned
about the environmental problems of waste disposal. The *Mobro* traveled six
thousand miles before being towed back to New York Harbor on May 16.
After sitting four months in Brooklyn's Gravesend Bay, officials decided to
burn the trash and bury the ash at the Islip landfill.

The apostle Paul considered everything to be worthless garbage compared with the priceless gain of knowing Christ Jesus as Lord. Before he met
Jesus, Paul put his confidence in his standing as a Jew. Born into a pure-
blooded Jewish family, he was a zealous Pharisee who meticulously obeyed
the law. After experiencing Christ, Paul trusted in him alone for salvation
and discarded the other works as rubbish (Philippians 3:4-9).

Isaiah calls the righteous acts that we regard with pride as nothing but
filthy rags (Isaiah 64:6). Even though Jesus Christ gave up his life to secure our
salvation, sometimes we focus on our own performance or ability to follow
rules. We obsess over how much time we spend doing things such as attending
church activities or studying the Bible. Or we begin to take pride in the things
we have given up. If we could see our own efforts at goodness next to Christ's
sacrifice, it would look like a barge piled with tons of smelly garbage.

What are you depending on for your salvation?

March 23

* * *

No one lights a lamp and then puts it under a basket. Instead, a lamp is placed on a stand, where it gives light to everyone in the house.
MATTHEW 5:15

I n March 1960, American physicist Theodore H. Maiman received a patent for the first laser, a device producing a powerful beam of light that can travel over long distances or be focused to an extremely small diameter. The special qualities of laser beams make them ideal for a wide variety of functions: They are narrow, they spread little, and they can be focused very precisely. A tightly focused beam can drill two hundred holes on a spot as small as the head of a pin. A large laser system can trigger a small nuclear reaction.

Since the early 1970s, the field of laser technology has exploded. Lasers function in equipment in homes, offices, hospitals, factories, and libraries. The capacity of lasers to record, store, and transmit information has led to a new era in communications and computer technology. Today the laser is one of our most versatile and valuable tools.

Jesus told his followers that they were like lamps on a stand, shining for everyone to see. Just as people don't light a candle or lamp and then hide it, God doesn't put his light within us so we can keep it hidden away. We are to be open about sharing our Christian experience and knowledge of his Word. The power of the gospel should light up our life so that others can see God's love and truth.

Our focus in living a holy lifestyle is not to draw attention to ourselves but to direct people's eyes to God. We should let our good deeds shine so that people will see them and praise our heavenly Father, instead of us (Matthew 5:16). We may feel like we are giving off a tiny, feeble beam, but in a dark world a feeble light can set off a powerful reaction.

March 24

* * *

Those who oppress the poor insult their Maker, but helping the poor honors him.
PROVERBS 14:31

B orn in 1910 in Skopje, Macedonia (the former Yugoslavia), Agnes Gonxha Bojaxhiu (Mother Teresa), the daughter of an Albanian grocer, took her vows as a nun on this day in 1937. In 1946, Sister Teresa received her "call within a call," which she considered divine inspiration to leave the convent and devote herself to the poor and the sick. She moved into the slums she had observed while teaching at a high school in Calcutta, India.

Mother Teresa founded the Order of the Missionaries of Charity. The group organized schools, operated centers to treat the blind and the aged, established a home to allow terminally ill people to die with dignity, and built a leper colony. When Mother Teresa died in 1997, missions of her order had spread to more than ninety countries and included four thousand nuns and hundreds of thousands of laypeople.

Mother Teresa left behind a life of comfort to live among the most rejected and destitute people in the world. She followed the example of Jesus, who voluntarily became poor for our sakes (2 Corinthians 8:9). She did what the rich young man in Matthew 19:16-22 was unable to do. When Jesus told him to sell all his possessions and give the money to the poor, the man went away sad.

Everyone isn't called to take a vow of poverty and give up all worldly wealth. We *are* all called to respond to the poor as God gives us opportunity. Proverbs 28:27 shows that shirking this responsibility is serious: "Those who close their eyes to poverty will be cursed." Proverbs 19:17 explains that when we help the poor, we are lending to God, and he will repay us. Charity is a call we all must answer.

March 25

* * *

You are the fountain of life.
PSALM 36:9

M any sources say that when Spanish explorer Juan Ponce de León set sail in March 1513, he was looking for the legendary Fountain of Youth. While serving as governor of Puerto Rico from 1509 to 1512, he had heard the Indians talk about an island called Bimini, the location of a miraculous spring that supposedly restored youth to those who bathed in or drank its water. When Ponce de León's political rivals removed him from office, King Ferdinand of Spain commissioned him to find and colonize the island of Bimini.

Ponce de León's search led him to explore several previously unknown islands in the area of the Bahamas. In April 1513, his expedition landed at Florida. Thinking it was another island, he claimed it for Spain and explored the eastern shoreline, the southern tip, and part of the western coast. He sailed to Spain in 1514 with news of his explorations but no information on the elusive Fountain of Youth.

Humanity has longed for immortality since the beginning of time. After the Fall, God gave us Jesus to provide eternal life. Jesus told the woman at the well that he had living water that bestowed eternal life (John 4:14). He scolded the Jewish leaders for searching the Scriptures for eternal life. Even though the Scriptures pointed to Jesus, the religious leaders refused to come to him to receive eternal life (John 5:39-40).

Today, many people are searching for ways to hold onto their youth, without giving a thought to the free gift of eternal life that God offers. He could not make the offer any plainer: "Anyone who believes in God's Son has eternal life" (John 3:36). Instead of hoping for a "fountain of youth," we should be leading others to the Fountain of everlasting life.

March 26

* * *

All who are victorious will be clothed in white.
I will never erase their names from the Book of Life.
REVELATION 3:5

I n March 1958, the patent office issued the first U.S. patent for a pencil with an attached eraser to Hyman L. Lipman of Philadelphia, Pennsylvania. He had his pencil manufactured in the usual way except that one-fourth of its length contained a small piece of glued-in India rubber. Trimming one end exposed the lead for writing, and cutting the other end exposed the India rubber.

People originally called the eraser a "rubber" because it was made of tree resin that "rubbed out" the marks of a pencil. Today's erasers are usually made from vinyl or synthetic rubber blended with pumice. Manufacturers blend raw material before putting it in a machine that forces it through a small hole to produce a long ribbon of eraser. They cut the lengths of eraser into three-foot strands, then chop the strands into bits called plugs with a rotary cutter.

When God judged the world's sin by sending the Flood, he "erased" all people and animals except for those on the ark (Genesis 7:23). Later, the entire nation of Israel came close to being blotted out of God's Book when the Israelites worshipped the golden calf (Exodus 32:32-33).

But what God likes to erase is sin. When David repented of his adultery with Bathsheba, he prayed for God to "blot out" the stain of his sin (Psalm 51:1). As believers under the New Covenant, we have God's promise that he will never again remember our sins once we repent, confess, and turn away from them (Hebrews 8:12). God doesn't necessarily remove all the consequences associated with our sin, but the sin itself no longer exists in his eyes. It's as though the sin has been rubbed out by a supernatural eraser.

What sins from your past still haunt you even though God has erased them?

March 27

* * *

I discipline my body like an athlete, training it to do what it should.
Otherwise, I fear that after preaching to others I myself might be disqualified.
1 CORINTHIANS 9:27

Since 2001, the National Athletic Trainers' Association (NATA) has designated March as National Athletic Training Month. The celebration has a twofold purpose: to increase awareness of the important role played by certified athletic trainers in schools, hospitals, corporations, the military, and sports settings and to educate the public on important health care issues.

A nonprofit organization, NATA represents and supports thirty thousand members of the athletic training profession through research and education. Certified athletic trainers specialize in the prevention, assessment, treatment, and rehabilitation of illnesses and injuries experienced by athletes and the physically active.

When Paul wrote to the Corinthians about the importance of discipline, he used the familiar imagery of rigorous gymnastic exercises among the Greeks that prepared them for the public games. Paul said that he lived a life of strict training, striving to practice self-control and subdue his natural inclinations. We can only be open to the Spirit's leading if we gain mastery over our corrupt nature. If we fail, it can mean our witness to the world becomes disqualified.

Paul used the same metaphor when he wrote to Timothy about spiritual training. While physical exercise is important for health, its value is short-term, for this life only. Training in godliness has much wider-reaching implications, bringing rewards in both this earthly life and our life to come (1 Timothy 4:8). The Greeks highly esteemed physical fitness, and it has become an obsession for many in our culture today. While it is important for Christians to have physical fitness to carry out God's work, it's much more important to be fit for heaven.

March 28

* * *

[Jesus said,] "Rejoice and be glad, because great is your reward in heaven."
MATTHEW 5:12, NIV

I n March 1967, ten thousand "hippies" flooded Central Park as they gathered for a "Be-In." Organizers plastered New York City with ads inviting everyone to "come as you are." Participants chanted "L-O-V-E" as they released balloons, bubbles, kites, and smoke rings into the air. Police reported no violence during the daylong celebration. Participants called the Be-In the joyful beginning of "the new epoch," a revolution of "human relations being developed within the youthful underground."

Organizers modeled the event after the "Human Be-In," also called "A Gathering of the Tribes," held the previous January at Golden Gate Park in San Francisco. More than twenty thousand people had attended the California event, which featured speakers and concerts. The press release called the event "a union of love and activism" for "Berkeley political activists . . . and San Francisco's spiritual generation and contingents from the emerging revolutionary generation."

God, too, invites people to come just as they are. But he doesn't want us to stay as we are. An encounter with Christ changes us forever. Once Jesus taught his followers the "Be-attitudes," listing the qualities in a person's life that bring spiritual blessing in this life and the next (Matthew 5:1-16). Some of the characteristics are in direct contrast with what our society thinks brings joy—Jesus applauded mourning, humility, and persecution. These conditions make us open to God's greatest blessings.

Jesus Christ was an activist. In three short years, he introduced a revolution in human relationships, with each other and with God. His radical teachings on love and forgiveness shook up all levels of society. Jesus didn't chant "L-O-V-E"; he lived it. His life of obedience to God and service to people showed us what a true child of God looks like. And that's the greatest generation to "Be-In."

March 29

* * *

*Please don't be so easily shaken and troubled by those who say
that the day of the Lord has already begun.*

2 THESSALONIANS 2:2, NLT-1

O n the night of March 29, 1848, both the American and the Canadian sides of Niagara Falls were silent—for the first time in recorded history. An ice jam formed on Lake Erie near Buffalo, New York, and blocked the water that flows along the Niagara River and over the falls. The next morning several thousand people gathered in the area to find the American falls slowed to a dribble and the Canadian falls stilled.

For many people, the sudden, eerie silencing of the falls caused great anxiety and fear. Believing that the world was coming to an end, many thousands attended special church services on both sides of the border. They were relieved when the ice jam broke apart the night of March 30, and the water flow returned to normal.

Paul wrote the second letter to the Thessalonians to clear up anxieties and misunderstandings about his teaching concerning the end times. He urged them to not be alarmed or fooled by those who claimed that the day of the Lord had already come. Although no one knows the timing of the return of Christ, that day will be preceded by recognizable events, such as a worldwide rebellion against God led by the Antichrist, who will exalt himself as God.

Throughout history there have been people who interpreted Scriptures and current events to predict a certain date for the end of the world. They have all been wrong. Believers should focus not on dates but on living holy, godly lives. Rather than being fearful, we are to look forward to the day when this world will come to an end (2 Peter 3:11-12). We can look forward by remembering that God is in control and that he has promised a new and better heaven and earth.

March 30

* * *

Heal me, O LORD, and I shall be healed.
JEREMIAH 17:14, NKJV

D octors' Day, celebrated March 30, commemorates the first use of anesthesia during surgery. Dr. Crawford W. Long used ether to painlessly remove a tumor from the neck of a patient in 1842. He continued to use ether but waited until 1849 to publish reports of his work. In 1846, William Morton, a dental surgeon, publicly demonstrated the use of ether in surgery. Although Morton received extensive publicity, doctors acknowledge Dr. Long as the first to use anesthesia during actual practice.

Eudora Brown Almond, wife of a physician, conceived the idea of a day of recognition for doctors. She chose March 30, to recognize Long's use of anesthesia in nearby Jefferson, Georgia. In 1933, Barrow County, Georgia, hosted the first celebration of Doctors' Day. The celebration grew in popularity, and Congress formalized the holiday in 1958 with a resolution from the House of Representatives and a congressional bill in 1990.

Those familiar with the Bible might remember that God was really the first to use anesthesia during surgery. He put Adam into a deep sleep before he removed a rib to make Eve (Genesis 2:21-22). When Jesus came to Earth, he healed people of all kinds of diseases wherever he went. He achieved his greatest cure, however, when he died on the cross to heal us of the fatal disease of sin (1 Peter 2:24).

All believers are to be involved in a healing ministry. The book of James instructs us to pray for one another's healing (5:16). Jesus taught that faith and healing go hand in hand, yet sometimes it's hard to know how to pray for someone who is suffering. But we can confidently pray for healing, knowing the outcome is in God's hands.

March 31

* * *

[Jesus said,] "We must quickly carry out the tasks assigned us by the one who sent us. The night is coming, and then no one can work."

JOHN 9:4

I n 1916, Germany and the United Kingdom put Daylight Saving Time (DST) into practice during World War I. The United States instituted DST on this day in 1918 in order to conserve fuel needed to produce electricity. Most areas reverted to standard time after the war. In 1942, the United States reinstated DST for the duration of World War II.

The Uniform Time Act of 1966 established a system of uniform DST throughout the country, except for states that voted to stay on standard time. Proponents of DST point out the reduction in energy consumption. Opponents claim that the benefit doesn't justify the adjustment of clocks twice a year and note that the disruption of sleep patterns in the spring corresponds to a spike in the number of serious auto accidents.

In the spiritual realm, this biannual changing of the clocks can serve as a reminder that we have a limited time on this earth. Jesus was keenly aware that he had only three years to carry out his earthly ministry. He tells his disciples that we need to be quick about carrying out the tasks assigned to us by God. Jesus made the most of his "daylight" and accomplished his mission before he died.

We live in the day of salvation when God's grace shines like the sun. We need to be about the business of bringing others into his Kingdom. But time is short. God has fixed the date, since the foundation of the world, when this present age will end. We don't know how brief our life will be. We must "redeem the time" by sharing the Redeemer with others until that day when we can no longer adjust our clocks to gain an extra hour.

April 1

* * *

Only fools say in their hearts, "There is no God."
PSALM 14:1

Many take advantage of April Fools' Day, or All Fools' Day, as a day for pranks and practical jokes. Some believe the origin of the holiday evolved as part of ancient spring festivals. Another common theory holds that the holiday began when countries adopted the Gregorian calendar in 1582, reformed from the Julian calendar, and the date for the New Year changed from April 1 to January 1. Without modern media, word spread slowly, and some people chose to ignore the change. Others called the reluctant changers "fools" and played practical jokes on them, such as giving them invitations to nonexistent parties.

People celebrate April Fools' Day in the United States, France, Great Britain, Germany, Canada, and other countries. The French call an April Fools' prank a *poisson d'avril* (April fish), and in Scotland it is an April gowk, or cuckoo. The usual practical jokes involve getting others to believe something that isn't true or sending them on a fool's errand.

The Bible has a lot to say about fools. Proverbs alone contains numerous verses that describe fools—that is, not people who lack intelligence but those who have character defects. Fools are quick-tempered, slanderous, unreliable, arrogant, and babbling. They feed on trash instead of truth. They despise their parents' correction and think doing wrong is fun. They have to be guided with a rod.

David cut to the chase in the first verse in Psalms 14 and 53 when he defined fools as those who don't believe in God. These people may be highly educated or have high IQs, but they live their life as if there is no God. As a result, they are not able to tell right from wrong. They rely on their own judgment, not realizing that to ignore God or deny his existence makes them fools—all year long.

April 2

* * *

They will reject the truth and follow strange myths.
2 Timothy 4:4, NLT-1

I n 1985, the Ringling Bros. and Barnum & Bailey Circus exhibited its most popular attraction—a "living unicorn." In April of that year, inspectors from the U.S. Department of Agriculture ruled that the unicorn was a goat with genetically engineered horn buds. When animal rights activists protested outside Madison Square Garden, the circus sent dozens of clowns to throw roses and chant, "I believe."

People have been fascinated with myths about unicorns for centuries. In the 1930s, a doctor from Maine "created" a unicorn. He transplanted the bits of tissue called horn buds from the sides of a calf's head to the middle of the skull, so that they touched each other. As the calf grew, the buds joined together and formed a single horn.

Paul warned Timothy that a time was coming when people would no longer listen to correct teaching and doctrine but would turn to strange myths. They would look for teachers who made them feel good instead of making them face the truth. We are definitely living in that time. Today, people take any kind of nonsense and promote it as spiritual.

Even some people claiming to be Christians perform "operations" on the truth. They take the idea of God and develop a belief system that doesn't demand anything of them. Others who claim to teach the Bible pull out a Scripture and transform it into something entertaining and pleasing but not doctrinally sound. But there is nothing more exciting than the story of a God who died in our place to give us an abundant life on Earth and then eternal life in a perfect place with him. Any other god is only a mythical creature.

April 3

* * *

Good news from far away is like cold water to the thirsty.
PROVERBS 25:25

R iders in the mail delivery service called the Pony Express could deliver mail on horseback from Missouri to California in ten days or less, compared to three weeks of travel by boat or stagecoach. The Pony Express operated from April 1860 until November 1861, with relays of men riding fast ponies to carry letters and small packages over a 1,966-mile trail between St. Joseph, Missouri, and Sacramento, California.

A California senator and a Missouri businessman collected four hundred fast horses and hired eighty riders, many of them teenagers. They set up 190 stations located ten to fifteen miles apart where riders could change horses in two minutes. A specially designed mailbag hung over the saddle, held by the rider's weight alone. Pony Express riders forwarded mail at the rate of more than two hundred miles per day. This era in history terminated when the transcontinental telegraph ended the need for the service.

God set up a relay system for delivering his Good News of love and forgiveness of sin. He sent prophets to preach the coming of a Savior. Then he sent the Savior, who went throughout cities and villages announcing the Good News about God's Kingdom (Matthew 9:35). After his death, Jesus' followers spread the news to far countries, having been scattered because of persecution.

Paul describes himself as a "special messenger" sent to bring the Good News to the Gentiles (Romans 15:16). Now it is our turn to take the message of salvation everywhere we go. But we are not working alone. Jesus said the gospel would be preached all over the world before the end comes. We all have a part to play in forwarding this greatest of news—until Jesus' return makes our service unneeded.

What role are you playing in spreading the Good News?

April 4

* * *

We were filled with laughter, and we sang for joy. And the other nations said,
"What amazing things the LORD has done for them."
PSALM 126:2

In 1976, Larry Wilde, director of the Carmel Institute of Humor and author of fifty-three books on the subject, initiated National Humor Month. He chose April because it begins with All Fools' Day, the weather is still bleak in many places, and taxes are due on April 15. According to Wilde, the purpose is "to heighten public awareness on how the joy and therapeutic value of laughter can improve health, boost morale, increase communication skills, and enrich the quality of one's life."

In 1979 Norman Cousins' book *Anatomy of an Illness* claimed that laughter was an essential part of his healing from cancer. Scientific research since then confirms that laughter can promote healing and relieve stress and burnout. Many tout the curative power of laughter as one of the most important medical discoveries of our time.

God has a sense of humor and wants his children to have one, as well. When God promised that Sarah would have a son when she was ninety and Abraham was a hundred years old, Sarah laughed in disbelief. A year later, she laughed in joy as she named her son Isaac ("he laughs"). She said, "God has brought me laughter. All who hear about this will laugh with me" (Genesis 21:6).

God has tried to show us that laughing and having a merry heart are like good medicine (Proverbs 17:22). Christians should laugh more than anybody. Our past is forgiven and our future is secure. We are protected and cherished by a wonderful God. As the Israelites returned from captivity in Babylon, they were so full of joy that other people took note. Perhaps if people saw Christians laughing more often they would want to know the God who gives us our joy.

April 5

* * *

In peace I will lie down and sleep, for you alone, O LORD, will keep me safe.
PSALM 4:8, NLT-1

T he National Sleep Foundation (NSF) sponsors National Sleep Awareness Week the first week in April to coincide with the return to Daylight Saving Time. The campaign highlights the importance of quality sleep for health, safety, and productivity. According to the NSF, before the invention of the lightbulb, Americans slept an average of 10 hours a night. The organization's 2005 polls indicate that, on average, Americans now sleep 6.8 hours on weeknights and 7.4 hours on weekend nights.

NSF polls show that 70 million Americans suffer from intermittent or chronic sleep problems, such as insomnia, sleep apnea, restless legs syndrome, narcolepsy, and daytime drowsiness. Sleep deprivation costs Americans an estimated $100 billion annually in lost productivity, medical expenses, and property damage. The National Highway Traffic Safety Administration estimates that sleepy drivers cause 100,000 crashes each year, resulting in more than 1,500 fatalities and 71,000 injuries.

Some people suffer from insomnia. The Tabernacle musician Asaph was too troubled to sleep when he wrote Psalm 77 (v. 4). Other people sleep too much. Proverbs contains many warnings that excessive love of sleep results in poverty (6:9-11; 19:15; 20:13; 24:33-34). Some people sleep at the wrong time. When Jesus was facing the horror of the cross, Peter, James, and John were unable to stay awake and keep watch with him for an hour as he had requested (Matthew 26:38-40).

While fleeing from his son Absalom, David was able to sleep peacefully because he trusted in God for his safety. Asaph found relief by meditating on God's wonderful works and deliverance—a good habit to form at night, when our problems look bigger. Many sleep disorders require medical treatment, but it helps to be aware that whether we are sleeping soundly or are awake with insomnia, God is watching over us. And he never sleeps (Psalm 121:3-4).

April 6

* * *

Everyone who competes in the games goes into strict training. They do it to get a crown that will not last; but we do it to get a crown that will last forever.

1 CORINTHIANS 9:25, NIV

I n 1894, French educator Pierre de Coubertin suggested that the Olympic Games of ancient Greece be restored as a way to contribute to a more peaceful world. As a result, the modern Olympic Games began in Athens, Greece, on this day in, 1896. About three hundred athletes from fewer than fifteen countries competed in forty-three events covering nine sports. In 2004, the Summer Olympics returned to Athens and included 202 countries with more than ten thousand athletes competing in twenty-eight different sports.

The ancient Olympic Games date from 776 B.C. and were held in the summer every four years in the sanctuary of Zeus at Olympia. Competitions included footraces, boxing, wrestling, long jumping, discus, and javelin throwing. Victors received crowns of wild olive. Roman emperor Theodosius I ended the Games around A.D. 393.

In order to be in top form for the Games, Greek athletes endured an unbelievably strict training regimen of exercise, personal discipline, and self-denial. Once they entered competition, they risked serious injuries from the rough sports. Christians, also, need to exercise their faith and develop self-discipline to live a life of godliness. We risk injury every time we contend with the world or with Satan in spiritual battle unless we are protected by prayer and the armor God has provided.

The comparison of the Games to the spiritual life ends with the prize. Greek athletes competed for a wreath that began to wither even before the athlete won the crown. Their reward was temporary; ours is eternal. We work for a prize that will never fade away—eternal life and a heavenly inheritance. When our competition is over, we will be rewarded with a crown that lasts forever, and we will receive it from the One who wore a crown of thorns for us.

April 7

***

Clothe yourselves with the Lord Jesus Christ,
and do not think about how to gratify the desires of the sinful nature.
ROMANS 13:14, NIV

I n April 1974, the streaking fad began on campuses in Florida and California and soon spread to colleges across the nation. Some students claimed they were expressing their "personal liberation." Others simply thought it was fun. Students running naked through public places became so commonplace that the shock value faded and the fad soon ended.

Streakers still occasionally show up at public events throughout the world. In the United States, an online casino has started to use streaking as a marketing tool, with the company's URL painted on the back of streakers who disrupt major sporting events. On a freezing day in 2004, three young men, after streaking in a Washington restaurant, discovered that a thief had stolen their car—with their clothes inside!

Hopefully, Christians don't do things like streak in public, but we sometimes forget that we need to "dress" our soul as well as our body. In Romans 13:12-13, Paul gives a list of specific sinful behaviors that believers must put aside. In the next verse he gives the secret to living a godly life with just a few words: "clothe yourself with the presence of the Lord Jesus Christ." *To be clothed with a person* was a common Greek phrase that meant "to take on the interests of someone, to imitate him, and to copy his spirit."

We were clothed with the righteousness of Christ at the time of our salvation. Now we must make the choice daily to clothe our spirit with the character of Christ. We do this by imitating his lifestyle of love and service, and by obeying his commands. In every decision we make, we try to conform to the qualities he modeled. As we pick out the right "clothing" day after day, people will begin to see more than a streak of godliness in us.

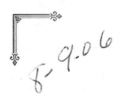

April 8

* * *

"The day is coming," says the LORD, "when I will make a new covenant
with the people of Israel and Judah."

JEREMIAH 31:31

One important part of President Franklin Roosevelt's New Deal was approved by Congress on this day in 1935. The Works Progress Administration (WPA) provided jobs in the construction of streets, bridges, highways, parks, and other public works projects designed to have long-range value. The WPA also created jobs for actors, musicians, writers, and artists. An estimated eight and a half million Americans found work through the WPA.

When Roosevelt became president in 1933, the Great Depression had brought business to a standstill and left one out of four workers unemployed. Many Americans had lost homes or farms, and panic had spread across the nation. As Roosevelt accepted the Democratic presidential nomination, he promised, "I pledge you, I pledge myself, to a new deal for the American people."

On the night of his crucifixion, Jesus inaugurated a new covenant based not on works but on grace. As he shared the Passover meal with his disciples, he called the wine the token of God's new covenant sealed by his blood, which he would pour out as a sacrifice (Luke 22:20). The old Mosaic covenant was now out of date and ready to be replaced by something new and far better (Hebrews 8:13).

The new covenant is possible because of Christ's death and the indwelling of the Holy Spirit in all believers. Now God's law is inside us, written on our heart and mind instead of stone tablets. Since the new covenant made Jesus our High Priest, we can approach God directly instead of going through earthly priests. The new covenant is eternal not temporary. It brings forgiveness instead of condemnation. When we observe communion, we are not just celebrating a "new deal," but the greatest deal ever offered.

April 9

***

Do not despise these small beginnings, for the LORD rejoices to see the work begin.
ZECHARIAH 4:10

R ay Kroc worked as the distributor of a machine that mixed five milk shakes at a time. When a business in California ordered eight of them, Kroc visited their hamburger stand. He found the McDonald brothers serving fifteen-cent hamburgers, ten-cent fries, shakes, and pies wrapped in paper, accompanied with plastic utensils. They filled orders in less than sixty seconds. The visit gave Kroc a vision of a nationwide chain of similar hamburger stands, and the first McDonald's franchise opened in Des Plaines, Illinois, in April 1955. That first day's revenues were $366.12.

Today, McDonald's is the world's leading food service retailer and serves forty-seven million customers every day. The corporation includes more than thirty thousand restaurants in 119 countries. When a McDonald's opened in Kuwait City in 1994, fifteen thousand customers lined up the first day. The line at the drive-thru was seven miles long.

In God's hands, too, small beginnings expand to great things. God grew an old man with a barren wife into a great nation that blessed the entire world. Jesus compared the Kingdom of God to a tiny mustard seed that grows into the largest tree in the garden and to yeast that expands bread dough. He multiplied a small lunch into an all-you-can-eat meal for thousands, with leftovers. His twelve disciples grew into a worldwide network of believers.

Sometimes our contribution to the Kingdom of God seems small and insignificant in our eyes. But humble beginnings do not mean that a ministry will not accomplish great things. When God gives us a vision, our part is to make a start and leave the results to him. In his hands, something small can grow into a "chain" of blessings.

What "small beginning" does God want you to offer him?

April 10

* * *

Now you can have sincere love for each other as brothers and sisters because you were cleansed from your sins when you accepted the truth of the Good News.

1 Peter 1:22, NLT-1

The tragic deaths of her brother and sister led Claudia A. Evart to found the Siblings Day Foundation, a nonprofit corporation working to promote the love of brothers and sisters and to establish a national day of recognition for siblings. Since 1996, twenty-two governors have signed state proclamations designating April 10 as Siblings Day.

Siblings Day serves as a reminder of the special bond between brothers and sisters and offers a chance to remember those who have passed away. And by telling their brothers and sisters they love and appreciate them, the siblings are strengthening family relationships.

When we accept Jesus as our Savior, God becomes our Father. That means we have a new family—a big family with lots of brothers and sisters. We have our local family within our church and our extended family throughout the world. When it comes to believers, there is no such thing as an only child. The bond shared by siblings who have shared a home and grown up together is a strong one. But the bond forged by a common faith in Christ is even more powerful.

Just like all parents, God wants his children to love one another. Just like all siblings, we sometimes argue and have trouble getting along. Relationships take work, but God is pleased when we nurture our connections with fellow believers and treat them like family. We are all growing up together. When we are with our brothers and sisters in Christ, we need to remember that we are related by blood—his blood—and we will share a home for all eternity.

April 11

* * *

My God will supply all your needs according to His riches in glory in Christ Jesus.
PHILIPPIANS 4:19, NASB

T he Revolutionary War left the American monetary system in disorder. Therefore, in 1789, the Constitution gave Congress the sole power to coin money and regulate its value. The Coinage Act, in April 1792, established the first U.S. federal mint in Philadelphia, Pennsylvania. The mint made ten-dollar gold coins called eagles, silver dollars, and other coins. Americans continued to use foreign coins along with the new currency until Congress passed a law in 1857 to remove all foreign coins from circulation.

Today, coins are minted in Philadelphia, Pennsylvania; in Denver, Colorado; and on a temporary basis, in San Francisco, California. Paper money is produced in Washington, D.C., at the Bureau of Engraving and Printing. Historians believe that coins were first made during the 600s B.C. in Lydia, a country in West Asia Minor. Gradually the use of coins spread throughout the rest of the world.

Paul thanked the Philippian believers for giving to him financially in his time of need. He promised that God would generously repay them by fully supplying their needs from his inexhaustible wealth. They could share in God's wealth because of their relationship with Jesus Christ, the channel of all spiritual blessings.

We think we can provide for our own needs, but all wealth is owned and regulated by God. We need to trust in his generosity and provision more than our job, our savings account, or the U.S. mint. God usually meets the needs of his children through other people. The only way to ensure that our own needs are met is to be obedient in sharing with others as God leads us. Then all kinds of physical and spiritual blessings will be in circulation.

Are you trusting God or your paycheck to meet your needs?

April 12

* * *

God's ways are as hard to discern as the pathways of the wind.
ECCLESIASTES 11:5, NLT-1

On the morning of April 12, 1934, weather surveyors at Mount Washington Observatory in New Hampshire recorded the highest velocity wind ever measured on the planet. The day before, a high-pressure system had forced a coastal storm inland. The barometer started to fall and the wind velocity began to climb. The "Big Wind" reached a speed of 231 miles per hour, and people commemorate the historic event each year.

Meteorologists consider Mount Washington one of the windiest places on Earth due to a unique combination of geographic and atmospheric conditions. Today, the observatory is a scientific and educational facility that records and disseminates weather information, conducts severe weather research, tests and develops instruments, and studies icing, cloud, and atmospheric phenomena.

In the Old Testament, wind played an important role in God's protection and deliverance of his people. He sent a wind to cause the floodwaters to recede to save Noah's family. One of the plagues that secured the Israelites' release from Egypt was a swarm of locusts brought by a wind. And God opened up the Israelites' escape path through the Red Sea with a strong east wind.

In the New Testament, wind is a symbol of God's Spirit working among his people. When Jesus appeared to his disciples after his resurrection, he breathed on them and said, "Receive the Holy Spirit" (John 20:22). Later, when the believers were filled with the Holy Spirit at Pentecost, a sound like a roaring windstorm filled the house (Acts 2:2). We know wind is present when we see its effects, but it is unpredictable and we can't control it. Nor can we predict what direction God will take, but we know he is working, whether subtly like a soft breath or dramatically like a "big wind."

April 13

* * *

You have been taught the holy Scriptures from childhood, and they have given you the wisdom to receive the salvation that comes by trusting in Christ Jesus.

2 TIMOTHY 3:15

T wenty-one-year-old Tiger Woods thrilled golf fans on this day in 1997, when he became the youngest player to win the Masters tournament. Woods smashed previous records by winning with the lowest total score (270) and the widest margin of victory (12 strokes). Woods set other golfing records as the youngest player to win the four Grand Slam tournaments and as the first golfer to hold all four Grand Slam titles at the same time: the Masters, the U.S. Open, the PGA Championship, and the British Open.

Woods's father began preparing him for a career in golf as an infant by letting his son watch him hit balls into a net in the family garage. Woods began playing as soon as he could walk, and he appeared on television at age two putting with Bob Hope. When he was three, he shot 48 for nine holes and later dominated the junior ranks in every age group.

In the Old Testament, Jewish children were trained in the law from their earliest days. Although Timothy's father was Greek, his Jewish mother had made sure Timothy learned the Scriptures. Paul commended him for having the faith of his mother, Eunice, and his grandmother Lois (2 Timothy 1:5). Later in the letter, Paul encouraged Timothy to avoid the influence of false teachers by holding fast to the truths he had been taught as a child (literally, "from an infant").

Today, children's ministries sometimes emphasize fun and entertainment and fail to ground children in the Word. If we come to Christ as an adult or lack a solid foundation, it is our responsibility to build one. When we are baby Christians, God will train us in the Scriptures like a parent. We may never win a Masters tournament, but we will win praise from the Master.

April 14

* * *

Deeper and deeper I sink into the mire; I can't find a foothold.
PSALM 69:2

T he *Titanic* was the largest, most luxurious ocean liner of its time, and called "unsinkable" by many. During its first voyage from England to New York City, the British steamer sideswiped an iceberg around 11:40 p.m. on April 14, 1912. Two and a half hours later, it broke apart and sank. The ship carried enough lifeboats for only half of its 2,200 passengers and crew. Approximately 1,500 people lost their life.

Many assumed that the iceberg had ripped a long gash in the ship's hull. When the wreck was recovered in 1985, no such tear was found. Researchers learned that the hull was made of steel that became brittle in the frigid North Atlantic waters, causing it to fracture easily during the collision. Some suspect that the *Titanic* was traveling too fast for an area where there was a possibility of icebergs.

One night, Jesus walked on water, and his disciple Peter wanted to join him. Peter left the boat and was doing fine until he looked around at the high waves. Then he became terrified and started to sink (Matthew 14:25-30). Like Peter, we may be accomplishing great things with God's help until we look around at our frightening circumstances. Then our faith starts to waver, and we get more than a sinking feeling.

At other times, we start to look at our successes and ignore the need to safeguard our spiritual growth. We may start to feel unsinkable, like the *Titanic*. But there are always hidden dangers that can wreck our witness and ministry. The only way to safely navigate life is to keep our eyes on Jesus, not on ourself or the circumstances around us. He will help us complete our voyage, and that's only the tip of the iceberg.

April 15

* * *

The LORD hates cheating, but he delights in honesty.
PROVERBS 11:1, NLT-1

Accordingto a July 2003 Roper poll conducted for the IRS Oversight Board, 81 percent of Americans claimed that no amount of cheating on their income taxes is acceptable. In an unofficial online poll, around 76 percent said they have never cheated. In the Roper poll, 12 percent considered cheating on taxes "a little here and there" acceptable.

Cheaters might be a minority, but they do significant damage to the economy. In a 2003 report to Congress, National Taxpayer Advocate Nina E. Olson estimated that in 2001 the gap between what taxpayers owed and what they actually paid was $311 billion. The IRS believes that hundreds of thousands of Americans use offshore credit, debit, and charge cards to hide taxable income. And that's only one form of tax evasion.

The Pharisees tried to trap Jesus by asking if they should pay taxes to the government that held them in subjection. They were sure Jesus' answer would make him appear either to be siding with the Romans against Israel or to be a rebel opposed to Rome's authority. Jesus took a coin stamped with Caesar's image and told them to give to the government everything that belonged to it. Then he added that they must give to God what is rightfully due him (Matthew 22:15-22).

Cheating the government is bad enough, but God told Israel that they had been cheating him by not bringing their tithes and offerings (Malachi 3:8). Believers today are not bound by the legal tithe system, but we can still cheat God. We may give our own wants and needs first priority instead of his work. We may avoid a nudge from his Spirit to give to a special offering or share with someone in need. Cheating a "little here and there" is never acceptable to God—and he does audit us.

April 16

* * *

As pressure and stress bear down on me, I find joy in your commands.

PSALM 119:143

T he Health Resource Network (HRN), a nonprofit organization formed in 1982, is a group of health professionals, educators, and health promotion experts dedicated to developing successful programs to improve health and prevent disease. The group also schedules National Stress Awareness Day each year on this day, after taxes are due.

Since 1993, the HRN has designated April as Stress Awareness Month to promote understanding of the causes and cures for our nation's stress epidemic. It encourages health-care professionals and organizations to distribute educational materials and sponsor discussion groups, seminars, and other community activities. The goal is to inform the public of the dangers of stress, share effective coping strategies, and dispel misconceptions about stress.

Moses knew about stress as he tried to settle all arguments for the entire nation of Israel from morning to evening. Moses' father-in-law advised him to appoint judges to help carry the load, since the burden was too heavy for one person (Exodus 18:13-26). Sometimes we create stress by taking on more than we can handle or not letting others share the load. Sometimes we try to take on things that are God's job.

David's life was filled with stress, but even as he was surrounded by enemies trying to kill him, he declared, "I wait quietly before God" (Psalm 62:1). Instead of focusing on the quickest way to escape the stress, he concentrated on God's power to help him deal with the cause. Too much stress is physically and emotionally harmful. It also crowds out God's voice and makes us more vulnerable to Satan's temptations. The most effective coping strategies are prayer, quiet trust, and letting God be in control.

April 17

* * *

Never seek revenge or bear a grudge against anyone.
LEVITICUS 19:18, NLT-1

This day in 1985 marked the official end of what was probably the longest war in history. During England's Civil War in the 1640s, Parliamentarianism spread throughout mainland England until it reached the last Royalist stronghold, the Isles of Scilly. The Netherlands sent ships to support the Parliamentarians. The Royalist navy did so much damage to the Dutch navy that the Dutch declared war on the Isles in 1651.

Before the Dutch fired a shot, Admiral Robert Blake arrived in Scilly with the Parliamentarian fleet, and the Royalist stronghold fell. The war was over, but no peace treaty was signed. In 1985, a local historian decided to check out the rumor that Scilly was still at war with the Netherlands, and the Dutch embassy in London confirmed its accuracy. The Dutch ambassador was invited to the Isles and the peace treaty was signed 335 years after the war had been declared.

It's part of human nature to hold a grudge when we've been attacked, wronged, or hurt, even after the argument or battle has ended. Some people bear a grudge against another person until the day they die. God instructed the Israelites to not bear grudges against one another (Leviticus 19:18). The "love chapter" in 1 Corinthians lists one quality of genuine love as not keeping a record of being wronged (13:5).

According to Jesus, one condition for answered prayer is not holding a grudge against anyone (Mark 11:25). God expects us to forgive others as he has forgiven us. Holding onto a grudge is unhealthy physically, emotionally, and spiritually. It destroys relationships and hinders our prayer and ministry. We can't be in a right relationship with God if we have some unsettled dispute with another believer. We can't afford to put off signing a peace treaty.

What old grudges are you still holding onto?

April 18

* * *

Warn the surrounding nations and announce to Jerusalem:
The enemy is coming from a distant land.
JEREMIAH 4:16

O n this day in 1775, Paul Revere made his most famous ride, signaling the approach of the British by having lanterns placed in a church steeple: "One if by land and two if by sea." In 1774, members of the Continental Congress had designated silversmith, engraver, and patriot Revere as an official courier to deliver information by horseback to the northern colonies. Revere served as the principal rider for Boston's Committee of Safety.

Along with William Dawes and Samuel Prescott, Revere rode out at midnight to warn the colonists in the Massachusetts countryside that the British army was on the march. Revere slipped past British troops and reached Lexington but was captured before he arrived at Concord. Prescott got through in time, and the colonists were prepared when the British attacked the next day.

In the Old Testament, the watchman on the city walls had the job of alerting the people of approaching enemies. If he failed to sound the alarm, he was responsible for their death. God appointed Ezekiel as a spiritual watchman for Israel to warn them about the danger of sin and coming judgment (Ezekiel 33). God said he would hold the prophet responsible if he failed to pass on the warnings.

Believers are to watch as well: We are to keep watch over our lifestyle and doctrine (1 Timothy 4:16). Believers are to warn and admonish one another so we won't be deceived by sin (Hebrews 3:13). And we are to warn about God's judgment of sin so unbelievers will repent (Colossians 1:28). We may be tempted to keep our mouth shut or to avoid imposing our beliefs on others, but the enemy is on the march and preparations need to be made.

April 19

* * *

Sanctify the Lord God in your hearts, and always be ready to give a defense to everyone who asks you a reason for the hope that is in you.

1 Peter 3:15, NKJV

In the American Revolution, minutemen fought side by side with the regular militia in the historic battles at Lexington Green and Concord Bridge on April 19, 1775. Although the concept of minutemen in America can be traced back to the seventeenth century, the title was formally adopted the year before the American Revolution began. They were the first to arrive at or await a battle, ready to fight at a minute's notice.

Minutemen were a small, elite force chosen from militia muster roles by their commanding officers. They were usually twenty-five years old or younger and selected on the basis of reliability, enthusiasm, and physical strength. Minutemen met regularly and trained hard in order to be prepared to turn out for battle in sixty seconds. They played a crucial role in the patriots' opposition to the British army but ceased to exist after Congress authorized a Continental army.

God expects believers to be ready at a minute's notice to do battle for the gospel. If we are living our life for him, it's inevitable that we will be asked to defend our faith and the reason for the hope in our life. To do this, we must carefully and prayerfully think through what we believe and why we believe it. God will provide opportunities based on our reliability, enthusiasm, and spiritual strength.

The apostle Peter explains that we are to give our answer with gentleness and respect, not belligerence or arrogance. Unbelievers aren't bullied or shamed into God's Kingdom. If we train hard and serve faithfully as God's minutemen and minutewomen, then sixty seconds can make a difference for all eternity.

How prepared are you to explain your faith?

April 20

* * *

We are Christ's ambassadors, and God is using us to speak to you.

2 CORINTHIANS 5:20, NLT-1

O n this day in 1934, Shirley Temple's film *Bright Eyes* debuted to great acclaim. Beginning at age three, Shirley Temple sang and danced her way into the hearts of Americans; fans saw her as one of the most famous child movie stars of all time. By the late 1930s, she was Hollywood's biggest box-office attraction. "Little Curly Top," or "Dimples," won a special Academy Award for *Bright Eyes*, one of her first films, in which she performed her most famous song, "The Good Ship Lollipop."

Temple retired from acting in her early twenties, and in 1950, she married businessman Charles Black. She later held several diplomatic posts, beginning as U.S. representative to the United Nations General Assembly from 1969 to 1970. The first woman to be appointed White House Chief of Protocol and as a foreign affairs officer in the State Department, Black also served as U.S. ambassador to Ghana in 1974 and ambassador to Czechoslovakia in 1989 and 1992.

Since an ambassador is an official sent from one sovereign or government to another, usually for a specific time, the ambassador needs to live in a foreign culture with different traditions and language. Yet, the ambassador speaks for the one who sent him or her and safeguards the sending country's honor. While Jesus Christ was on earth, his mission was to represent his Father. Our mission is to be ambassadors for Christ.

God has entrusted us with the message of reconciliation. Through us he issues his invitation to others to have their sins forgiven, as though Christ himself were pleading with them (2 Corinthians 5:20). There is no greater honor or responsibility than representing Christ to a lost world. By our words and actions, we help shape what others think of him. It's time to stop playing around on "The Good Ship Lollipop" and start taking our role as Christ's ambassador seriously.

April 21

* * *

Let us run with perseverance the race marked out for us.
HEBREWS 12:1, NIV

Although cases of cheating pop up regularly in the Boston Marathon, one of the most famous episodes occurred on this day in 1980. Twenty-three-year-old Rosie Ruiz was the first woman to cross the finish line, clocking the third-fastest time ever recorded for a female. As she stepped up to the winner's podium, looking relaxed and sweat-free, race officials began to question her.

Neither the monitors at the various checkpoints nor any of the other runners remembered seeing her during the race. She didn't show up in any of the many photographs taken. A few observers in the crowd eventually revealed that they had seen her join the race in its final half mile. Officials also found evidence that when Ruiz qualified for the Boston race by participating in the New York Marathon, she achieved her time by riding the subway.

The New Testament often compares the Christian life to a race. God is the race official, and he allows no cheating. We start at the beginning as new believers and persevere to the end, until we become like Christ. The course is sometimes difficult, with obstacles and twists and turns, but there is no shortcut in the process of spiritual growth.

We all have our own race that God has marked out just for us—including service, ministry, trials, victories, and disappointments—to achieve his purposes for our life. Sometimes we may not like how our path is laid out, but we have to run our own race, not someone else's. It helps to remember that Jesus is running alongside us to encourage and strengthen us. We strive to someday be able to say with Paul, "I have finished the race, and I have remained faithful" (2 Timothy 4:7).

April 22

* * *

All the earth is the LORD's, and he has set the world in order.

1 Samuel 2:8

Since April 22, 1970, Earth Day has been an annual event to celebrate Earth and focus on the environmental health of our planet. Former Wisconsin senator Gaylord Nelson initiated the idea of a nationwide demonstration to show support for environmental causes. On the original Earth Day, approximately twenty million Americans in schools and communities throughout the nation participated in rallies and demonstrations, making environmental protection a major national issue.

Earth Day is now a worldwide observance with events scheduled in late March or April. An estimated one thousand groups and five hundred million individuals take part in programs designed to call attention to local and global threats to the environment and discuss possible solutions. Volunteers join in activities such as picking up litter, cleaning up streams, and restoring parks.

The biggest threat to our planet's environment is sin. The prophet Isaiah says that "the earth suffers for the sins of its people" and their refusal to obey God's laws (Isaiah 24:5). Paul writes that from the beginning, all creation has been groaning from the curse of sin and wanting to be set free (Romans 8:22). Sin has distorted God's perfect world along with the human population.

God created the earth, and his glory fills it. He preserves it, and someday he will judge it and then renew it. We are responsible to be good stewards of the earth, taking good care of it while being careful to not worship it instead of its Creator. While there *are* practical environmental problems that need to be solved, the most important issue to work on is the spiritual health of our planet.

April 23

* * *

[Jesus said,] "Even the Son of Man came not to be served but to serve others and to give his life as a ransom for many."
MATTHEW 20:28

S ince 1974, National Volunteer Week has recognized and celebrated the efforts of nearly ninety million volunteers who improve our communities and enrich others' lives. Businesses, government agencies, hospitals, schools, and faith-based organizations simultaneously sponsor thousands of service projects in their communities during Volunteer Week each April, usually the third week of the month.

Award ceremonies honor millions of volunteers for their contributions during the past year. Each year, *USA Weekend* announces its Make a Difference Day winners and gives awards to the ten most-outstanding service projects. In 2004, a new national awards program gave presidential recognition to "people of all ages who have demonstrated a sustained commitment to volunteer service." It is hoped that the President's Volunteer Service Award will encourage more people to help meet our country's critical needs.

Jesus set the ultimate example as a volunteer. He existed as God in heaven, but came to Earth as a servant. He did not seek his own glory or honor, but he sought to serve others. He devoted all his actions to meeting people's needs, whether turning water into wine, giving sight to the blind, teaching the truth about God, confronting sinners, or simply showing love. Jesus' commitment to serve others led him to give up his life as payment for our sin.

As believers, we are to consider others as more important than ourselves and look out for their interests, as well as our own (Philippians 2:3-4). This kind of selfless thinking is opposite of the human perspective. But the Christian life calls for us to be personally involved in meeting the needs of others. We can't serve God without voluntarily serving other people. We may not win an award, but we *will* make a difference in our world.

April 24

* * *

Do not add to or subtract from these commands I am giving you. Just obey the commands of the LORD your God.

DEUTERONOMY 4:2

S chools celebrate Mathematics Awareness Month every April to increase appreciation for and understanding of mathematics. The observance began in 1986, when a proclamation by President Ronald Reagan highlighted the declining enrollment in math programs at all levels of the American educational system, despite the importance of mathematics in diverse career fields.

The first year's observance focused on national events such as the opening of an exhibit at the Smithsonian Institution. In recent years, organizers have focused on the local, state, and regional levels with activities designed to increase the visibility of mathematics as a field of study and to communicate the usefulness of mathematics in many fields. Organizers plan activities around a different theme each year and enlist the assistance of thousands of teachers, students, parents, businesspeople, and public policy leaders.

Some things the Bible teaches just don't add up. God + Jesus + the Holy Spirit = 3 as well as 1. When a man and a woman marry, two become one. If we try to keep our life, we will lose it; if we give it up for Christ, we will find it. Whoever wants to be first must be last. These things may not make sense to us, but that doesn't subtract from their truth.

We may try to make God fit into our own neat little formula, but God's wisdom is not like ours. He says his thoughts and "ways are far beyond anything [we] could imagine" (Isaiah 55:8). Our job is to obey his commands, not necessarily to understand how they work. As we grow closer to God and study his Word, he will multiply our understanding, but we will never have complete understanding of him. We can rest assured that he is the sum of all things and be glad that nothing can subtract from his love for us or divide us from him.

April 25

* * *

A person without self-control is like a city with broken-down walls.
PROVERBS 25:28

O n April 26, 1986, the worst nuclear accident in history occurred at approximately 1:23 a.m. at the Chernobyl power plant near Kiev in Ukraine. An explosion ripped apart a reactor and resulted in a fire that burned for days and sent large amounts of radioactive material into the atmosphere. Three months after the accident, Soviet officials reported that thirty-one people had died from burns or radiation sickness and that more than two hundred people had suffered serious injuries.

The Chernobyl reactors lacked an enclosure built in most Western reactors to prevent radioactive isotopes from escaping. The radioactive material spread to parts of what are now Ukraine, Russia, and Belarus, and even spread into northern and central Europe by the wind. Experts predicted a sizable increase in cancer deaths among those who lived in the vicinity.

As a result of the Chernobyl disaster and the Three Mile Island accident in Pennsylvania, the Nuclear Regulatory Commission tightened its control of nuclear power plants in the United States. One thing we all need to tighten is our self-control, one of the fruits of the Spirit. Paul included lack of self-control in a list of character traits that will increase and contribute to society's breakdown as the tribulation period draws nearer (2 Timothy 3:3, NIV).

Our culture promotes self-gratification rather than self-control. People think they have a right to say or do whatever they want. They see no need to restrain their actions and reactions. Everyone suffers the consequences. A lack of self-control damages relationships and kills marriages. It promotes an atmosphere of violence and leads to an increase in child abuse. A failure to let the Holy Spirit control our "reactor" can lead to disaster, and the deadly fallout affects everyone in our vicinity.

How does your life demonstrate self-control?

April 26

* * *

Let God weigh me on the scales of justice.
JOB 31:6

Some calendars list April 26 as Richter Scale Day in honor of Charles Richter, the American physicist and seismologist whose research led to the earthquake magnitude scale and who was born on this day. The Richter magnitude is a number that indicates the strength of an earthquake based on data obtained from a seismograph, which records back-and-forth movements of the ground. Calculations based on the Richter scale measure the amount of energy released by an earthquake.

More than a thousand earthquakes with a Richter magnitude of at least 2 occur on a daily basis. Earthquakes measuring 5 or less rarely cause serious damage, but a magnitude of 7 or more can result in great damage and many deaths. To measure the largest earthquakes, seismologists today use the moment magnitude scale, which utilizes data recorded by more-sensitive instruments.

Wouldn't it be helpful if we had a scale to measure the magnitude of our spiritual growth, the intensity of our devotion to Christ? It would need to be a sensitive instrument to detect the slightest movement away from God. That's exactly what the Word of God does. The Bible is so penetrating that it not only judges our behavior, it also discerns our thoughts, attitudes, and motives (Hebrews 4:12).

The image of a plumb line is used several times in the Old Testament as a symbol of God judging his people. The Word serves as our plumb line to see how our lives measure up to God's standards. Just as the plumb line detects the slightest deviation from a straight line, Scripture shows us when we are not aligned with God's desires. If we are measuring our life by the world's scale, we are using the wrong tool. Only the Bible can measure a shift away from God—and any movement in that direction is of great magnitude and always results in damage.

April 27

* * *

[Jesus said,] "The servant who received the five bags of silver began to invest the money and earned five more."

MATTHEW 25:16

The most recent auction of the world's rarest stamp was in April 1980. The one-cent British Guiana 1856 Magenta was issued as a provisional stamp because a shipment of stamps coming from Great Britain had been delayed. It depicts a three-masted ship with a Latin inscription above and below: *Damus Petimus Que Vicissim* ("We give and expect in return").

The stamp has no market price, since only one exists. Supposedly, a young man discovered the stamp when looking through some family papers in 1873. He sold it to a collector for six shillings. The stamp changed hands a number of times, and in 1970 a syndicate purchased it for $280,000. In 1980, chemical heir and multimillionaire John E. DuPont bought the 1856 Magenta at an auction for more than $900,000.

Not many of us own a rare stamp, but we all have things that should appreciate in value. Jesus told a parable about a man who gave bags of gold to three servants in proportion to their abilities (Matthew 25:14-30). While the man was gone on a trip, the first two servants invested his money and doubled it. The third servant buried the money. When the master returned, he praised the first two for using well what they had been given and gave them more. He called the third servant useless, gave his money to one of the other servants, and threw him out.

God didn't give us all equal resources, but he does demand that we be productive and make wise use of what we have. We are to look for the best investment of our time, money, energy, and abilities, pouring ourself into ventures that will have eternal rewards. The gospel is the rarest treasure of all with the ultimate appreciation in value.

How are you using the resources that God has entrusted to you?

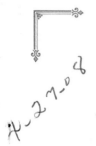

April 28

* * *

*They will act as if they are religious, but they will reject the power
that could make them godly.*

2 TIMOTHY 3:5, NLT-1

O ne night in April 1975, a group of friends began to talk about pets. Gary Dahl announced that he thought animal pets were too much trouble. He claimed that he had a pet rock that was cheap, easy to deal with, and didn't make a mess. Over the next few weeks, Dahl wrote a training manual for pet rocks and bought rounded gray pebbles for a penny each. He packed them in gift boxes shaped like pet carrying cases.

Dahl introduced the Pet Rock at gift shows in San Francisco and New York. The buyer for the Neiman Marcus store placed an order for five hundred rocks. *Newsweek* ran a story about the fad. By the end of October, Dahl was shipping ten thousand rocks a day, selling two-and-a-half tons by Christmas. He sold one million rocks for $3.95 each, making Dahl an instant multimillionaire.

Paul warned that in the last days there would be more and more people with a "pet rock" type of religion—cheap, easy, and no mess. These people have an appearance of godliness, but inside they lack and even deny the life and power of the gospel. They proudly go through the rituals of religion but want nothing to do with the demands of following Christ.

Even true believers can slip into a "pet rock" mentality. We may be diligent about church attendance but not diligently attending to our daily walk. We may proudly display a Bible on the coffee table but not go to the trouble of studying it. We may concentrate on the latest "Christian" fad instead of nurturing our faith. This approach to our faith will cause us to miss out on opportunities to grow, minister to others, and be blessed by God. There is no substitute for a real relationship with the Rock of Ages.

April 29

* * *

Rescue those being led away to death; hold back those staggering toward slaughter.
PROVERBS 24:11, NIV

The first Nazi concentration camp established in Germany, Dachau became the model for all SS-controlled camps. More than two hundred thousand prisoners ended up at Dachau or its branches in southern Germany and Austria. Prisoners suffered slave labor under inhumane conditions. Many died from cruel medical experiments. Untold thousands died from starvation, sickness, exhaustion, beating, torture, or execution by hanging, shooting, injections, or in gas chambers.

As the Allied troops advanced into Germany near the end of World War II, the SS began to evacuate the camps. The number of prisoners in Dachau had increased to the point of horrendous overcrowding, triggering a typhus epidemic that killed thousands. On this day in 1945, U.S. Army troops liberated thousands of prisoners from Dachau.

According to Proverbs 24:11, it is our duty to do whatever we can to deliver those who are being unjustly oppressed or condemned. Every day sin leads people away to death and destruction. Even though the condemnation for sin is just and fair, God offers deliverance through Jesus' death. How can we hesitate to share the liberating message of the gospel with those in sin's deadly grip?

We won't be reluctant to witness to unbelievers if we remember how God lifted our own death sentence. When we point others to God's truth or give our testimony of being set free from sin's condemnation, we are allies with the Holy Spirit in his work of deliverance. Those who choose to leave the death camp of sin will feel as one Dachau survivor, who wrote: "For the rest of my life I will celebrate this day as my second birthday. The day I received the gift of my new life" (Edgar Kupfer-Koberwitz).

April 30

* * *

The LORD God planted all sorts of trees in the garden—
beautiful trees that produced delicious fruit.
GENESIS 2:9, NLT-1

U sing his position as editor of Nebraska Territory's first newspaper, and later as secretary of the territory, J. Sterling Morton shared his enthusiasm for trees by suggesting a tree-planting holiday in 1872. Morton began Arbor Day in Nebraska—a state that was once a treeless plain. Trees were especially needed in the area as windbreaks to hold soil in place, for fuel and building materials, and for shade from the sun.

Volunteers planted more than a million trees in Nebraska that first Arbor Day. Other states began to observe Arbor Day, and it became a nationwide tradition in schools in 1882. The most common date is the last Friday in April, but individual states observe Arbor Day to coincide with the best weather for planting trees.

When God made a garden to be Adam's home, he planted all kinds of beautiful trees with delicious fruit (Genesis 2:9). God often compares Israel to an olive tree and speaks to the Israelites in metaphors involving cedars of Lebanon and palm trees. Jesus compares faith to the seed of a mustard tree (Luke 17:6).

The psalmist in Psalm 1:3 compares believers to trees planted by the riverbank. If we drink in God's Word, we will consistently bear fruit in the proper season. Our leaves will never wither, and we will prosper in all we do. In the new Jerusalem, a river will run down the main street with a tree of life on each side, bearing leaves for healing the nations and producing a fresh crop of fruit each month (Revelation 22:2). If we let God nourish and prune us, we will be fruitful and have a healing effect on our world right now.

May 1

*** * ***

Do not let kindness and truth leave you; bind them around your neck.
PROVERBS 3:3, NASB

Writer and poet Don Blanding thought Hawaii should have a holiday centered on the custom of wearing leis. Fellow writer Grace Tower Warren suggested May 1 and coined the phrase, "May Day is Lei Day." A few people first observed Lei Day in 1927 in Honolulu. Its popularity grew, and Lei Day was declared an official holiday in the territory in 1929.

Today May 1 is celebrated on all the major Hawaiian Islands with festivals featuring adult and youth lei contests, demonstrations, exhibits, and entertainment. Many schools and institutions sponsor pageants, electing a lei queen along with a court of eight princesses to represent the eight islands and their respective leis. In Honolulu, the day includes draping leis on tombs and crypts in the Royal Mausoleum.

It can be said that we all wear something around our neck. Proverbs advises us to wear kindness and truth like a necklace (3:3) and to tie our parents' teaching around our neck (6:20-21). In contrast, the description of wicked people in Psalm 73:6 says that "they wear pride like a jeweled necklace." People see visible outward evidence of what is going on inside us.

Pharaoh hung a gold chain around Joseph's neck when he rewarded him for interpreting his dream (Genesis 41:42). Belshazzar gave Daniel a gold chain for reading the mysterious writing on the wall from God (Daniel 5:29). If we pursue godliness and knowledge of God's Word, he will reward us by hanging his wisdom and love around our neck for all to see. We choose whether we want to wear God's beautiful, fragrant "lei" or something smelly and unattractive, such as pride.

What have you been wearing around your neck?

May 2

* * *

Be sure that everything is done properly and in order.

1 CORINTHIANS 14:40

Robert's Rules of Order Day commemorates the May 2 birthday of the author of the standard manual on parliamentary procedure in the United States. Henry Martyn Robert graduated from West Point and was commissioned in the U.S. Army Corps of Engineers. While attending a church meeting, he was unexpectedly asked to preside. His embarrassment made him determined to educate himself on parliamentary law before ever attending another meeting.

Robert searched out and studied the books available on the topic. His interest increased as he was periodically transferred to different parts of the United States. He found that people from different parts of the country had different ideas of correct procedure for meetings. Wanting to bring order out of chaos, Robert eventually authored the manual known as *Robert's Rules of Order*.

There can be no doubt that God is a God of order. Genesis describes how he took a formless place of chaos and created a world of amazingly detailed order. When God brought the Israelites out of Egypt, he gave specific instructions for all their activities including marching, setting up camp, and worshipping. Paul's letters often contain principles and guidelines for the conduct of church services in dignity and orderliness.

Isaiah said that God "made the world to be lived in, not to be a place of empty chaos" (Isaiah 45:18). He doesn't intend for our life to be a place of chaos and confusion, either. If we think that our life is chaotic, we may be feeling the effects of living in a sinful world opposed to God's rule. Or we may not be able to see the order that he is bringing out of our circumstances. Or maybe we just need to spend more time in God's rule book.

May 3

* * *

Do not join them in their rebellion. Open your mouth, and eat what I give you.

EZEKIEL 2:8

On this day in 1981, imprisoned Irish-Catholic militant Bobby Sands slipped into a coma after refusing food for more than two months. In an earlier conviction because of his Irish Republican Army (IRA) activities, Sands had been given "special category status" in a prison that allowed some freedoms. In 1976, Britain enacted a policy of "criminalization" of Irish militants. Sands was convicted in 1977 of gun possession near the scene of a bombing and imprisoned as a dangerous criminal instead of as a political prisoner.

On March 1, 1981, Sands began a hunger strike to protest this policy and was soon joined by several other prisoners. Around the end of April, Pope John Paul II sent a message urging Sands to end the strike. Sands' death on May 5 triggered extensive rioting in Belfast and led to some reforms in the treatment of IRA prisoners.

Sometimes we go on a spiritual hunger strike, refusing to take in God's instruction. We may think parts of his Word are too hard to obey, or we may be rebellious and want to do things our own way. God told Ezekiel to open his mouth and eat whatever message God gave him. God expects us to take in his Word as food and digest it. It may not be what we would have chosen, but it will nourish our souls.

God told Amos that since Israel had rebelled and rejected his words through his prophets, they would experience a famine of hearing God's words (Amos 8:11). They would urgently call on him, but he would not answer them. We can't take lightly the privilege of feeding on God's Word for strength, guidance, comfort, and spiritual growth. If we refuse to take in his Word, he may withdraw it.

May 4

* * *

*I will be your God throughout your lifetime—until your hair is white with age.
I made you, and I will care for you. I will carry you along and save you.*

Isaiah 46:4

I n 1963, there were only seventeen million Americans aged sixty-five or older. Approximately a third of them lived in poverty, and the nation had few programs to address their needs. In April, President John F. Kennedy met with the National Council of Senior Citizens and later designated May as Senior Citizen Month, encouraging Americans to recognize past and present contributions of older persons to our country.

President Jimmy Carter changed the title to "Older Americans Month" in 1980. Every president since 1963 has issued a formal proclamation asking the country to honor older members of their communities. Today forty-four million people are age sixty years or older—one in six Americans.

Most Americans dread getting older, but aging has a positive connotation in the Bible. The Old Testament uses phrases like "ripe old age" and "good old age." Proverbs assures us that gray hair is "a crown of glory" (16:31) and "the splendor of the old" (20:29). Besides their natural gifts and abilities, older believers have accumulated a wealth of knowledge and experience. They are an invaluable asset to the body of Christ when we are wise enough to honor them.

God promises his people that he will carry us from our conception through our death. If we trust him to watch over us, there is no need to fear growing older. It seems appropriate that Older Americans Month is celebrated in the birth month of Robert Browning. Some of the British poet's best-loved lines are: "Grow old along with me! The best is yet to be." If we are a child of God, the best truly is yet to be.

May 5

* * *

He may have a great army, but they are merely men.
We have the LORD our God to help us and to fight our battles for us!
2 CHRONICLES 32:8

C inco de Mayo ("Fifth of May" in Spanish) commemorates the Mexican army's defeat of French forces on this day in 1862. The French army, one of the most highly regarded fighting forces in the world, expected to conquer Mexico City with little resistance. However, under the command of General Ignacio Zaragoza, the greatly outnumbered Mexican army confronted the French troops at the city of Puebla. The French withdrew after two hours of fierce fighting.

Although the French returned and conquered the country the next year, the heroism of the Mexican forces at the Battle of Puebla became a symbol of Mexican pride and patriotism during the four years of French occupation. Cinco de Mayo is a national holiday in Mexico and is also celebrated in certain regions of the United States.

In 2 Kings 6, the army of Aram surrounded the city of Dothan, where the prophet Elisha was staying. Elisha assured his terrified servant there was no need to fear: "For there are more on our side than on theirs!" (2 Kings 6:16). When Elisha asked God to open his servant's eyes, the servant saw the Lord's army of horses and chariots of fire surrounding the Aramean army.

When Judah was under attack, King Hezekiah reminded the people that the Assyrian army was made up of mere men, while they had a "power far greater" on their side (2 Chronicles 32:7-8). Sometimes we feel like we're outnumbered by a powerful army—when our troubles seem greater than our resources or when we're surrounded by people hostile to God. At those times we need to remember that the Spirit who indwells us is far greater than any force trying to conquer us.

May 6

* * *

[Jesus] replied, "What is impossible for people is possible with God."
LUKE 18:27

O n this day in 1954, a twenty-five-year-old British medical student named Roger Bannister became the first person in history to break the four-minute-mile barrier. So many athletes had tried and failed to run a mile in under four minutes that it was considered a physical impossibility. Bannister prepared himself by researching the mechanics of running and developing scientific training methods. In spite of windy conditions, he achieved a time of 3 minutes 59.4 seconds.

When the officials announced his time, the onlookers wildly erupted after the words *three minutes*. Bannister's record, however, was broken less than two months later by an Australian athlete. Because of improvements in training and running techniques, more-accurate timing devices, and controlled conditions in competition, top runners today routinely run the mile in less than four minutes.

God is in the business of doing the impossible. Over and over, he revealed himself to the Israelites as an omnipotent God who is able to accomplish all things. The angel Gabriel reminded a young virgin of this when he announced that she would conceive a son: "For nothing is impossible with God" (Luke 1:37). That woman's Son, Jesus, reminded his followers that although salvation is impossible from a human perspective, God can accomplish it (Luke 18:27).

We all need to be reminded of God's power to do impossible things in our life. He will accomplish his purposes in spite of our weaknesses and limitations. How can we doubt that any natural circumstances could prevent his supernatural plan from unfolding? If we are running in the center of his will, we can break all kinds of barriers.

**What "unbreakable" barrier in your life is holding you back
from fully serving God?**

May 7

* * *

Blessed be the LORD, who daily bears our burden.
PSALM 68:19, NASB

In May 1884, construction began on the building that is considered the country's first skyscraper. The Home Insurance Company Building in Chicago included nine stories plus a basement and stood 138 feet tall. The architect was William Le Baron Jenney, who is credited with designing the first load-carrying structural frame. A steel frame carried the entire weight of the building instead of the walls bearing the building's weight in the usual method.

The steel skeleton revolutionized American architecture and allowed greater numbers of people to live and work in downtown areas. The term *skyscraper* originally referred to buildings of ten to twenty stories but now is applied to high-rise buildings with more than forty stories.

Jesus' birth revolutionized life by removing the burdens of the law and sin. Isaiah compares the Messiah's coming to the lifting of burdens from people's shoulders (Isaiah 9:4). The gift of salvation means we no longer have to carry the weight of our sin or the law's demands.

If we feel overburdened, it's because we are bearing a load we aren't meant to carry. God never meant for us to have the weight of the world on our shoulders. It's his job to be in control of the universe. God also doesn't want us to carry around the backbreaking load of our past. Our sins are forgiven and forgotten if we have repented. Jesus offers to take our heavy burdens and give us an easy and light one—a life of following him (Matthew 11:28-30). When we let Jesus bear our heavy burdens and we concentrate on loving and obeying him, then the sky's the limit on how far we can go in our spiritual life.

May 8

* * *

"Come now, let us reason together," says the LORD.
ISAIAH 1:18, NIV

I n 1952, a congressional resolution signed into law by President Harry Truman officially established the National Day of Prayer (NDP). In 1988, President Reagan amended the law to designate the first Thursday in May as the NDP. The observance is based on the constitutional rights of freedom of speech and religion and is meant to be celebrated by all Americans. Thousands of activities are planned nationwide.

A number of groups have recently labeled the NDP as "an annual abuse of the Constitution" and a threat to religious liberty. Groups including humanists, atheists, agnostics, and "freethinkers" have designated the first Thursday in May as the National Day of Reason. They intend this alternative celebration to promote reason and critical thought. One Web site states that thinking has proven to be "a much more effective and worthwhile endeavor than prayer."

Do we really need to choose between praying and reasoning? At age twelve, Jesus amazed the scholars in the Temple with his understanding. As an adult, he often stunned the educated religious leaders with his answers to questions designed to trap him. At the same time, Jesus was continuously in communication with his Father.

Paul was another brilliant example of critical thinking and prayer blended together. His great reasoning powers are exhibited in his letters, which are masterfully laid out to refute doctrinal errors. These same letters reveal that Paul was devoted to prayer; he exhorts us to "never stop praying" (1 Thessalonians 5:17). Many of the great scientists and thinkers of the Western world were also people of great faith and prayer. Being a Christian doesn't mean we stop thinking. It means we don't worship thinking.

May 9

* * *

Truthful words stand the test of time, but lies are soon exposed.

PROVERBS 12:19

S candal hit the *New York Times* in the spring of 2003 when it was discovered that a reporter had plagiarized and fabricated dozens of stories. Using a laptop computer and cell phone, Jayson Blair had apparently pretended to be at the scenes of big stories when he was not. He also made up information from fictional unnamed sources and used material from articles in other newspapers.

After Blair resigned from the paper in May, a team of *New York Times* reporters began to examine each one of the 673 stories he had submitted during his four years of employment. The newspaper's investigation revealed that a number of colleagues and editors had become suspicious and had questioned Blair's reporting. As a result of the investigation, two of the paper's top editors were also forced to resign.

Lying is rampant in our culture today, with the mind-set that the end justifies the means. Being less than truthful is sometimes considered clever if it leads to personal gain. Many people think there is a difference between big lies and "harmless little white lies." God makes it clear that he detests lying. When God was about to judge Israel in Micah's time, he said that the people were so used to lying that their tongues could no longer tell the truth (Micah 6:12).

Deceitfulness has no place in a believer's life. Proverbs 12:19 contrasts truth, which lasts forever, with lies, which can be detected. Besides God's judgment, there are other serious consequences, including a loss of trust. If we want to be a credible witness for Christ, we'd better keep our mouth and our life free from any traces of deceitfulness.

The costs of lying aren't worth it for any amount of temporary gain, fame, or attention.

May 10

* * *

[Jesus said,] "What is the price of two sparrows—one copper coin? But not a single sparrow can fall to the ground without your Father knowing it."

MATTHEW 10:29

In Japan, officials designate one week each May as Bird Week to encourage people to appreciate and protect birds in their country. Activities for the week include bird-watching, exhibitions, and lectures focusing on the habitat of wild birds and how they coexist with the natural environment. An estimated seven hundred species of wild birds inhabit Japan, including ninety species considered endangered.

In 1946, a number of ministries, academic societies, and other organizations jointly formed what is now the Japanese Society for Preservation of Birds. The action reflected the people's concern about damage done to birds' natural habitat during World War II as huge numbers of trees were cut down for fuel. The Japanese first observed Bird Day in 1947; a few years later officials expanded the observance to Bird Week.

God is a bird-watcher. In biblical times, sparrows were the least expensive bird and considered of little value. Yet Jesus said that God is aware of what happens to every single sparrow on the earth. Nothing in creation is too trivial to escape his attention. Nothing happens without his knowledge and permission.

If God pays such close attention to sparrows, how closely is he watching over the lives of his children? Jesus assured his disciples that they were much more valuable to God than a whole flock of sparrows. God is so involved in the details of our life that he even knows the exact number of hairs on our head (Matthew 10:30-31). We don't ever have to worry about any circumstance in our life taking him by surprise. With such close attention from our heavenly Father, we will never be endangered.

May 11

* * *

He holds the whole body together with its joints and ligaments,
and it grows as God nourishes it.

COLOSSIANS 2:19

The most famous set of conjoined twins was born on this day in 1811. Doctors coined the term *Siamese twins* because Chang and Eng were born to Chinese parents in Siam, present-day Thailand. Chang and Eng were joined at the chest by a band of flesh.

The twins left Siam as teenagers to begin a world tour and later became one of P. T. Barnum's most famous attractions. In the late 1830s, Chang and Eng decided to become U.S. citizens, adopted Bunker as their last name, and settled in North Carolina, where they lived until their death in 1874. After their death, doctors discovered that they could have easily been separated.

Followers of Jesus Christ are bound together more tightly than Siamese twins. In Colossians 2:19, Paul explains that we all form a single body, with Christ holding all the parts together. On the other hand, in 2 Corinthians 6:14, Paul warns against teaming up with unbelievers. Paul doesn't mean that we should avoid contact with unbelievers or leave unsaved spouses if we're already married. But we are to avoid forming binding, intimate relationships with unbelievers.

Inappropriate ties with unbelievers can weaken our commitment to godliness and tempt us to divide our loyalties between Christ and the world. The only way to keep ourselves separated from the world's belief system and its influence is to stay connected to Christ and his body, where we experience true fellowship. We are joined with other followers of Christ so tightly that separation would be painful. It's more than a band of flesh that holds us together—it's *his* flesh.

May 12

* * *

I will comfort you there in Jerusalem as a mother comforts her child.

ISAIAH 66:13

I n the seventeenth century, England celebrated "Mothering Sunday" to honor all mothers. Many of the country's poor worked as servants and lived in the homes of their employers. On Mothering Sunday, the servants were given the day off to return home and spend the day with their mothers. They often took a "Mothering Cake" to mark the day.

In the United States, Mother's Day is the result of a campaign by Ana Jarvis, whose mother had expressed a desire to see such a holiday. In 1907, Ms. Jarvis arranged a memorial service at her mother's church in West Virginia on the second anniversary of her mother's death. Ms. Jarvis worked to promote a national holiday through public speaking and writing letters to politicians, businessmen, and clergymen until 1914, when President Woodrow Wilson officially proclaimed the second Sunday in May as Mother's Day.

God makes it clear that mothers are to be respected. The fifth commandment to honor fathers and mothers carries the promise of a long and fruitful life for the nation as a reward. According to the law, anyone who struck or cursed his or her parents was put to death. In the New Testament Jesus modeled obedience, respect, and honor in his relationship with his mother.

God compares his love for Israel to a mother's love. Even if it were possible for a mother to forget her nursing child, he would never forget his people (Isaiah 49:15). As Jesus grieved over Jerusalem's rejection of its Messiah, he said he had often wanted to gather his people together as a mother hen protects her chicks under her wings (Matthew 23:37). In God we have the perfect parent. No matter what our relationship with our earthly mother, we can be assured that our heavenly Father loves us with a perfect mother love.

May 13

* * *

O my Strength, I watch for you; you, O God, are my fortress.
PSALM 59:9, NIV

Although reports of a strange creature living in Scotland's Loch Ness can be traced back to A.D. 565, the modern legend began with a newspaper article in May 1933. A local couple had allegedly seen "an enormous animal rolling and plunging on the surface" of the lake. The report caused media frenzy, with newspaper correspondents rushing to Scotland and a circus offering a reward for the beast's capture.

Sightings increased, and a famous 1934 photograph convinced many that "Nessie" was a survivor of a dinosaur species thought to be long extinct. The photo was revealed as a hoax in 1994, but amateur investigators have kept a continual vigil. Since the 1960s, a number of scientific expeditions have searched the waters using sonar and underwater photography. Their results have been intriguing but not conclusive.

Why is it that many get so caught up in a legendary creature that *may* exist yet not bother thinking about God, who *does* exist? Some people get obsessed with reading and studying the latest phenomenon and never open the Book that reveals our phenomenal God. The Bible is far deeper than the eight-hundred-foot-deep Loch Ness and contains conclusive evidence of God, his thoughts, and his plans.

The possibility of a living dinosaur-like creature is fascinating, but we should be watching for God. We don't have to sneak up on him or take surprise photographs to see him. He is at work in the world around us and in the details of our personal life. If we keep a vigil for him, we will have "God-sightings" every day. We need a lot less Loch Ness excitement and a lot more interest in the God who created dinosaurs in the first place.

How will you watch for God at work in your life today?

May 14

* * *

They share freely and give generously to those in need.
PSALM 112:9

T he Rockefeller Foundation was chartered on this day in 1913 to "promote the well-being of mankind throughout the world." John D. Rockefeller was at one time the world's richest person, having made a fortune in the oil business. He felt a strong sense of stewardship about his financial empire and became famous for his philanthropy.

Rockefeller provided an initial endowment of $100 million for the foundation and later increased it to more than $183 million. By the end of 2001, its endowment was estimated to be $3.1 billion. Today, the Rockefeller Foundation describes its mission as "a commitment to enrich and sustain the lives and livelihoods of poor and excluded people throughout the world."

Godly people share their resources with those in need. When they do, God promises that he will remember their generosity forever and give them honor (Psalm 112:9). Paul urges us to remember some of Jesus' words not recorded in the Gospels: "It is more blessed to give than to receive" (Acts 20:35). Our natural tendency is to accumulate wealth for our own selfish uses. Receiving is a lot of fun, but generous people discover the greater joy in giving to others.

We don't have to be rich to be charitable, just attentive to the needs of those God has placed in our path. He doesn't consider the amount as much as the spirit of our giving. In return for our obedience, he honors us for sharing what he gave us in the first place, and we gain the lasting pleasure that comes from meeting others' needs. With such a great deal, we can all feel like the richest people on earth.

May 15

* * *

No good thing does He withhold from those who walk uprightly.
Psalm 84:11, NASB

T he American Chiropractic Association designates May each year as National Correct Posture Month. The observance seeks to educate people about the consequences of poor posture and to train people in how to maintain a healthy posture. Chiropractors explain that poor posture can lead to a number of long-term problems including muscle strains, chronic pain, spinal problems, decreased lung capacity, digestive problems, and conditions such as carpal tunnel syndrome.

If not stopped in time, habitual poor posture can result in permanent damage as the bones remold themselves and the bad posture becomes permanent. This can eventually lead to loss of flexibility and mobility. Doctors suggest plenty of exercise as one way to improve posture.

God wants his people to have good posture—to walk uprightly. The biblical use of the word means to live a life of integrity. He frequently called the Israelites to holy living: "You must be blameless before the LORD your God" (Deuteronomy 18:13). Peter echoes this command by reminding believers that we must be holy in everything we do, just as God is holy (1 Peter 1:15).

Physical slouching and slumping may feel comfortable at first, but in the long run it leads to pain and problems. We are also tempted to *spiritually* slouch, to make little compromises that don't seem like a big deal at first. But habitual compromising results in serious problems as our character molds itself around these little lapses in integrity. The condition can eventually become permanent. We will never achieve perfection in our earthly life, but we should be progressing toward Christlike holiness each day. We need to heed God's advice to "stand up straight," or we will have more problems than a pain in the neck.

May 16

* * *

You died to this life, and your real life is hidden with Christ in God.
Colossians 3:3

I n May 1578, laborers discovered the most famous catacombs in the world when they opened a sepulchral chamber while digging on the outskirts of Rome. Early Christians had cut the catacombs into the soft rock, building a network of connecting passageways and rooms that covered more than six hundred acres. Graves were cut into the wall and sometimes closed off with brick or marble slabs.

The catacombs date back to approximately the third century, when Christians used them for burial and memorial services. During periods of persecution, the Christians hid in the catacombs. When Christianity became the established religion of the Roman Empire, Christians no longer needed the catacombs. People forgot about their existence until laborers discovered them in 1578.

The catacombs were a place of concealment and safety for the early Christians. Paul implies both of these elements when he says our real life is "hidden with Christ in God." Just as Christ died an earthly death, we died to the world and its influences. Now our true life, our eternal life, is hidden from the world. The world doesn't recognize it because it doesn't recognize the invisible Christ. This treasure is safely hidden away with God in heaven where nothing and no one can take it away.

The next verse reminds us that our real life won't always be hidden. When Christ is revealed to the whole world in all his glory, we will share in that glory (Colossians 3:4). The world will see him and us as we truly are. Living in a hostile world can make us wish we could escape and hide in our own catacombs, but we are living for that day when what is hidden will be revealed.

May 17

* * *

The message of the cross is foolish to those who are headed for destruction! But we who are being saved know it is the very power of God.

1 CORINTHIANS 1:18

I n May 1968, city planners formally dedicated the Gateway Arch in St. Louis, Missouri. The stainless-steel-clad Arch is the tallest monument in the United States, with concrete foundations sunk sixty feet into the ground, reaching into bedrock. Designed to sway up to nine inches each way, the Arch was built to withstand earthquakes and hurricane-force winds.

The Arch is part of the Jefferson Expansion Memorial on the Mississippi riverfront honoring Thomas Jefferson and the Louisiana Purchase. The Arch represents the spirit of the pioneers who settled the West. Visitors can ride a unique tram system to the top, where a viewing area holds up to 160 people and offers a view as far as thirty miles in any direction on clear days.

For Christians, the most beloved memorial is the Cross. The Cross of Christ reaches into heaven and spans the distance from the beginning of time to eternity. Its foundations are sunk into the bedrock of God's love and mercy. It can withstand the fiercest demonic attacks and sway the most hard-hearted sinners. There is room for an infinite number of people to visit the Cross and come away changed forever.

Sometimes the cross is used merely as a cultural icon or a fashion accessory, even worn by those who oppose what it stands for. Familiarity can dull our senses to the power behind the symbol of Christ's agonizing death, which opened up the way for us to be accepted by God. We need to visit there daily. The best view is not found at the top of some earthly monument but at the foot of the Cross.

May 18

* * *

"Don't sin by letting anger control you." Don't let the sun go down while you are still angry, for anger gives a foothold to the devil.

EPHESIANS 4:26-27

On this day in 1980, Mount Saint Helens erupted when an earthquake triggered a massive landslide that took off the top of the mountain. Picturesque Mount Saint Helens in southwestern Washington had been dormant for more than a hundred years before a bulge in its north face indicated renewed activity in early 1980. The landslide uncorked the column of magma that had been building up, and pressurized gases within the volcano were released in a tremendous explosion.

Within a few minutes, a vast, gray landscape replaced the forested slopes, and the mountain's elevation decreased from 9,677 feet to 8,365 feet. The landslide killed countless animals, and reports listed sixty people dead or missing. Winds carried volcanic ash across 57,000 square kilometers of the western United States, causing travel disruptions, economic loss, and other problems.

The Old Testament frequently uses volcano-related images to describe God's anger against sin and those who rebel against his authority. In anger, God explodes and bursts out in fury, surrounded by thick, rising smoke. The Lord's righteous anger shakes the heavens and moves the earth (Amos 1:2). This picture warns us against God's anger and also demonstrates what a powerful force anger is.

Trusting Jesus saves us from God's anger but not from our own. Sometimes our anger might be legitimately directed at sin, but we are warned against letting anger control us (Ephesians 4:26). This happens when we react in the heat of the moment, or when we let the pressure of anger quietly build until we suddenly explode and devastate those around us. The only way to prevent an eruption is to not let a day end with unresolved anger in us, whether active or dormant.

How are you guarding against eruptions of anger?

May 19

* * *

Evil people and impostors will flourish.
They will deceive others and will themselves be deceived.

2 TIMOTHY 3:13

In 1910, Earth made the most intimate contact with a comet in recorded history. As Halley's Comet neared the sun, astronomers announced that Earth would pass through its tail during May. Some people saw this as impending doom because several years earlier astronomers had discovered that comets contain cyanogen, a highly poisonous gas. Scientists explained that there was no danger because the gas molecules in the tail were so spread out.

Many newspapers published doomsday stories but did not follow up with the assurances of safety from the astronomers. Opportunists took advantage of the panic that arose in some cities and sold "comet pills" to counter the effects of the cyanogen. At least one doctor became wealthy from prescribing pills to be taken every hour until the comet passed.

A lot of deception happens in the world today, much of it opposite to the "comet pill" scam. Some people teach that hell is a myth and that there is no danger from personal sin. Some pastors claim to believe the Bible but teach that God is a God of love only, not judgment. They assert that if someone doesn't accept Christ while alive, God extends grace to him or her after death.

As believers, we need to be bold about countering this deception with the truth. God is a God of love *and* holiness. He promises forgiveness and eternal life for those who accept Christ's sacrifice, and judgment and condemnation for those who reject it. We need to give people the good news *and* the bad news. Hell is very real, and living for Christ is the only way to counter that danger.

May 20

* * *

Be still in the presence of the LORD, and wait patiently for him to act.
PSALM 37:7

O n this day in 1899, Jacob German became the first person ever arrested for speeding. Observers noted that the taxicab driver for the Electric Vehicle Company in New York City was driving at the "breakneck" speed of twelve miles per hour. Officers held German in jail but did not take his license: The state of New York did not require a driver's license or registration until two years later.

Speed has reached epidemic proportions in the United States. Some statistics demonstrate that speed is a factor in more than 30 percent of all fatal auto accidents, and on average, one thousand Americans die each month in speed-related crashes. Polls indicate that drivers mistakenly believe that speeding is not as serious as other traffic violations and does not pose a serious threat to safety.

We don't speed just on the highway; sometimes we get in a hurry on our spiritual journey as well. We may get impatient when nothing seems to be happening and try to speed things up and help God out. Sarah got impatient when she remained barren after so many years. She decided to speed up the fulfillment of a promised son by offering her Egyptian servant to Abraham (Genesis 16) to father a child. Sarah later regretted her hasty action.

A large part of the Christian life is waiting on God to act. We wait for him to provide guidance in our life, to fulfill his promises, and to right wrongs. We need help from the Holy Spirit to trust God to come through, rather than taking things into our own hands. But the danger in spiritual speeding is that we might rush right out of God's will and into sin. If we don't voluntarily slow down, he may have to "pull us over."

May 21

* * *

You alone are my hope in the day of disaster.

JEREMIAH 17:17

On this day in 1881, Clara Barton organized the American Association of the Red Cross in Washington, D.C. During the Civil War, Barton had distributed supplies to injured soldiers. After the war she headed the agency that tracked down information on almost twenty-two thousand soldiers. Barton modeled the American humanitarian organization after the International Red Cross but added disaster relief to battlefield service. Barton served as president until 1904.

Volunteers lead the Red Cross and work to help people prevent, prepare for, and respond to emergencies. The American Red Cross offers health and safety training to the public and provides emergency services to U.S. military families. In the event of a disaster such as an earthquake, tornado, flood, fire, or hurricane, it provides relief services to communities across the country.

Disasters have occurred since Adam and Eve's sin warped the perfect world God created. God sent the Flood during Noah's time and often threatened to send disasters as judgment for sin. He identifies himself as the One who sends both good times and bad times (Isaiah 45:7). Disasters can also result because this world is under the power and control of Satan (1 John 5:19), even though God ultimately determines the extent of that power.

The best way to prepare for disaster is to remember that God is always in control and to use the good times to grow a strong faith and vibrant prayer life. Then when the bad times come, we can continue to trust him to keep us safe and provide for our needs. If we are believers, we have already avoided the ultimate disaster that no one can provide relief from—dying without having accepted the gift of forgiveness for our sin.

May 22

* * *

I will refuse to look at anything vile and vulgar.
PSALM 101:3

On May 21, 1980, President Carter declared a state of emergency at Love Canal in Niagara Falls, New York. For several years there had been public concern about the dangers of toxic chemicals in the area. Hooker Chemicals and Plastics had used the abandoned canal as a dumping site between 1942 and 1953. The company later sold the property, and the new landowners built homes and schools on the land.

Studies showed that some residents had suffered chromosome damage and other health problems caused by the buried toxic chemicals seeping through the ground into their home. Approximately seven hundred families were evacuated and temporarily relocated. Love Canal became a symbol to many of the threat of hazardous wastes in modern society.

Today our society is in a state of emergency because of the toxic effects of pornography. For years, magazines, films, and now the Internet have spread harmful images and material. The results have been damaged families, increased crime rates, unhealthy relationships, and wasted lives. Pornography doesn't just demean women—it degrades the human race and distorts something that God planned to be a beautiful expression of love within marriage.

Even Christians are not immune to the harmful and addictive effects of pornography. What was once considered taboo is now accepted in mainstream magazines, television programs, and movies. King David knew the importance of protecting himself from evil. He vowed to never look at anything vile or vulgar (Psalm 101:3). David was determined to have nothing to do with anything that might lead him away from righteousness. Until we relocate to our pure, permanent home, we are responsible to guard against what seeps into our earthly home.

May 23

* * *

There is salvation in no one else! God has given no other name under heaven by which we must be saved.

ACTS 4:12

C arolus Linnaeus was born on this day in 1707. Many consider Linnaeus the originator of modern scientific classification of plants and animals and often refer to him as the father of classification. He studied botany and medicine and taught both. The first to lay down principles for defining genera and the species of organisms, Linnaeus also developed a uniform system for naming them.

In May 1753, he published the first edition of his two-volume *Species Plantarum*. Five years later, his tenth edition of *Systema Naturae* applied this system to animals as well. These two works are considered the foundation of binomial nomenclature. Linnaeus classified 4,400 species of animals and 7,700 species of plants.

After God formed all the birds and animals from the ground, he gave the first man, Adam, the privilege of picking names for them (Genesis 2:19). God brought them to Adam and let him choose a name for each one. Adam even got to pick a name for his wife (Genesis 3:20).

We get to name our children and pets. Some people choose nicknames for their spouses and even name their cars. But we *don't* get to pick the name of our Savior. When Peter and John were arrested for preaching and were questioned by the Sanhedrin, Peter declared that there is salvation in no name except that of Jesus of Nazareth. In our diverse society, people want to name their own method of getting to know God. They may call a person, a group, or some philosophy their savior. But salvation from sin comes only from faith in the name that was already chosen before the world was created.

May 24

✳ ✳ ✳

They think the whole world revolves around them!
EZEKIEL 38:12

I n the early sixteenth century, Nicolaus Copernicus, a Polish astronomer, developed a mathematically strong heliocentric, or sun-centered, system of astronomy, rejecting the Ptolemic theory of the earth as the center of the universe. Copernicus argued that all the planets revolve around the sun and that the earth rotates on its axis once every day. Because of his groundbreaking work many consider him to be the father of modern astronomy.

Copernicus knew his theory would upset leaders who could have him punished or even killed, but his supporters urged him to publish his writings. By the time his masterpiece, *On the Revolutions of the Heavenly Spheres*, was released, Copernicus was on his deathbed. He died on May 24, 1543, escaping the severe penalties suffered by some of his supporters.

False religions revolve around something other than God. They may revolve around nature, self, a philosophy, a set of rules, or a prophet. Christianity is centered on the person of Jesus Christ, who is God in the flesh. But even believers have to struggle against our human nature, which thinks that the world revolves around us.

Once we become Christians, we are to be God-centered, no longer motivated by our wants and needs. We work for his glory instead of our own. We serve God for who he is, not for what we get from him. He is at the center of our desires, goals, and choices, even though our culture and our old sin nature nudge us back to a "me-centered" life. Christ must be at the center of our life before we can truly love God and others or carry out his will. Only then are things in the proper order.

What does your life revolve around?

May 25

* * *

*Together with them, we who are still alive and remain on the earth
will be caught up in the clouds to meet the Lord in the air.
Then we will be with the Lord forever.*

1 THESSALONIANS 4:17

O n this day in 1991, a massive airlift called Operation Solomon brought 15,000 Ethiopian Jews to live in Israel. Only those directly involved knew about the Sabbath day mission. Any airplane that could fly the distance brought loads of passengers who disembarked, dropped to their knees, and kissed the ground. An earlier mobilization had transported 14,500 Ethiopian Jews to Israel between November 1984 and January 1985, but many had been left behind.

In 1877, Professor Joseph Halevi studied and wrote about the Falasha ("strangers"), as other Ethiopians called the Jews in their country. Besides the Jewish holidays, the Falasha observed a day of mourning fifty days after Yom Kippur. All the villagers gathered at the highest point of a mountain and spent all day praying that God would bring them to Zion, or Jerusalem.

God has scheduled his own airlift, more massive than anything the world has ever seen. First, believers who have died will rise with their new, eternal bodies. Then, living believers' bodies will be transformed "in the blink of an eye" (1 Corinthians 15:52). Both groups will be caught up in the clouds to be united with Christ and with each other.

Only God knows when Operation Rapture, as some call it, will happen, but he wants us to live each day looking forward to the event. No matter how bad things get, we know that our rescue is already planned. We live as "Falasha" in a world hostile to our faith, but at the right time we will be air-lifted out of here and will drop to our knees before our Savior.

May 26

* * *

[God said,] "He who overcomes shall inherit all things."
REVELATION 21:7, NKJV

The major networks in Britain and the United States initially rejected the concept behind the television series *Survivor*. When Swedish television developed the idea into *Expedition Robinson* in 1997, it was an instant hit. In May 2000, *Survivor* premiered in the United States to major ratings success. The American version airs around the world.

In each *Survivor* episode, sixteen contestants appear in a remote, harsh environment, although the conditions are not life-threatening. Divided into teams, they vote someone out of their tribe every three days. The two tribes eventually merge, and each person then competes individually for reward and immunity. The last remaining survivor wins one million dollars.

God leaves believers in a harsh environment, although our souls are never in any danger. We can gain rewards for service and obedience, and we have been freely given immunity from the penalty of sin. Best of all, we are members of one huge tribe, and no one ever gets voted off the island, although some days we may wish we had that option.

God doesn't expect us to merely survive; he calls us to be overcomers. If we are children of God, our faith in Christ has already overcome the world (1 John 5:4-5, NIV). In Revelation 2 and 3, Jesus tells what is in store for overcomers: They eat manna and fruit from the tree of life; they sit with him on his throne and have authority over the nations; and the Savior himself announces them before God and the angels. What we have to look forward to at the end of our "episode" is far greater than a measly million dollars.

Are you living like an overcomer or merely surviving?

May 27

* * *

Are you amazed and incredulous? Don't you believe it?
ISAIAH 29:9

R obert LeRoy Ripley died on this day in 1949. Ripley was an American cartoonist who gained fame for his cartoon panel titled "Believe It or Not." The panel contained illustrations describing strange facts, events, and oddities Ripley had collected during his extensive travels around the world. At one time, the cartoon had an estimated daily newspaper audience of eighty million readers.

Ripley also used the material to develop lectures, radio and television shows, books, movies, and museums. In 1933, he opened his first Odditorium in Chicago, Illinois. Today, there are nineteen Ripley's Believe It or Not! Museums in the United States and eight in other countries.

When it comes to the gospel, we have the same two choices—to believe it or not. God makes it clear that those who reject him have willfully refused to believe. The consequences are serious. Anyone who refuses to believe the gospel will be condemned at the final judgment (Mark 16:16). During the Tribulation, God will allow unbelievers to be deceived by the Antichrist because they have rejected the truth (2 Thessalonians 2:10-11).

Anyone who chooses to believe and accept the gospel is given salvation. But while we are on earth, we still struggle with doubts. Our lack of faith can cause God to limit his work in our life, just as Jesus did not perform many miracles in his hometown because of the people's unbelief (Mark 6:5). God wants to help us with our doubts, but he requires honesty. Like the father who wanted Jesus to heal his son, we can admit, "I do believe, but help me overcome my unbelief!" (Mark 9:24).

May 28

* * *

[Jesus said,] "Those who accept my commandments and obey them are the ones who love me."

JOHN 14:21

T he National Spelling Bee finals are held each year on the Tuesday, Wednesday, and Thursday after Memorial Day. The event began in 1925 with nine contestants. Today, newspapers and other sponsors send 240 to 250 students to the finals. Out of the eighty-one national champions, forty-two are girls and thirty-nine are boys.

The sponsors organize spelling bees in their communities, usually with help from local school officials. Individual champions advance to the finals in Washington, D.C. Students are eligible if they are younger than sixteen at the time of the national finals and eighth grade or lower during their school's final competition. Rewards for the champion include a reference library, a set of encyclopedias, a savings bond, and cash prizes, which totaled seventeen thousand dollars in the 2005 spelling bee.

God has a different way of spelling *love* than we do. He spells it o-b-e-y. Jesus said that if we love him we will obey his commandments. He set the perfect example by loving God through obedience even to the point of dying on the cross. John wrote that we can tell who is a child of God and who is a child of the devil by seeing if they live righteously (1 John 3:10). God judges our love not by our words but by our lifestyle.

Our culture confuses love with sentiments and feelings. Love is not something we "fall into," but something we choose to do. God is not impressed by our warm, fuzzy feelings when we are refusing to live as he wants us to. Biblical love requires great commitment and sacrifice, but the rewards are also great. We have no excuse for not knowing how to love God. He has spelled it out for us in his Word.

May 29

He makes me as surefooted as a deer, enabling me to stand on mountain heights.

2 SAMUEL 22:34

O n this day in 1953, at 11:30 a.m., Edmund Hillary of New Zealand and Tenzing Norgay, a Sherpa guide from Nepal, became the first people to reach the summit of Mount Everest, the highest point on Earth. They approached the mountain from the south side, which had been labeled unclimbable. Since Hillary and Norgay's success, hundreds of climbers have successfully reached the top of the world.

Mount Everest sits on the crest of the Great Himalayas in Asia, on the border between Nepal and Tibet. With the summit at about the cruising altitude of jets, climbers must contend with very low oxygen levels, deadly cold temperatures, and unpredictable, dangerous weather.

We all have mountains in our life. They loom ahead of us, blocking our path and preventing us from reaching our goals and dreams. We can't go around the mountains and we can't go over them. Or can we? Jesus said that a tiny amount of faith like a mustard seed can move a mountain (Matthew 17:20). He wasn't talking about moving physical mountains, but about following God's will. Within his plan, our small faith combined with his power has the potential to accomplish anything.

Once we reach the summit of our "mountain," we need to have the same attitude as David. Both Psalm 18 and 2 Samuel 22 contain his song of praise after he had victory over his enemies. David gave God credit for everything he accomplished, even his agility in the high, rocky places where he often fled for refuge. If God allows us to reach the top of the world, we need to remember who guided us there.

5-26-01
for memorial Day

May 30

* * *

[Jesus told his disciples,] "Do this to remember me."
LUKE 22:19

Memorial Day, formerly known as Decoration Day, was instituted to honor the Civil War dead. Local observances were held as early as 1866, many of them in the South where most of the war dead were buried. The first official and large observance took place on May 30, 1868, at Arlington National Cemetery, which held the remains of twenty thousand Union soldiers and several hundred Confederate dead. Five thousand people attended the ceremony.

New York was the first state to declare the holiday, in 1873; other states quickly followed. After World War I, citizens expanded the observance to honor those who died in all American wars. In 1971, Congress declared Memorial Day a national holiday and changed the date to the last Monday in May. In recent years, many use the occasion to decorate the graves of loved ones.

Under God's direction, the Israelites had "Memorial Day" celebrations to help them remember major events in their history. They celebrated Passover each year to commemorate their miraculous deliverance from slavery in Egypt. When Jesus ate his last Passover meal, he instituted a new memorial to commemorate the deliverance from slavery to sin that he would accomplish for all believers through his death. As he shared the bread and wine with his disciples, he instructed them to eat and drink in remembrance of him.

The speaker at the first official Memorial Day service urged the audience to tend the graves of the dead soldiers to testify that our country had not forgotten the cost of a free, undivided republic. When we take part in the Lord's Supper we are testifying that we remember the cost of our salvation. We are celebrating a "Memorial Meal" in honor of the One who won the war against death and sin.

May 31

* * *

"For I know the plans I have for you," says the LORD. *"They are plans for good and not for disaster, to give you a future and a hope."*

JEREMIAH 29:11

Thousands of graduation ceremonies are held across the United States in late May and early June. Many schools have two ceremonies: the baccalaureate, or religious service, held in a church; and the commencement exercises, when the class valedictorian and salutatorian give speeches and the diplomas are handed out.

Historians believe that graduation exercises were first held by European universities during the Middle Ages. Today, American educational institutions still retain many of the European graduation traditions. The customary long robes and flat, tasseled mortarboards are derived from European academic dress.

When we become Christians, in a sense we are also "graduating." Our name is called out and recorded in the Lamb's Book of Life. Instead of rental gowns, we get permanent robes of righteousness and a helmet of salvation (without the hassle of a tassel). Our "diploma" is the Good News, which God entrusts to us so that we can share it with others.

Like a new graduate, we may wonder what our future holds. While God's Word doesn't give us specific details of how our life will play out, it does give us assurance about our future. Before we even knew him, God had a custom-made spiritual career planned for us. He has equipped us with exactly what we need to travel that path. We can know that our future is secure in his hands as we wait for that final "graduation," when our name will once again be called and we will walk across the stage where eternity waits on the other side. And then our real future will begin.

June 1

* * *

Sing to the LORD; praise his name. Each day proclaim the good news that he saves.
PSALM 96:2

C able News Network (CNN) went on the air for the first time on this day in 1980. Ted Turner created the network to offer live news broadcasts around the clock, using satellites to transmit reports from news bureaus throughout the world. The station gained attention with its 1991 coverage of the Persian Gulf War. Turner's company also operates two other news channels: Headline News and CNN International.

Paul considered his ministry of telling the Good News a sacred trust from Jesus Christ himself. Paul said that his life was worthwhile only if he used it for doing the work that the Lord Jesus assigned him: "the work of telling others the Good News about the wonderful grace of God" (Acts 20:24). As he traveled toward Jerusalem, the Holy Spirit revealed that trials and suffering awaited him there and that his life would soon end. Yet Paul focused on his ministry and used every opportunity to share the news of God's saving grace wherever he went.

We aren't all appointed to be missionaries, pastors, or teachers. But we are all assigned the task of spreading the news about salvation. David said he had not kept the news of God's love, faithfulness, and saving power hidden in his heart but had told everyone in the assembly (Psalm 40:10). No matter what our gifts are, or what our job is, or where we live, God places someone around us who needs to hear his message of love and forgiveness from our mouth. Sometimes we focus solely on "lifestyle witness" and forget that non-believers need to hear the words too. If we are willing and stay tuned in to God's Spirit around the clock, we will find opportunities to broadcast the most important news throughout our world.

How are you helping to spread the Good News and God's grace?

June 2

* * *

Who are those who fear the LORD? He will show them the path they should choose.
PSALM 25:12

The American Hiking Society sponsors National Trails Day on the first Saturday of June. People first observed this special day in 1993. It draws thousands of outdoor enthusiasts for trail dedications, educational exhibits and workshops, gear demonstrations, and trail work projects.

National Trails Day also highlights the work of volunteers, land managing agencies, and businesses that support the development and maintenance of our nation's trails. The American Hiking Society hopes to increase the public's awareness of trails and the benefits of hiking, including improved health and weight management.

We need to be careful of what trail we hike on. Jeremiah warned Judah of the danger of straying from the old paths of godliness and righteousness. The people had left God's ways to follow new paths of idolatry and apostasy. Today our society encourages us to turn aside from the "old paths" laid out by God in his Word to try "new" roads to self-fulfillment and enlightenment. But only his way is good, and when we follow it, we will find rest for our soul (Jeremiah 6:16).

In Matthew 7:13-14, Jesus contrasted two trails that we all choose between. The way to hell is a broad highway, easy to travel with a wide gate. The road to God's Kingdom and eternal life is narrow with a small gate. The road to salvation may be narrow, but it is well-marked by God's Word, well-lit by the Light of the World, and well-worn by the saints of old. It is our duty to make others aware of this trail and its benefits, which are out of this world.

June 3

O death, where is your victory? O death, where is your sting?
1 CORINTHIANS 15:55

The 1989 Tiananmen Square Protest was the peak of a series of student-led prodemocracy demonstrations in China. In early May, around one hundred thousand students and workers marched in Beijing to demand democratic reforms. On June 3 and 4, the People's Liberation Army crushed the protesters, killing and injuring an undetermined number. Although the Chinese government had suppressed similar protests for years, the brutal measures taken at Tiananmen Square brought international condemnation.

One powerful symbol of the protest came from a famous photograph taken of a solitary figure standing in front of a row of advancing tanks, halting their approach. The unidentified protester stood defiantly in front of the tanks for half an hour until a bystander pulled him out of the way. *Time* magazine named him "The Unknown Rebel" and included him in their list of "100 Most Influential People of the 20th Century."

Two thousand years ago, a solitary figure hung on a cross to defeat death. As God in the flesh, Jesus was the only one who had the power to break the curse of sin that leads to eternal separation from God. When Jesus offered himself as a sacrifice on our behalf and then rose from the dead, he stopped death in its tracks and broke sin's tyrannical grip.

No one could pull Jesus out of the way of the cross, although Peter tried. When Jesus predicted his death, Peter took him aside and said, "Heaven forbid, Lord. This will never happen to you!" Jesus responded, "Get away from me, Satan!" He scolded Peter for "seeing things merely from a human point of view, not from God's" (Matthew 16:22-23). Jesus had to submit to death in order to defy it. Each time we are obedient to God, we are staging our own protest against Satan and sin.

June 4

* * *

My lover said to me, "Rise up, my darling! Come away with me, my fair one!"
SONG OF SONGS 2:10

T his day in 1798 saw the posthumous publication of the twelve-volume autobiography of Giacomo Girolamo Casanova. Born in Venice, Italy, in 1725, Casanova's actor parents planned for him to enter the priesthood, but at age sixteen he was expelled from a seminary for misconduct. After that, Casanova worked as a secretary, a soldier, a preacher, an alchemist, a gambler, a violinist, a lottery director, and a spy. He became chiefly known for his reputation as a seducer of women.

Casanova was continually involved in political and amatory plots. While traveling throughout Europe, he gained the friendship of many important people and won fame for his wit and charm with women. He is often referred to as the greatest romantic lover of all time.

Our society seems obsessed with the idea of romantic love, but unfortunately, the word *lover* usually refers to an immoral relationship. Song of Songs gives a beautiful picture of pure love. The two lovers anticipating their marriage describe the physical, emotional, and spiritual joys of love between a man and woman. It's sad that the concept of love has been so twisted that this God-ordained poetry embarrasses many Christians.

In a world of couples, and singles looking to be couples, it's easy to forget that our most important love relationship is with Jesus Christ. He gave up his life to become, as many writings and songs say, the "lover of my soul." For our part, we are to act as his lover—putting him first and finding joy and fulfillment in him. If we look at who he is and what he has done for us, we will agree with Matthew Henry: "What, not love the most glorious lover in the world!"

June 5

* * *

[Jesus said,] "You will grieve, but your grief will suddenly turn to wonderful joy."
JOHN 16:20

O n this day in 1998, Arizona Congressman Bob Stump stunned his colleagues in the House of Representatives when he reported, "It is with great sadness I announce that Bob Hope has died." Within seconds of his speech, worldwide media rushed to prepare tributes to the beloved entertainer.

Bob Hope's daughter Linda immediately called news agencies and told them her father was at home in Pasadena, California. "It's not true," she said. "He's happily having his breakfast." Congressman Stump later explained that he had seen the story on the Associated Press Web site. AP blamed the erroneous obituary on a technical problem. Bob Hope didn't die until July 2003.

On the third day after Jesus' crucifixion, two of his followers were walking to the village of Emmaus. A stranger joined them and asked why they were so sad. While sharing a meal with him, the two men were suddenly stunned to recognize that Jesus was alive and was the stranger (Luke 24:13-34)! Just as Jesus had predicted, his followers' grief turned to wonderful joy as they saw that he had risen from the dead.

There have always been people who acknowledge the life and death of Jesus but deny his resurrection. In 1 Corinthians 15:12-34, Paul explained that the Resurrection is the core of our faith. If Christ has not really been raised, then our faith is useless and we are still condemned for our sins. But just as surely as death entered the world through Adam, resurrection from death began through Jesus Christ. We all physically die because we are related to Adam, but if we are related to Christ, we receive new life. When we die, our obituary may be accurate on earth but it will be invalid in heaven.

June 6

* * *

Not forsaking our own assembling together, as is the habit of some.
HEBREWS 10:25, NASB

Richard Hollingshead opened the world's first drive-in movie theater in Camden, New Jersey, on this day in 1933. He had wanted to invent something that pertained to his two main interests: cars and movies. So he experimented in his driveway with a projector on the hood of his car, a screen nailed to trees in his backyard, and a radio set behind the screen. After diligent testing and modification, he was ready for the first public screening, charging twenty-five cents per person plus twenty-five cents for the car.

The idea was an instant success, and Hollingshead and his cousin developed a drive-in movie franchise throughout the United States. The popularity of drive-ins peaked in the 1950s, with five thousand scattered across the country. Their success gradually tapered off during the 1970s because of higher real estate costs and competition from cable television and video rentals. Today there are approximately five hundred drive-in theaters in the United States.

Some people treat church like a drive-in movie. They want to park in their own pew, watch the service, toss something in the offering plate, and not be bothered again until the next "showing." Some Christians think their Sunday spiritual fix is enough and don't get involved in the ministry of the church or other members' lives. The New Testament paints a totally different picture of the church.

The early Christians met together in homes, shared meals and material possessions with one another, and functioned like a family. Hebrews urges us to keep the habit of gathering together on a regular basis to give and receive strength and encouragement. We are to study the Bible together, pray together, and grow together. The only similarity in a drive-in movie and church is that in both we get a preview of coming attractions—in church we get a little taste of heaven as we worship the Lord together.

June 7

***

L eonardo da Vinci suggested the concept of a parachute about 1495, but the first practical one was not invented until the 1780s. In 1785, French aeronaut Jean Pierre Blanchard dropped a dog attached to a parachute from a hot-air balloon. Twelve years later, Andre-Jacque Garnerin used a cloth parachute to jump from a hot-air balloon in Paris. Parachutes soon became standard equipment for balloonists and later were adopted as life-saving devices for airplane pilots and passengers.

When nylon was patented in 1937, its benefits as parachute material quickly became apparent. Researchers used dead weights for testing until Adeline Gray made the first jump in the United States, using a nylon parachute, in June 1942. Ms. Gray, who worked as a parachute rigger at the Pioneer Parachute Company, jumped from an aircraft flying out of Brainard Field in Hartford, Connecticut.

A parachute is a good illustration of faith. The employees at the Pioneer Parachute Company most likely believed that nylon parachutes worked, but Adeline Gray demonstrated trust that the parachute would hold her up. The word *believe* is used almost a hundred times in the book of John alone. The biblical use of the words *believe* and *faith* mean much more than having an opinion or mere intellectual agreement.

John 8:30-59 states that some people believed Jesus' words without making a commitment of faith in him. He called them children of the devil (8:44). Just because we believe the message is true doesn't mean we are born again. Belief in Christ means to place confidence in him to save us. We are persuaded of God's truth, we have surrendered to him, and our lifestyle demonstrates that trust. We don't just believe that the gospel is true; we have taken a leap of faith and it's holding us up.

June 8

* * *

When the woman saw that the fruit of the tree was good for food and pleasing to the eye, and also desirable for gaining wisdom, she took some and ate it.
Genesis 3:6, NIV

On this day in 1937, a specimen of the world's largest flower bloomed in the United States at the New York Botanical Garden. The giant Sumatran Titan Arum (*Amorphophallus titanum*) measured eight and a half feet high with a four-foot diameter. Visitors were repelled by its putrid, rotting-corpse fragrance. The plant is native to the Sumatran jungles of Indonesia, where it is called the "corpse flower."

The first Western botanist to find the Titan Arum was Dr. Odoardo Beccari of Italy. He sent his patron seeds and supervised their cultivation in Italy. Fom there, shipments of the "corpse flower" were sent to other countries.

Eve decided that the fruit from the tree of the knowledge of good and evil looked delicious and pretty and would make her wise. But when she and Adam disobeyed God's command and ate from the forbidden tree, it was as if the fruit became "corpse fruit." For the first time, the stench of death and decay entered God's perfect garden. They were repelled by the results and expelled from the garden.

We play out that same scene anytime we give in to sin's pull. A habit seems harmless, an activity appears pleasurable, or a relationship looks attractive, so we ignore the Spirit's nudge that this is not in line with God's will. Eventually what seemed harmless blooms into full-blown sin, with a putrid fragrance of death and destruction. The results may be the death of a dream or ministry, or even physical death. We need to remember that just because a flower has a large, colorful bloom doesn't mean it smells good. And just because a decision looks harmless doesn't mean that we won't be repelled by the results.

June 9

* * *

He rescued us from the domain of darkness,
and transferred us to the kingdom of His beloved Son.
COLOSSIANS 1:13, NASB

I n early June 1995, Air Force pilot Captain Scott O'Grady was shot down while helping to enforce the NATO no-fly zone over Bosnia. When the surface–to-air missile struck his F-16, O'Grady parachuted into hostile territory. Serbian forces immediately began searching for the pilot to capture him and use him as a bargaining tool.

O'Grady slept during the day, covered with camouflage netting, and traveled between midnight and 4 a.m. He soaked up rainwater with a sponge and ate grass and bugs. Even though armed Serbs were never far away from him, O'Grady managed to avoid capture for six days, when members of the U.S. Marine Corps carried out a daring rescue mission and plucked the young captain out of enemy territory.

We have all been in enemy territory. We are born with a sin nature and come into a world under the influence of Satan. He is armed with lies, traps, and temptations to keep us under his dominion. Satan desperately tries to capture our soul. But God carried out a daring rescue mission on our behalf. He sent his Son, Jesus Christ, into the middle of hostile territory, where he knew Jesus would be rejected, persecuted, and crucified.

Through Christ's sacrificial death, God rescued us from Satan's kingdom of darkness and brought us into Christ's kingdom of light and love. God's plan was carried out before we were born, but we have to make the choice to be rescued. Once we are delivered into Christ's Kingdom and get a taste of the abundant life he offers, we wonder how we ever survived on the spiritual equivalent of grass and bugs.

June 10

Confess your sins to each other and pray for each other so that you may be healed.
JAMES 5:16

O n this day in 1935, two men with serious drinking problems, a New York City stockbroker and an Ohio physician, formed a program they called Alcoholics Anonymous. Today A.A. includes more than eighty thousand local groups in the United States and an estimated two million members worldwide. Others have started similar addiction support groups using A.A.'s twelve-step program.

The A.A. program prescribes total abstinence as members refrain from alcohol "one day at a time." The first step for new members is to admit they have a drinking problem by standing up at a meeting and confessing, "I am an alcoholic." Members share their experiences and learn to draw strength from one another to break their addiction. Participants are urged to admit they are "powerless over alcohol" and to surrender their lives to "the care of God."

The first step to becoming a believer is for us to admit that we have a problem with sin. We have to understand our natural state as a sinner before we can come to the Cross and confess, "I am a sinner." Once we name our disease, we can accept the cure that Jesus offers.

After we accept Christ, we still have a problem with sin. His death has paid the penalty for our sin and assured us of acceptance by God. But we still struggle against our old nature, which daily tempts us to give in to sin's pull. Many Christians think they have to look perfect and hide their struggles, but James 5:16 urges us to confess them to fellow believers and pray for one another. As we humble ourselves and draw strength from God and from one another, we will break sin's addiction "one day at a time."

June 11

*[Jesus said,] "The standard you use in judging is the standard
by which you will be judged."*
MATTHEW 7:2

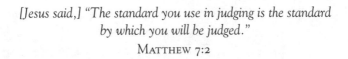

merican Idol: The Search for a Superstar premiered on this day in 2002
and was an instant sensation. The show followed the same formula
as the original British version, *Pop Idol*. Judges traveled across the nation and
auditioned thousands of hopeful singers, then chose thirty to perform on the
series. Viewers voted by phone to narrow the group to nine plus a "wildcard"
picked by the judges. Each week these finalists performed and faced a new
round of critiquing before one was ejected. The final winner nabbed an RCA
recording contract.

Many people consider judge Simon Cowell to be the secret to the show's
success. The British BMG Records executive was nicknamed "Mr. Nasty" by
British viewers. Cowell critiques most performances with embellished put-
downs and insults, once advising a contestant to hire a lawyer and sue her
voice teacher. Some people, upset by his harsh comments, are so vocal about
it that he has hired a security guard.

In 1 Corinthians 5:12, Paul says that it is our job to judge people within
the church in regard to sin. The problem is our tendency to be hypocritical
and readily judge a fellow believer's life without examining our own. Jesus
compared it to seeing a speck of sawdust in someone's eye but not noticing
the log in our own eye (Luke 6:41).

Jesus warned that we should stop judging others so that we would not be
judged (Matthew 7:1). He obviously didn't mean that we should not form
opinions or make judgments about situations or people. It is our duty to distinguish between good and evil, but we don't need to be habitually judgmental on issues that don't relate to sin. And we should never harshly criticize or
hastily condemn others. Believers should never earn the nickname "Mr." or
"Ms. Nasty."

When do you have a tendency to be overly critical or judgmental?

June 12

* * *

*Some people have deliberately violated their consciences; as a result,
their faith has been shipwrecked.*

1 TIMOTHY 1:19

I n June 1981, the Centers for Disease Control and Prevention
(CDC) reported that five homosexual men in California had a rare
form of pneumonia found only in patients with weakened immune systems.
These cases were later identified as acquired immunodeficiency syndrome
(AIDS), a viral disease that weakens the immune system, destroying the
body's ability to defend itself from disease. AIDS leaves an infected person
vulnerable to infections that are harmless to healthy people.

AIDS quickly became a worldwide epidemic, with an estimated forty million people living with HIV infection or AIDS by 2003. The United Nations
estimated that between 1981 and the end of 2003, around twenty million people had died worldwide because of AIDS and associated illnesses. The United
States Department of Health estimates that by the end of 2002, approximately
half a million people in the United States had died from AIDS.

Just as a weakened immune system makes a person susceptible to disease
and infection, a weakened conscience leaves a person vulnerable to sin. Paul
told Timothy that some people had shipwrecked their faith by violating their
conscience. Later in the first letter to Timothy, Paul warned against false
teachers who were liars and hypocrites. They pretended to be religious, but
their conscience was dead, literally "seared" or "branded" as with a hot iron
(1 Timothy 4:2).

When people's conscience is seared, they have a hard time discerning
right from wrong and no longer feel remorse when they sin. The results can
easily be seen in our society: Casual sex is viewed as the norm. Abortion no
longer seems wrong. We debate over whether marriage is between a woman
and man. To ignore or resist our conscience is to weaken our God-given protection against the infection of sin.

June 13

* * *

Don't you realize that if even one person is allowed to go on sinning,
soon all will be affected?
1 CORINTHIANS 5:6, NLT-1

The worst accident in racing history occurred on this day in 1955, at Le Mans, France. In Europe's classic sports car race, the winner is the car that travels the greatest distance in a twenty-four-hour period around an 8.3-mile circuit. The course was originally laid out for slower cars, leading driver Pierre Levegh to complain about the need for a signal system with the faster speeds.

As the 1955 race entered its third hour, an Austin-Healey swerved to avoid a Jaguar making a pit stop. Levegh's Mercedes clipped the Healey at 150 miles per hour and shot into the air like a rocket. His car burst into flames and disintegrated, scattering components into the crowd of 250,000 spectators. Within a few seconds, approximately eighty people died, including Levegh, and a hundred were injured, many of whom were seriously maimed.

Just as an out-of-control car does a lot of damage in a crowd of spectators, one person who is blatantly sinning can do a lot of damage in a congregation. In 1 Corinthians 5, Paul scolds the Corinthian believers for tolerating one of their members who is involved in an immoral relationship. He says they even boast about their spirituality while allowing this sin in their midst.

Paul instructs them to exclude the man from intimate fellowship with other members until he repents. Corrective action was necessary for the man's sake as well as the rest of the congregation. Today we hear a lot about loving acceptance and tolerance but not much about church discipline. But tolerated sin eventually affects bystanders. It's imperative to take action when someone is out of control, whether it is a fellow believer or us.

June 14

***

I am not ashamed of the gospel, for it is the power of God for salvation to everyone who believes, to the Jew first and also to the Greek.

Romans 1:16, NASB

O n this day in 1777, the Continental Congress passed a resolution that "the flag of the United States be thirteen alternate stripes red and white" and that "the Union be thirteen stars, white in a blue field, representing a new Constellation." As new states were added to our nation, new stripes and stars were added to the flag. In 1818, Congress restored the thirteen original stripes and declared that only stars would be added to represent new states.

Citizens observed the first Flag Day in 1877 on the one-hundredth anniversary of the adoption of the Stars and Stripes. Congress instructed that the flag be flown from all public buildings. Several states continued the annual tradition, and in 1949 Congress designated June 14 as a national observance.

Many Americans proudly fly the Stars and Stripes year-round, but they take particular care when displaying the flag on Flag Day and other patriotic holidays. What a witness it would be if we Christians were as bold in displaying our faith. We worry too much about what the world will think—if someone will be offended or consider us intolerant.

Paul was never ashamed of being a believer in the gospel of Jesus Christ, no matter where he was or whose company he was in. He urged Timothy to "never be ashamed to tell others about our Lord" (2 Timothy 1:8). The gospel is true, and it alone has the power to save. We never need to apologize for being followers of Christ. It's a wonderful privilege to live under the American flag, but it's a greater honor to show that our allegiance is to God's Kingdom. If we had a little more spiritual patriotism, maybe more would join us.

June 15

Jesus answered him, saying, "It is written."
LUKE 4:4, NKJV

John Bartlett was born in June 1820 in Plymouth, Massachusetts. He started his career as a clerk in the University Book Store in Cambridge, which he later bought. While working there in 1855, he compiled the book for which he is chiefly known, *Familiar Quotations*.

Bartlett had little formal education, but his book of quotations has become one of the most widely used reference works in the English language. *Familiar Quotations* was published in nine editions during Bartlett's lifetime and numerous editions after his death. It is still published under his name today and contains over twenty-two thousand quotations.

The best text to quote is something believers should find very familiar—Scripture. As preparation for his ministry, Jesus spent forty days fasting in the wilderness. Satan tempted him physically, emotionally, and spiritually. As recorded in the fourth chapters of Matthew and Luke, the only words spoken by Jesus were verses from Deuteronomy 6 and 8. Satan soon left him alone.

Memorizing Scripture is an effective tool for spiritual growth and a powerful weapon in spiritual warfare. We need to have God's Word hidden in our heart so we can avoid sinning (Psalm 119:11). When we're in the middle of a trial or temptation, it's not always convenient to run for our Bible and search for a specific passage. But it's not enough just to be able to roll verses off our tongue. We have to study the whole Word of God and depend on his Spirit to teach us. Then when the devil tempts us to sin we can follow Jesus' example and remind Satan of what is written.

June 16

* * *

Jesus knew their thoughts, and said to them:
"Every kingdom divided against itself is brought to desolation,
and every city or house divided against itself will not stand."
MATTHEW 12:25, NKJV

O n this day in 1858, over a thousand Republican delegates gathered for the Republican State Convention in the statehouse at Springfield, Illinois. By early evening, they had chosen Abraham Lincoln as candidate for the U.S. Senate to oppose Democrat Stephen Douglas. At eight o'clock, Lincoln accepted the nomination with a memorable speech noted for a paraphrase of a verse from Matthew 12.

Acknowledging the issue of slavery that was tearing the nation apart, Lincoln declared, "A house divided against itself cannot stand. I believe this government cannot endure permanently." Lincoln's friends thought his speech was too radical, and his law partner believed it was politically incorrect. Lincoln lost the Senate campaign, but his skillful debates with Douglas led to his successful bid for the presidency in 1860.

Some people accused Jesus of healing a demon-possessed man by the power of Satan. Jesus pointed out that if Satan were casting out Satan, then he was fighting against himself and his kingdom would not stand. But if Jesus was casting out demons by the power of God, then God's Kingdom had arrived among them. He then challenged the people to make a clear-cut choice, to either work with him or against him.

History has shown that no city, kingdom, or country can escape destruction from internal war. The same is true of a church body or a household when divisive issues take the focus off Jesus, our leader. Even our mind can experience internal strife until we resolve to be 100 percent for Christ. Only then will our "house" stand.

June 17

* * *

The LORD is watching everywhere, keeping his eye on both the evil and the good.
PROVERBS 15:3

O n this day in 1994, millions watched live television coverage of a white Bronco traveling down Los Angeles freeways. Earlier that day, actor and former football star O. J. Simpson had learned that he would be charged with the June 12 murders of his ex-wife and her friend. Police located Simpson fleeing in the Bronco being driven by his friend, former football player Al Cowlings.

In a cell-phone conversation, Simpson told police that he was suicidal and had a gun to his head. Reporters learned of the escape attempt and began live television coverage of the Bronco flanked by police cars, using news heli-copters. After nine hours on the Los Angeles highways, the vehicle returned to Simpson's estate. Simpson surrendered after a ninety-minute standoff in the driveway. Police recovered the gun, a mustache and goatee disguise, and his passport.

Sometimes we feel no one is watching us, but there is no escape from an omnipresent God. He sees every action no matter how we try to hide. His eyes go beyond any television camera to see every thought and motive. There is no such thing as a secret from God. We can easily fool ourselves, but not him.

The watchfulness of God will either frighten us or comfort us. While God sees every "hidden" sin, he also sees every good deed that goes unno-ticed by the rest of the world. He sees every wrong and injustice done to us. He knows every need that concerns us and every sorrow that burdens us. And because he is a God of love and mercy, he will take care of all those things. As God's children, we never have to fear his piercing, far-reaching eyes.

What have you been trying to hide from God?

June 18

* * *

We who have fled to him for refuge can take new courage,
for we can hold on to his promise with confidence.
HEBREWS 6:18, NLT-1

Most critics considered Rudolf Nureyev the greatest male dancer of the twentieth century, if not of all time. Nureyev's overpowering stage presence and superb athletic skill and grace mesmerized audiences. As a national ballet star, Nureyev enjoyed the rare freedom of travel outside the Soviet Union until Soviet officials took away this privilege for disciplinary reasons.

Early in 1961, the Soviet ballet company selected Nureyev to replace an injured dancer in a Paris performance. In June, Soviet authorities decided to send Nureyev home after he broke the rules and mingled with foreigners. Knowing he would probably not be allowed abroad again, Nureyev broke from his Soviet guards at the airport and ran toward Paris policemen begging, "Protect me!" Nureyev's request for asylum was granted, and he began a new life of personal and professional freedom.

God set aside cities of refuge for the Israelites (Numbers 35). If a person killed someone accidentally, he could flee to one of these cities to escape the vengeance of the victim's relatives. The person was given asylum in the city until his case was judged by the community. Israelites could also secure sanctuary and protection by grasping the horns of the brazen altar in the Tabernacle courtyard (1 Kings 1:50).

The author of Hebrews applies this familiar concept of asylum to Jesus Christ (6:18). He is the only place of refuge where sinners can flee to escape the vengeance of the law, which demands judgment and death for sin. Christ's sacrifice satisfied God's justice and demonstrates his mercy. Once we choose to break away from our bondage to sin and cry out for Jesus to protect us, he will grant the ultimate asylum. And we will begin a new life of freedom.

June 19

* * *

The LORD is like a father to his children, tender and compassionate
to those who fear him.

PSALM 103:13

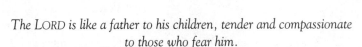

Sonora Dodd of Spokane, Washington, held the first Father's Day celebration for her father on this day in 1910. Dodd first had the idea of Father's Day while listening to a Mother's Day sermon in 1909. She wanted a day to honor her father, William Smart. The Civil War veteran's wife had died while giving birth to their sixth child. Smart raised the children by himself on a farm in Washington State.

President Calvin Coolidge supported the idea of a national observance for fathers. In 1966, President Lyndon Johnson signed a proclamation designating the third Sunday in June as Father's Day.

All believers have a loving and compassionate heavenly Father. Since he always has our best interests in mind, the relationship involves discipline. According to Proverbs 3:12, the fact that God corrects us shows that he loves us, just as an earthly father will correct a child he delights in. We can always count on God to give us compassion when we need it and discipline when we're asking for it.

In a prayer for mercy and pardon for the nation of Israel, Isaiah called on God as Father. "Surely you are still our Father! Even if Abraham and Jacob would disown us, LORD, you would still be our Father" (Isaiah 63:16). Because of our connection with Jesus, we have a more personal relationship with God than Israel did. Nothing can ever sever our bond with him. Father's Day is a good time to focus on our perfect heavenly Father and his love for us.

June 20

* * *

[Jesus said,] "The cares of this world, the deceitfulness of riches, and the desires for other things entering in choke the word, and it becomes unfruitful."

MARK 4:19, NKJV

U ntil June 1974, the traditional method for aiding choking victims was slapping them on the back, which tended to push the foreign objects farther into the airways. Dr. Henry Heimlich used the journal *Emergency Medicine* to introduce a technique that he called "subdiaphragmatic pressure." The person giving aid uses his fist in a firm upward thrust just below the choking victim's rib cage to force air and the food or object from the victim's lungs. Three months later, the method was named the Heimlich maneuver by the *Journal of the American Medical Association.*

Most people would not hesitate to use the Heimlich maneuver to help someone who is choking, but too often we don't lift a finger when sin has a stranglehold on someone. Jesus listed things that can choke the truth before it bears fruit. Believers sometimes slide into bad attitudes, harmful habits, or wrong actions that choke and hinder God's work in their life. During those times we may be tempted to stand by and watch, but God expects us to come to their aid. He wants us to love one another enough to confront someone who is behaving in a harmful or ungodly way.

When confronting, we have to make sure we use the correct "maneuver." Gossiping to others worsens the situation. Legalistic condemnation is ineffective. Self-righteousness guarantees deaf ears. We need to follow a basic two-step technique: prayer and speaking the truth in love. They may reject our message or get angry, but we have to be obedient. When someone's life or ministry is being choked by sin, the worst action we can take is to give them a friendly slap on the back and pretend that nothing is wrong.

June 21

*** * ***

*[Jesus said,] "Salt is good, but if it loses its saltiness,
how can it be made salty again?"*
LUKE 14:34, NIV

O n this day in 1961, President Kennedy pressed a button in his office in Washington, D.C., and dedicated the country's first practical sea-water conversion plant. Located in Freeport, Texas, the plant was operated by the Office of Saline Water, part of the U.S. Department of the Interior.

It produced approximately one million gallons of water a day at a cost of about $1.25 per thousand gallons. Today, reverse osmosis, made possible by the development of special polymers that make effective filtering membranes, has replaced the large-scale evaporation method of conversion.

God has a different kind of conversion process going on. When we become believers, he makes us salty. Jesus says that his followers are the salt of the earth (Matthew 5:13). But he warned that if the salt loses its saltiness, it is no longer good for anything. We should have something distinctive about our life that sets us apart and reveals God to other people. If we get to the point where we blend in with the rest of the culture instead of displaying godliness, we are no longer useful for God's work.

Some people think that Jesus compared believers to salt because we have a preserving influence on society: Through the indwelling Holy Spirit and our prayers, our presence helps to restrain the evil rampant in the world. Others believe that we are called salt because we make others thirsty to know God. If others see something different in us, they want to know more. Seawater has to have its salt removed before it is good for drinking, but we have to retain our saltiness so that we can give others the Living Water.

What are you doing to make sure you retain your "saltiness"?

June 22

* * *

All who listen to me will live in peace and safety, unafraid of harm.
PROVERBS 1:33, NLT-1

T he National Safety Council (NSC) designates June as National Safety Month. The goals are many: to offer safety and health solutions for the home, workplace, and community; to raise awareness of living safely both on and off the job; and to decrease the number of accidental injuries and deaths. The NSC provides daily safety tips throughout the month of June.

The mission statement of the NSC is "to educate and influence society to adopt safety, health, and environmental policies, practices, and procedures that prevent and mitigate human suffering and economic losses arising from preventable causes." The organization estimates that each year over twenty million Americans sustain disabling injuries at work, at home, during transportation, or in their community. Each day an estimated 270 people die from preventable injuries in the United States.

Believers should certainly embrace practical safety information and use common sense to avoid preventable injuries. But we know that our safety ultimately comes from our relationship with God. Proverbs 29:25 defines *safety* as "trusting in the Lord." If we submit to his leading, he promises to keep us safe and secure.

The world has been a dangerous place ever since Adam and Eve's fall into sin, but the threats to our safety seem to be multiplying daily. We face high crime rates, increasing health risks, and threats of terrorism. In such a time, we can look for encouragement from David. He faced many perils in his life, but he trusted God to lead him to "a place of safety" (Psalm 18:19). Even when he walked through the dark valley of death, David trusted in the Lord's presence and protection (Psalm 23:4). Regardless of our location or circumstances, the safest place to be is in God's powerful and loving hands.

June 23

* * *

*I have learned the secret of being content in any and every situation. . . . I can do
everything through him who gives me strength.*

PHILIPPIANS 4:12-13, NIV

On this day in 1884, America's first gravity-powered roller coaster
opened at Coney Island in New York City. LaMarcus A. Thompson's
Switchback Railway traveled at six miles per hour on a six-hundred-foot
track. The thrilling attraction was a huge success. Within four years, he had
built fifty more coasters across the nation and in Europe.

By the 1920s, North America had about two thousand roller coasters.
The popularity of amusement parks waned during the Depression and World
War II, when money was scarce and wood and rubber were needed for the
war effort. Roller coasters experienced a rebirth when the nation's first
Disneyland theme park opened in 1955. Today's roller coasters boast speeds
up to one hundred miles an hour on increasingly complex tracks that have
twists, loops, and drops.

People like roller coasters for the thrill of the ride. Sometimes our life
seems like a roller coaster, but we're *not* thrilled. In this world we will always
have ups and downs, highs and lows. We are on the mountaintop one day
and down in the valley the next. Our emotions can quickly plunge from
ecstasy to agony.

The apostle Paul had a roller-coaster kind of life, yet he declared that he
had learned to be content regardless of his circumstances, whether he was in
need or had plenty (Philippians 4:11-12). In another letter he linked contentment with godliness (1 Timothy 6:6). Since contentment is something that can
be learned, we have no excuse for riding on an emotional roller coaster. Our
life may not always be a walk in the amusement park, but even in hard times
we can trust in Christ's strength and provision. And that's a thrilling thought.

June 24

I will praise You, for I am fearfully and wonderfully made.
PSALM 139:14, NKJV

I n June 2000, researchers announced that they had decoded the set of genetic instructions that govern our body's assembly and function. Scientists presented a working draft of the human genome code after more than ten years of research. The success was the result of the work of thousands of researchers plus immeasurable hours of work by hundreds of robotic sequencing machines in labs operating around the clock.

The twenty-four different human chromosomes can't be seen by the eye, but each set contains 3.1 billion base pairs, or a code written in 3.1 billion "letters." Scientists compare the amount of data to the contents of two hundred telephone books, each one five hundred pages long. They estimate that reading this data aloud would take more than nine years.

In Psalm 139:13-16, David expresses awe at God's creation of the human body. He praises God that he "knit together" all the inner delicate parts of his body. God watched as David was being woven together (literally, "embroidered") in the dark of his mother's womb. David had only a tiny fraction of the knowledge we have today about how the human body is constructed, but he knew who designed it.

Maybe all our advancements in science and technology have dulled our sense of wonder. We forget that every day we walk around inside one of God's most intricate creations. We spend too much time and energy working to change our body instead of marveling at its complexity. Every time we look in the mirror, we see one of God's "embroidered" masterpieces, and we should agree with David, "Your workmanship is marvelous—how well I know it" (Psalm 139:14).

June 25

The LORD will hold you in his hand for all to see—
a splendid crown in the hand of God.

ISAIAH 62:3

I n June 1973, Secretariat became the first horse since 1948 to win the Triple Crown (the Kentucky Derby, the Preakness Stakes, and the Belmont Stakes). Secretariat set records in both the Kentucky Derby and the Belmont Stakes, where he won by an unprecedented thirty-one lengths.

In his two-year career, Secretariat came in first place sixteen times, second place three times, and third place once. Many racing fans regard him as the greatest Thoroughbred in history. Secretariat appeared on the covers of *Newsweek*, *Time*, and *Sports Illustrated*. A bronze statue of him was erected at Belmont Park in Elmont, New York.

God likes to award crowns, and not just to Thoroughbreds. When Paul knew that his death was near, he looked forward to his prize—the crown of righteousness that the Lord will give to everyone who eagerly looks forward to his glorious return (2 Timothy 4:8). James writes that we can patiently endure testing because God has promised a crown of life to those who love him (James 1:12). Solomon writes that if we embrace wisdom, "she will present [us] with a beautiful crown" (Proverbs 4:9).

Any crown we receive is made possible by the crown Jesus wore just before his crucifixion. After the Roman soldiers flogged him, they put a crown of long, sharp thorns on his head and then hit and mocked him (John 19:1-5). Jesus submitted to humiliation, suffering, and a painful death so that we can be exalted by God. But the next time Jesus comes to Earth, he will come as the King of kings to lead the armies of heaven and judge the world for sin (Revelation 19:11-16). On his head will be many crowns—none made of thorns.

June 26

* * *

He will assess its value, and his assessment will be final.
LEVITICUS 27:12

On this day in 1974, at 8:01 a.m., a checker swiped a package of Wrigley chewing gum across the first checkout scanner at the Marsh Supermarket in Troy, Ohio. The package became the first product ever logged under the new Universal Product Code (UPC) computerized recognition system. A committee of grocers and food manufacturers formed in the United States in 1970 had recommended the use of bar codes.

IBM invented the UPC, a 12-number bar code that represents the manufacturer's identity and an assigned product number. This information is read within nanoseconds by a laser beam moving approximately ten thousand inches per second. The data is then transferred to the store's database computer for pricing and inventory management. Today, bar codes keep track of everything from cattle to freight cars.

God doesn't need a scanner to keep track of who belongs to him. Once we accept Christ as Savior, we are marked with his Holy Spirit. Our names are logged into the Lamb's Book of Life. God instantly recognizes his children among the billions of people in the world. The presence of his Spirit living in us is invisible to the world, but it identifies us more reliably than any bar code.

God also doesn't need a scanner to tell him our value. Jesus asked his followers, "Is anything worth more than your soul?" (Mark 8:37). All the riches in the world don't come close to the value of eternal life with God. He purchased our soul at an immense expense through the death of his only Son. Our worth is not determined by a bar code but by the blood of Christ (1 Peter 1:19).

**Are you living as though you are valuable to God or
like you're not worth much?**

June 27

* * *

Jonah got up and went in the opposite direction to get away from the LORD.
JONAH 1:3

I n June 1884, William Tecumseh Sherman refused the Republican nomination for president. Sherman was the Civil War general most remembered for "Sherman's march to the sea," when he led a force of sixty thousand handpicked men from Atlanta to Savannah, Georgia. Determined to bring the war to an end, his soldiers pillaged the areas they passed through, devastating family farms, homes, and railroads along with military resources.

When the war ended in 1865, Sherman served as a lieutenant in the regular army. Once General Ulysses Grant was elected president, he promoted Sherman to the rank of full general and gave him command of the entire U.S. Army. Sherman retired in 1883. In 1884, when he refused the Republican nomination for president he said: "I will not accept if nominated, and I will not serve if elected."

The prophet Jonah had a similar attitude when God told him to go to the great city of Nineveh to warn of impending judgment if the people did not repent of their wickedness. Jonah responded by buying a ticket on a ship that was going the opposite direction of Nineveh. It took a violent storm and three days in the stomach of a big fish to teach Jonah that he couldn't run away from the mission God had planned for him.

God has good works planned for every believer, not to earn salvation, but to bring God glory and to give evidence of our new life in Christ (Ephesians 2:10). If we try to run away from what God wants to do in us and through us, we set ourselves up for misery and troubles. God doesn't nominate us for works, he appoints us to them. And the wisest thing we can do is to accept and serve.

June 28

* * *

The LORD God said, "It is not good for the man to be alone;
I will make him a helper suitable for him."
GENESIS 2:18, NASB

O n this day in 1778, a famous heroine of the War of Independence earned her nickname by bringing soldiers water from a spring at the battle of Monmouth. Molly Pitcher was born Mary Ludwig, and in 1769 she married John Hays, who later enlisted as a gunner in the First Pennsylvania Artillery.

Like many soldiers' wives, Molly went to camp with her husband and helped by cooking, washing, and other work. According to some accounts, when her husband collapsed from heatstroke during the Battle of Monmouth, Molly took his place at the cannon and fought the rest of the battle. In 1822, the Pennsylvania state legislature recognized her heroism with a yearly pension.

When God created a wife for Adam, he was making Adam's "other half." God made Adam from the ground, but Eve was created from Adam's side. She was his counterpart, someone to be his helper. The two were perfect companions for each other, meant to operate as one. Sadly, like all the other parts of God's perfect world, the marriage relationship has been distorted by sin. Husbands and wives often fight against each other instead of operating as one.

Cooking dinner and taking out the trash are important, but a more important way couples can help one another is to help fight each other's battles. Christian husbands and wives have a common enemy, Satan. He works hard to destroy their relationship and hinder their spiritual growth. If couples are honest and open with each other about their struggles, they can join forces. When one grows weary of the battle, the other can take the weapon of prayer and fight on their spouse's behalf.

June 29

* * *

*When you make a promise to God, don't delay in following through, for God takes
no pleasure in fools. Keep all the promises you make to him.*

ECCLESIASTES 5:4

M ost cases involving breach of promise are brought by women, but a
man filed the first breach of promise suit in America in June 1623.
Rev. Greville Pooley proposed marriage to the twice-widowed Cecily Jordan
and she accepted. Later, Mrs. Jordan's neighbor, William Farrar, asked her to
marry him and she agreed. The jilted minister sued the wealthy widow for
breach of promise.

The case drew a lot of attention in Virginia and in London. Rev. Pooley
eventually withdrew his suit and was forced to post bond that he would never
have any claim to Mrs. Jordan or her property. Virginia soon passed a law that
made it illegal for a woman to be engaged to more than one man at a time.

People have a hard time keeping their word. Promises are broken every
day between friends, business associates, and spouses. We make promises easily but have a hard time keeping them. Solomon warned against taking our
vows to God lightly. When we make a promise to him or anyone, he expects
us to keep it (Ecclesiastes 5:4).

In contrast to our unfaithfulness, God always keeps his promises, whether
they are promises of blessings or judgment. David declared "God's way is perfect" and all his "promises prove true" (Psalm 18:30). We can count on God
because "[his] promises are backed by all the honor of [his] name" (Psalm
138:2). It would be against his holy character to break his word. As individual believers, we can rely on his promises of provision, protection, and guidance. As a church, we have his promise to be our bridegroom—and he will
never jilt us.

June 30

* * *

There is no longer Jew or Gentile, slave or free, male and female.
For you are all one in Christ Jesus.
GALATIANS 3:28

T wenty-eight women attending the Third National Conference on the Commission on the Status of Women formed the National Organization for Women (NOW) in June 1966. Today, NOW has 550 chapters throughout the country campaigning for equality among women and men through demonstrations, protests, lobbying, litigation, and civil disobedience.

NOW's main objectives are to increase employment, educational, and political opportunities for women; end violence against women; support legalized abortion and access to birth control; and abolish discrimination based on sex, race, or sexual orientation. Within the last two decades, major focuses have been legalizing same-sex marriages, protecting the rights of lesbians, and increasing the number of women in policy-making positions in government, businesses, and other institutions.

In the past, women have been considered as nothing more than property or slaves with no rights at all. Some cultures today still see women as inferior to men. Jesus challenged the views of his time by treating women with respect and dignity. Many of his followers were female, and his ministry was supported largely by a group of wealthy women.

Christianity revolutionized the relationship between the sexes. While Scripture lays down differing roles for husbands and wives, it always places responsibility on both sides—a radical new concept in biblical times. Peter describes husbands and wives as equal partners in "God's gift of new life" (1 Peter 3:7). The New Testament makes it clear that women have equal value and deserve equal honor.

July 1

* * *

"A host always serves the best wine first," he said.
"Then, when everyone has had a lot to drink, he brings out the less expensive wine.
But you have kept the best until now!"

JOHN 2:10

T he world's first television commercial aired on this day in 1941, when NBC ran a ten-second advertisement for Bulova watches and clocks. The ad showed the picture of a clock and a map of the United States with a voice-over announcing, "America runs on Bulova time." The commercial cost the company less than ten dollars and was aired before a baseball game.

Bulova had previously broadcast the first radio commercial in 1926. Bulova broke new ground again in 1956 when it cosponsored *The Jackie Gleason Show*. This was the first time that a company of its type had ever made such a large sponsorship commitment.

Every day advertisements inundate our minds; ads appear everywhere— on television, on radio, on the Internet, in newspapers, in magazines, on sweatshirts, and even on the sides of buses. Deception has become standard practice in the world of advertising. That great deal may be an introductory offer, with the price going up after the first few months. There may be additional fees and charges beyond the advertised price. If we don't carefully read the fine print, we can end up with less than we bargained for.

God has a totally different approach to his offer of salvation. He tells us up front that when we accept Christ, we will have trials and sorrows. The world will hate us and persecute us. We will have to take up a cross and die to self. While we do experience incredible joys and benefits on earth, the best is coming later. Like the guests at the wedding where Jesus turned water into wine, we will be astonished that God saved the best for last.

July 2

* * *

Who are these that fly along like clouds?
ISAIAH 60:8, NIV

On this day in 1982, thirty-three-year-old Larry Walters fulfilled his dream of twenty years. The Vietnam veteran and truck driver, with no pilot or balloon training, filled forty-five weather balloons with helium, tied them to an aluminum lawn chair, and took off from the roof of a house in San Pedro, California. The balloons took him up faster than expected, and Walters soon drifted sixteen thousand feet above Long Beach.

As he approached a municipal airport, two mystified airline pilots notified air traffic controllers about what seemed to be a man floating across the sky in a chair. After Walters shot several balloons with a pellet gun, he descended, but the descent left him entangled in power lines ten miles from his takeoff point. Walters' instant celebrity status failed to recoup the estimated four-thousand-dollar cost of his flight, which included a fifteen-hundred-dollar fine from the Federal Aviation Administration.

We all sometimes wish we could just take off and fly away, far from our troubles and trials. When David was betrayed by a close friend, he cried, "Oh, that I had wings like a dove; then I would fly away and rest!" (Psalm 55:6). He yearned to escape the pain and sorrow of his situation.

We get into trouble when we try to take flight without waiting for God to give us wings. Isaiah said that those who trust in the Lord will find renewed strength and "soar high on wings like eagles" (Isaiah 40:31). The original readers of this passage were weary of waiting for deliverance from captivity. God promised to lift them up so they would not only endure, but soar. By trusting in God and waiting for him to act, we will also soar high above our circumstances—and we won't even need balloons or a lawn chair.

July 3

* * *

[Jesus said,] "You will know the truth, and the truth will set you free."
JOHN 8:32

I sraeli soldiers carried out a daring rescue mission on this day in 1976. Just a week earlier, on June 26, Palestinian terrorists had hijacked an Air France airliner on its way to Paris from Tel Aviv. The hijackers flew the plane to Entebbe, Uganda, and freed those passengers who did not appear to be Israeli. They held the 106 Israelis hostage to negotiate the release of fifty-three fellow terrorists in prisons in Israel, Kenya, West Germany, and other places.

Israel responded on July 3 by dispatching four cargo planes carrying approximately two hundred soldiers escorted by Phantom jet fighters. After flying the twenty-five hundred miles from Israel to Uganda, the commando unit rescued the hostages within an hour after the Israelis landed. During the operation, all seven hijackers, twenty Ugandan soldiers, and three hostages were killed.

Today, America is in a hostage situation. Our once great nation has been hijacked by those who insist that faith has no place in politics or the marketplace. Students no longer learn the true history of our country or the beliefs that led our Founding Fathers as they formed a government unlike any that had ever existed. Christians are intimidated and ridiculed when they speak out about the issues our society struggles with. It's hard to believe that America was founded on a belief in God and his standards of justice and righteousness.

Our country needs a daring rescue operation by believers who are willing to get involved in their neighborhood, workplace, and government. We have a powerful weapon in God's truth. Jesus said that the truth about salvation sets people free from bondage to sin. As we prayerfully and lovingly share God's truth, more people will experience that wonderful freedom, and our national hostage situation will be resolved as well.

July 4

* * *

My salvation and my honor depend on God.
PSALM 62:7, NIV

A mericans celebrate Independence Day, or the Fourth of July, as the birthday of the United States of America. It is the anniversary of the day on which the Continental Congress formally adopted the Declaration of Independence in 1776 at Philadelphia, Pennsylvania. A committee led by Thomas Jefferson wrote the Declaration, which is a powerful statement of the colonies' decision to become an independent nation and break ties with Great Britain.

The city of Philadelphia held the first celebration of Independence Day on July 8, 1776, just four days after the Declaration of Independence was adopted. Officials read the Declaration aloud, bands played, and city bells rang out. In 1941, Congress designated July 4 as a legal holiday to be observed in all states and territories.

Independence can be a good thing, but not when it comes to a relationship with God. In times of prosperity, the nation of Israel often became arrogant and the Israelites forgot their need for God. At other times they depended on Egypt or their own strength for security. Each time this happened, God warned of impending judgment: "I will bring an end to Israel's independence" (Hosea 1:4). He rebuked Israel for talking about depending on him but not living that way (Isaiah 48:1-2).

Perhaps our American spirit of rugged independence hampers our ability to fully rely on God. Sometimes we depend on God for our salvation but find it hard to look to him for daily guidance, strength, and material provision. Somehow we feel we should be earning our own way. But when we become believers, we adopt a declaration of *dependence* on God. Fully depending on him is the only way to break ties with Satan and sin.

When do you depend on something or someone other than God?

July 5

* * *

[Zophar asked Job,] "When you mock God, shouldn't someone make you ashamed?"

JOB 11:3

T he Church of the SubGenius developed with the 1980 publication of *SubGenius Pamphlet No. 1*. The group has been promoted on college campuses, among underground pop-culture figures, and on the Internet. Outsiders view the church as an elaborate mockery of organized religion. A 1950s clip-art drawing of a male smiling face smoking a pipe represents the SubGenius religion. "Bob" supposedly founded the church after seeing a vision of God, and "Bob" has been killed and resurrected many times. SubGenius gatherings, or Devivals, are usually held at nightclubs and feature "preachers" and rock bands.

On this day in 1998, a very important SubGenius event, X-Day, had been predicted by "Bob" as the date for the destruction of the world (except the SubGenius members) by aliens. Since this didn't occur, the church claims that it is obviously not 1998 yet. Members celebrate X-Day each year at a New York campground with bonfires, parties, and rock concerts.

Mocking the truth is nothing new. The first verse of Psalm 1 gives a progression of behavior we should avoid if we want to be blessed. The last step is joining in with mockers. Judah was judged for arrogance, even mocking the Holy One of Israel (Isaiah 5:19). Peter reminded his readers, "In the last days scoffers will come, mocking the truth" (2 Peter 3:3).

Today Christianity seems to be the preferred target for mocking. We identify with the Tabernacle musician Asaph when he cries out, "How long, O God, will you allow our enemies to insult you? Will you let them dishonor your name forever?" (Psalm 74:10). God waits for unbelievers to come to know him, but he will eventually judge those who scoff at the truth. When they mock Christianity, they are mocking him. It doesn't take a genius to figure out that's not a smart thing to do.

July 6

* * *

[God] wants everyone to be saved and to understand the truth.
1 TIMOTHY 2:4

O n the cover of *Leslie's Weekly*, on this day in 1919, "Uncle Sam" originally appeared. The picture carried the title, "What Are You Doing for Preparedness?" and went on to become "the most famous poster in the world" according to its creator, James Montgomery Flagg. More than four million copies were printed in 1917 and 1918 as the United States entered World War I.

Because of the enormous popularity of the illustration, recruiters later adapted it for use in World War II. Uncle Sam is still one of the most well-known personifications of the United States. Most people are familiar with the gentleman dressed in red, white, and blue who is staring into the viewer's eyes, with pointed finger, and saying, "I want you."

If we were to make a similar personification of God, he would also be saying, "I want you." God's desire is for the entire human race to come into a personal relationship with him through faith in Jesus Christ. Peter explained that one reason that Christ's return is delayed is because God "does not want anyone to be destroyed, but wants everyone to repent" (2 Peter 3:9). Jesus died to offer salvation to the entire world.

Because of low self-esteem or painful childhood experiences, some people feel that God could never desire them. Others think he would never forgive and accept them because of their sinful past. These are lies from Satan. God sees each and every person on the earth as someone worth dying for. And he did. Our poster of God would have him looking intently into our eyes, but not pointing. He would be holding his hands out to us, and they would be scarred by nailprints.

July 7

* * *

For the happy heart, life is a continual feast.
PROVERBS 15:15

I n July 1954, Britain celebrated the end of fourteen years of food rationing. The London Housewives' Association held a special ceremony in Trafalgar Square to observe Derationing Day. The Minister of Fuel and Power burned a large replica of a ration book at a gathering in his constituency.

Food rationing had begun in Great Britain in January 1940, four months after the start of World War II. Officials imposed limits on a number of essential and nonessential food items, including meat, butter, sugar, flour, and chocolate, and also on clothes, furniture, and fuel. Beginning in July 1948, three years after the war ended, officials gradually removed restrictions. The British saw the end of rationing six years later, when restrictions on meat and bacon ended.

Many people, including believers, live out a "rationing" religion. They limit their worship to Sunday mornings and their prayers to mealtimes and bedtime. They only open their Bible when they are in church services or else limit their reading to favorite, familiar Scriptures. They restrict their giving to what seems financially comfortable and their service to what easily fits into their schedule. They are spiritually depriving themselves without even realizing it.

This is not the kind of life that God intends for his children. God brought the Israelites to "a place of great abundance" (Psalm 66:12). Jesus came to give "a rich and satisfying life" to believers (John 10:10). God wants us to feast on his presence and his Word every day. Since his love, forgiveness, and mercy are unlimited, we can freely celebrate them every day and enjoy his blessings without restrictions.

July 8

* * *

You, brethren, have been called to liberty.
GALATIANS 5:13, NKJV

The Liberty Bell was rung in Philadelphia, Pennsylvania, on this day in 1776, after the first public reading of the Declaration of Independence. The following year, colonials moved the bell to Allentown, Pennsylvania, for safekeeping while British troops occupied Philadelphia. They returned the bell to Philadelphia in 1778, where bell ringers sounded it every July 4 and on every state occasion until 1835.

Scholars believe the crack in the bell appeared sometime between 1817 and 1846. There are several popular legends about when the bell cracked, but none of these are verified by newspaper accounts or documents. The Liberty Bell weighs 2,080 pounds and has a twelve-foot circumference at the lip. It bears the inscription: "Proclaim Liberty Throughout All the Land unto All the Inhabitants Thereof. Leviticus xxv:x."

Adam and Eve experienced perfect liberty in the Garden of Eden. They lived in a flawless environment free from worries about daily needs. In their innocent state, they did not know guilt or shame. Most importantly, they experienced an open, intimate relationship with their Creator. The moment they disobeyed God's command, sin took a heavy toll and a crack appeared in their liberty. The freedoms they had known were instantly taken away.

Thankfully, God had another plan. Although the perfect world of Eden was lost, he made a way for us to regain freedom from worry and guilt and to have an intimate relationship with him. Jesus came to restore the liberty we were meant to have. With him as our Savior, we don't have to worry about our future or the shame of past sins. We can enter into a personal relationship with our Creator. Like the Liberty Bell, we should be ringing out this news to proclaim the freedom found only in Christ.

*How have you experienced liberty through
your relationship with Christ?*

July 9

* * *

You are my hiding place; you protect me from trouble.

PSALM 32:7

I n 1933, Anne Frank's family moved from Germany to the Netherlands to escape the Nazi persecution of the Jews. In July 1942, her family, along with four other Jewish people, went into hiding in rooms in her father's office building in Amsterdam. Two years later, a neighbor betrayed the family to the Nazis, who arrested the group and sent them to concentration camps. Fifteen-year-old Anne died of typhus nine months later at the Bergen-Belsen camp.

Anne kept a record of her experiences during the twenty-five months spent in hiding. Her father published the diary in 1947 as *The Diary of a Young Girl*. Anne's diary has now been translated into sixty-seven languages and is still one of the world's most popular books.

In Isaiah 4:2-6, God describes a future time of restoration for Israel. Just as God's glory was visible to the Israelites during their exodus from Egypt, his presence will again be visible in Jerusalem. A canopy of smoke and cloud during the day and clouds of fire at night will cover the land. God's presence will be a shelter from heat and "a hiding place from storms and rain."

We all need a place to hide sometimes. We may not be looking for a way to escape persecution, but we may need a refuge from the storms of life. David praised God for being his hiding place in times of trouble (Psalm 32:7). We don't visibly see God's presence now, but his glory covers our life like a canopy. Regardless of the trials, stress, or pressures that are bearing down on us, we can draw close to God through worship, prayer, and the Word. He is the safest hiding place in the world.

July 10

* * *

A good name is to be more desired than great wealth.
PROVERBS 22:1, NASB

I ma Hogg was born on this day in 1882 into a wealthy Texas family. Ima's parents named her after the heroine of an epic Civil War poem written by her uncle. Despite rumors that Ima had a sister named Ura, she was the only girl in the family. Her parents chose ordinary names for her brothers—William, Michael, and Thomas.

Miss Ima, as she was known, enjoyed a privileged life but shared her wealth and resources with others. She became a leading philanthropist and is often referred to as the "first lady of Texas." Her contributions in the areas of education, mental health, history, the arts, and music left an enduring legacy that has enriched the lives of many people. Miss Hogg died at age 93 while vacationing in London.

Most people would agree that Ima Hogg had an ugly name, but that didn't stop her from living a life of beauty. The good name referred to in Proverbs is an honorable reputation based on admirable character, which is more valuable than great wealth. Miss Hogg had both wealth and a good reputation; people knew her as a lady of graciousness, compassion, and generosity.

These days Christians are called all sorts of unflattering names, some of them downright ugly. But our concern should be with what kind of reputation we are building by our actions and lifestyle. We can't always avoid being misunderstood, but how the world sees us influences how people see Christ. Our reputation will either contribute to or detract from God's work. We don't all have the resources to be great philanthropists like Ima Hogg, but we all have spiritual wealth to share with others, regardless of what the world calls us.

July 11

* * *

[Jesus said,] "You ignore God's law and substitute your own tradition."
MARK 7:8

O n this day in 1985, the Coca-Cola Company announced the return of the original formula for its flagship soft drink, now to be called Coca-Cola Classic. Two network newscasts featured the announcement as their major story that day, and it appeared on the front page of almost every prominent newspaper in the country. Company executives expressed surprise at the bond consumers felt with their drink and their outrage when the manufacturer tampered with it.

In April 1985, the Coca-Cola Company had introduced a new, sweeter version called New Coke. Although taste tests of two hundred thousand consumers had indicated a preference for the new formula, the change brought a public outcry. By June, fifteen hundred calls a day flooded the company's consumer hotline, compared to four hundred a day before the change. Some consumers panicked and hoarded cases of the old Coke in their basement until the company announced it would continue to manufacture the original Coke.

Throughout history people have tried to substitute a new "formula" for God's truth. Jesus criticized the religious leaders of his day for abandoning God's commands and teaching rules made by men instead. He called them hypocrites because they made an outward show of worshipping God but focused on their own traditions rather than worshipping him from their heart (Mark 7:6-8).

Many churches today do the same thing. Sometimes churches focus on rituals, rules, social causes, or entertainment more than the Word of God and its message of salvation. These things may be good and useful, but they become evil when they replace God's Word. Whenever anyone tampers with God's Word, there should be an outcry. It's the only "formula" that has the power to change lives. Only God's Word is "the real thing."

July 12

* * *

As to all my affairs, Tychicus, our beloved brother and faithful servant and fellow
bond-servant in the Lord, will bring you information.
COLOSSIANS 4:7, NASB

President Lyndon Johnson signed the Freedom of Information Act (FOIA) into law in July 1966. The first law of its kind to establish the right of individuals, FOIA allowed access to records in the possession of the federal government. The government reserves the right to withhold information relevant to the nine exemptions and three exclusions contained in the act.

Citizens, scholars, and reporters have used FOIA to obtain needed government information. President Bill Clinton signed the "Electronic Freedom of Information Act Amendments of 1996" in that year to make the ruling compatible with electronic information. Congress passed legislation to further amend FOIA in 2002 and 2003.

God believes in freedom of information. He has freely revealed himself to everyone through his creation and his Word. "Everything he does reveals his glory and majesty" (Psalm 111:3). He "reveals secrets" (Daniel 2:28) and "deep and mysterious things" (Daniel 2:22). God "reveals his thoughts to mankind" (Amos 4:13). He clearly wants us all to have free access to information about him.

God also wants believers to freely share information about him with others. Some people call their faith a private matter, but God doesn't see it that way. We all have someone in our life who needs to hear our testimony. Paul openly shared details of his faith journey. John the Baptist told everyone about the light so that they "might believe because of his testimony" (John 1:7). John the apostle "faithfully reported everything he saw" (Revelation 1:2). Rather than keeping our testimony and our beliefs private, we should offer free access to the information that can give others a new life.

July 13

* * *

I have become all things to all men so that by all possible means I might save some.

1 CORINTHIANS 9:22, NIV

Mel Blanc died in July 1989, at the age of eighty-one. Most children and adults would not recognize his face, but almost everyone in America knows his voice—or voices. Blanc created hundreds of unique voices for popular radio, television, and motion picture characters. He earned a reputation as the first great cartoon voice actor and the nickname "The Man of 1,000 Voices."

Blanc's break came when he secured an audition with a cartoon company and passed his oral test: "Can you do a drunken bull?" Providing the voice for Porky Pig became Blanc's first major role in 1937; Bugs Bunny followed a year later. Over time, Blanc accounted for the voices of 90 percent of the cartoon "stable" at Warner Brothers plus dozens of Hanna Barbera characters. He had an amazing versatility and the ability to create voices and personalities to match the characters and stories.

When it comes to the gospel, all of us should have more than one voice. We have one message but many ways of sharing it. Whenever possible, Paul conformed to the customs and sensitivities of whatever class or group of people he was around in order to win as many to Christ as possible. Jesus used different approaches with people, tailoring his teaching according to their background and their needs.

We must be careful to never change the content of the Good News, but we can be versatile and use creative approaches matched to the personalities of those we are trying to influence for Christ. Some people respond best to casual friendship evangelism. Others are more open to hearing a personal testimony. Some are reached by intellectual discussion. If we had a thousand voices, or techniques, we should use them all to win people to Christ.

***What different approaches are you using
to share the gospel with others?***

July 14

* * *

He sets the prisoners free and gives them joy.
PSALM 68:6

On this day in 1789, in Paris, France, an armed mob assisted by royal troops attacked and captured the Bastille, releasing its prisoners. The Revolutionary government later demolished the fortress. To the French, the storming of the Bastille represented the end of the former regime. Bastille Day has been celebrated on July 14 as a national holiday in France since 1880.

The Bastille was built around 1370 as part of the fortified east wall of the city. In the seventeenth and eighteenth centuries, officials used the fortress as a state prison, primarily housing political prisoners. Any citizen considered obnoxious to the royal court could be arrested by a secret warrant and detained indefinitely in the Bastille without accusation or trial. The stronghold became a symbol of royal tyranny.

When Jesus attended the synagogue in Nazareth, he got up and read a passage from Isaiah regarding the future Messiah. The passage explained that part of the Messiah's ministry would be releasing captives and freeing the oppressed. Jesus told his listeners that the Scripture had been fulfilled that very day (Luke 4:16-21). The Bible teaches that we are all "prisoners of sin" until we are released by faith in Jesus Christ (Galatians 3:22).

Even as believers, we can again slip under the tyranny of sin. When we habitually give in to a particular temptation, a pattern develops. This allows Satan to plant a stronghold in our life that oppresses us and hinders our relationship with God. The solution is to attack the stronghold armed with prayer, the Word of God, and the power of the Holy Spirit. Then we will enjoy the freedom that Christ won for us when he died. The only way to stay free from the tyranny of sin is to remain in the fortress of Jesus' name.

July 15

* * *

[Jesus said,] "My sheep listen to my voice; I know them, and they follow me."
JOHN 10:27

T he United States Patent Office registered one of the most famous trademarks in the world in July 1900. The RCA Victor Company based its logo on a painting called *His Master's Voice* by English painter Francis Barraud. In the picture Nipper, part bull terrier and part fox terrier, sits listening to an old-fashioned phonograph. He is looking into the "horn" speaker with a puzzled expression, as though trying to locate the source of his master's voice.

The Gramophone Company in England first adapted the painting for advertising and used it on needle tins, sales promotion novelties, company literature and letterheads, and eventually, record labels. After *His Master's Voice* was registered in the United States and Canada, the copyright was extended to Central and South America, the Far East, and Japan. It remains one of the world's most widely recognized and best loved logos.

In the tenth chapter of John, Jesus uses the illustration of sheep to show his relationship with his followers. Like a good shepherd, Jesus calls his sheep and gathers his flock. He walks ahead of his sheep, and they follow him because they know his voice. They will not follow a stranger whose voice they don't recognize (vv. 3-5).

Today we have many voices vying for our attention. Sometimes it's hard to distinguish the ones speaking truth from those spouting deception. Since Satan can disguise himself as an angel of light (2 Corinthians 11:14), his voice can sound deceptively spiritual. True believers should not be fooled by false teachers because they are familiar with Jesus' voice. We recognize his voice because it lines up with the Word of God. When we look for the source of *our* Master's voice, we look in the Bible, not a phonograph speaker.

July 16

* * *

Whoever claims to live in him must walk as Jesus did.
1 JOHN 2:6, NIV

Apollo 11, the first manned mission to land on the moon, launched on this day in 1969. Crew members Neil Armstrong, Edwin "Buzz" Aldrin Jr., and Michael Collins flew the spacecrafts *Columbia*, the command module, and *Eagle*, the lunar module. On July 20, Armstrong and Aldrin landed the Eagle at the fairly flat Tranquility site and spent two hours and thirty-one minutes walking and exploring the surface of the moon.

Besides making history with the first steps by humans on another planetary body, the astronauts evaluated the possibility of working on the moon's surface, installed instruments for scientific research, and collected forty-nine pounds of lunar rocks and soil. The historic flight paved the way for the Apollo lunar landing missions that followed. A total of twelve American astronauts have walked on the moon in six missions.

Trying to live like Jesus lived can seem like taking a walk on the moon. We still exist in the same physical world, but Christ asks us to live by a new set of laws totally alien to our human nature. He tells us to love our enemies and put others' needs before our own personal interests. Christ wants us to die to self and give up our desires and rights—all with the goal to live a holy life because our God is holy. How can we accomplish such a mission?

We can find the secret in Psalm 119:45: "I will walk in freedom, for I have devoted myself to your commandments." We must be so devoted to studying and applying God's Word that it becomes a part of us. Jesus paved the way for us by living a life of complete obedience to the Father. Following his example is the only way we can successfully complete our heavenly mission on Earth.

July 17

* * *

Forsaking the right way, they have gone astray.
2 Peter 2:15, NASB

American aviator Douglas Corrigan took off from New York on this day in 1938, supposedly headed for California. Twenty-eight hours and thirteen minutes later he landed safely—in Dublin, Ireland. Corrigan explained that he must have had a faulty compass, but no one believed the 180-degree wrong turn was an accident.

For three years, Corrigan had sought permission to make a solo flight from New York to Ireland. Authorities had refused permission for an ocean crossing because of the condition of his plane. After his rebellious trip to Ireland, American authorities suspended his pilot's license, but the public greeted "Wrong Way Corrigan" as a national hero upon his return to the United States.

Americans have always admired pioneers who forge a new way through the wilderness or discover a new route over oceans. However, that doesn't work in the spiritual life. Jesus made it clear that there is only one way to God: "I am the way, the truth, and the life. No one can come to the Father except through me" (John 14:6). The only route to forgiveness of sin and a relationship with God is through the Cross. We can enter God's presence only on the basis of Christ's sacrifice on our behalf.

Today our culture encourages us to appreciate the diversity of other religions and beliefs. God *does* expect us to treat everyone with respect and dignity. But any belief system based on something other than faith in Jesus Christ is a "wrong way." People who depend on a philosophy, an organization, rituals, or their own goodness are using a faulty compass. Pointing out the right way is not being intolerant, it's sharing truth. Whether others are going the wrong way out of rebellion or ignorance, they won't be greeted as heroes when they arrive on the other side of eternity.

July 18

* * *

*I don't mean to say that I have already achieved these things or
that I have already reached perfection.*

PHILIPPIANS 3:12

On this day in 1976, fifteen-year-old Nadia Comaneci was the star of the Montreal, Quebec, Olympics when she became the first gymnast in Olympic history to earn a perfect score of ten. After her performance on the uneven parallel bars, the Romanian athlete was awarded six more perfect scores in different events. Electronic scoreboards of the day were designed to display a maximum score of 9.99, so many pictures of Nadia show the scoreboard reading 1.00.

Comaneci retired after the 1980 Olympics and the 1981 World Student Games. She defected to the United States in 1989 and later married American Olympic medalist Bart Conner. The couple performs together in gymnastics exhibitions and offers clinics.

Jesus said that his followers are to be perfect as our Father in heaven is perfect (Matthew 5:48). With God's absolute holiness as the standard, how can we ever achieve perfection? Through the power of the Holy Spirit, God works his righteousness into our life. As we exercise our will to make godly choices, practice spiritual disciplines, and imitate Jesus' life of obedience, we gradually become transformed into his image.

We will never achieve total perfection while we are on the earth. After thirty years of knowing Christ, Paul had accomplished tremendous things. Yet he acknowledged that he had not yet reached perfection. "But I press on to possess that perfection for which Christ Jesus first possessed me" (Philippians 3:12). Someday our sanctification process will be finished. In the meantime, our performance may not always merit perfect marks, but we can be assured that we will "nail the landing."

How are you moving toward holiness in your life?

July 19

* * *

Remember that the Lord will reward each one of us for the good we do,
whether we are slaves or free.

Ephesians 6:8

I n July 1862, President Abraham Lincoln signed a bill creating the Medal of Honor, the highest award for valor in action against an enemy force that can be bestowed upon a person serving in the Armed Services of the United States. Since then, more than 3,400 people have been honored for distinguished actions during active military service that "involved extreme jeopardy of life or the performance of extraordinary hazardous duty."

In the "Purge of 1917," a review commission revoked the medals presented to 911 people. Several of these were reinstated decades later. In recent years, a number of medals have been awarded for actions during World War II that may have been overlooked because of racial prejudice.

Most people will never be honored with a prestigious medal, but Paul reminds his readers that God will reward all believers. We could never repay Jesus for the death he suffered to free us from the penalty of sin. Even if we spent every minute of our life in active service for him, it would not make us deserving of eternal life. Yet God promises to honor *us* for any service done in his name and out of gratitude to him.

Congressional Medals of Honor and other earthly awards will be left behind when we die. But the rewards that God will bestow are everlasting and will never be revoked. His judging is impartial and no one will be overlooked. In the heat of spiritual warfare, serving God often seems like "extraordinary hazardous duty," but we can hope for the greatest award possible—which will be to hear God say "Well done, my good and faithful servant" (Matthew 25:23).

July 20

* * *

Having chosen them, he called them to come to him.
ROMANS 8:30, NLT-1

Six weeks after the United States entered World War I, a universal draft went into effect. The names of the first ten thousand men were drawn on this day in 1917. Draft officials proclaimed it Lottery Day. The armed forces eventually drafted a total of 2,702, 687 men between the ages of twenty-one and thirty.

President Abraham Lincoln signed into law the first effective draft by the federal government on March 3, 1863. The legislation required all men between the ages of eighteen and forty-five to enroll in local militia units and be available to be called into national service. The responsibility for the actual drafting of men was given to individual states. Most used a lottery system.

God does not use a draft system to enlist people for his Kingdom. As our Creator, he has the right to force us to worship him and to submit to his will. But instead, he allows us to choose whether to obey or disobey him. Free will is very precious to God. He places people and circumstances in our life to guide us to a relationship with him, but gives us the freedom to accept or reject his love and forgiveness.

It's impossible for us to clearly see how God's sovereignty fits together with our free will. Paul writes that from the beginning of time, God chose us for salvation and called us to become his children. Yet we have the choice to disobey and refuse his call. God didn't make us mindless puppets with strings to pull, but he does tug at our heartstrings. It's not a lottery that calls us to repentance and submission to God's will; it's his kindness (Romans 2:4).

July 21

* * *

Teach those who are rich in this world not to be proud and not to trust in their money, which is so unreliable.

1 Timothy 6:17

O n this day in 2002, WorldCom filed for Chapter 11 bankruptcy protection, the largest filing in United States history. At one time, WorldCom was the second-largest long distance phone company in the United States. WorldCom expanded mainly by acquiring other telecommunications companies. An internal audit in June 2002 revealed improper accounting in the billions, and the U.S. Securities and Exchange Commission initiated an investigation.

The investigation estimated that the company's assets had been inflated by about $12 billion. The bankruptcy cost investors an estimated $200 billion. In 2004, WorldCom emerged from Chapter 11 bankruptcy with a new name (MCI) and $5.7 billion in debt.

All of us will experience bankruptcy in one of two ways. First, many people will be like the rich man in Jesus' parable. He kept building bigger and bigger barns to store all his crops and goods. "But God said to him, 'You fool! You will die this very night. Then who will get everything you worked for?'" (Luke 12:20). The man had acquired much material wealth, but when he died, he learned that he was destitute in the things of God. His soul was bankrupt.

We can see the other kind of spiritual bankruptcy displayed by the tax collector in another parable. The Pharisee prayed by boasting about his goodness. In contrast, the tax collector "beat his chest in sorrow, saying, 'O God, be merciful to me, for I am a sinner'" (Luke 18:13). Only when we understand that we come to God destitute, with nothing to offer him, can we enter into his riches. When we "file" this kind of bankruptcy, we emerge with an unpayable debt of love and gratitude to God—and incredible assets in him.

July 22

* * *

Don't let anyone think less of you because you are young.

1 TIMOTHY 4:12

On this day in 1989, eleven-year-old Tony Aliengena became the youngest pilot to fly around the world. The worldwide trip included good-will stops in the Soviet Union. The only problem during the trip occurred when Tony's father took the controls to give his son a rest. While attempting to take off from Alaska, Tony's father inadvertently crashed the Cessna 210 Centurion. Fortunately, neither Tony nor his father sustained injury.

The fourth-grader returned to John Wayne Airport in Orange County, California, after logging 21,567 miles in seven weeks. Tony had also made history early the previous year when at age nine he became the youngest pilot to cross the continental United States.

Sometimes we forget what amazing things children and young people can accomplish. As a young pastor, Timothy faced the difficulty of others' being overly critical of him because of his age. Even though he had trained for years, some doubted his maturity in leading because church leaders tended to be so much older. Paul advises him to not be intimidated by this attitude but to earn the respect of all believers by setting an example of godliness in his lifestyle, teaching, love, faith, and purity (1 Timothy 4:12-13).

God can use anyone in his work, regardless of age. Even young children can use their gifts to be a blessing to the body of Christ. In the same way, new believers who are young spiritually can fill important roles in the church. While children and new converts do need to concentrate on building a solid foundation for spiritual growth, as we all do, we should encourage them to actively participate in the work of God's Kingdom.

18 from Bowden

July 23

* * *

They invent new ways of sinning.
ROMANS 1:30

I nventure Place, a museum dedicated to the creative process, opened to the public on this day in 1995 in Akron, Ohio. The museum offers hands-on exhibits, special events, and interactive programs to help people "Discover the Inventor in You!" The National Inventors' Hall of Fame was organized in 1973 by the U.S. Patent and Trademark Office and what is now the National Council of Intellectual Property Law Associations.

Each year the selection committee of the National Inventors' Hall of Fame chooses inventors for induction from a list of people nominated by their peers and the public. Representatives from national technical and scientific organizations make up the committee. As of 2004, 221 inventors had been inducted into the Inventors' Hall of Fame.

We owe much to those dedicated, creative people whose inventions provide practical solutions to problems, improve the quality of daily living, or even save lives. Unfortunately, we have a tendency to carry the inventive spirit too far. Throughout history, humans have tried to invent their own morality, their own god. The results are always disastrous.

Our culture today has tried to replace God with man's invention of moral relativism. Schools teach our children that there are no absolute standards of right and wrong, only choices depending on the situation. Yet there *are* absolute standards and God has laid them out in his Word, from the Ten Commandments in the Old Testament to the commands of Jesus in the New Testament. Situational ethics may seem logical and appealing, but following anything other than God's standards of right and wrong amounts to no more than inventing ways to sin. And that won't get us inducted into a Hall of Fame.

July 24

***

His dynasty will go on forever; his kingdom will endure as the sun.
PSALM 89:36

I n July 1975, Chinese archaeologists announced one of the most significant finds of the twentieth century. While digging a well near the ancient capital of Xi'an, workers discovered the three-acre burial mound of Qin Shi Huang, China's first emperor. Over seven thousand life-size clay soldiers, horses, chariots, and even weapons arranged in battle formation faced east to guard the tomb. Experts have restored most of the lifelike figures and put them on display at the Museum of Qin Terra Cotta Warriors and Horses in Xi'an.

The emperor ascended to the throne in 246 B.C. at age thirteen. Hoping to extend his power to the afterlife world, he immediately began work on his mausoleum, which took eleven years to finish. The people believed that the burial of the "army" ensured that the emperor would have troops at his command after death.

However, no matter how hard they try to maintain power, all earthly authorities are only temporary, except for the dynasty of David through which the Messiah came. God made a covenant promise that David's line would last forever. Although there is no king from the house of David ruling today, someday Jesus Christ will return to sit on David's throne and rule the entire world.

Like the Emperor Qin Shi Huang, some people give much thought and take careful measures in preparing for death. They select just the right burial plot, make a detailed will, and even plan their funeral service. We need to *first* make sure our soul is secure in God's salvation. Moses told Israel, "The eternal God is your refuge, and his everlasting arms are under you" (Deuteronomy 33:27). The only "arms" we'll need in the afterlife are God's.

July 25

* * *

Look now; I myself am he! There is no other god but me!
I am the one who kills and gives life.

DEUTERONOMY 32:39

On this day in 1978, doctors in Great Britain announced the birth of the world's first successful test-tube baby. Many people celebrated the medical breakthrough that made the conception of Louise Joy Brown possible; others worried about future implications for possible misuse of this medical breakthrough. Today the process of in vitro fertilization is a commonplace procedure used by infertile couples around the world.

In July 1997, scientists announced the birth of Dolly, a sheep cloned from a cell of another sheep. Scientists had previously believed that mammals could not be successfully cloned. The news intensified the ongoing debate on whether cloning should be allowed in animals and humans.

We live in an amazing era of technology, when doctors are able to extend life and manipulate it beyond anything ever dreamed before. We need to remember that any knowledge or means we have comes from God, who holds "the life of every living thing in his hand" (Job 12:10). No matter how far we advance in medicine and science, God is the only one who ultimately possesses the power of life and death.

Scientists will never be able to give life like God does. Jesus explained to Nicodemus, "Humans can reproduce only human life, but the Holy Spirit gives birth to spiritual life" (John 3:6). God gives us the gift of life when we are conceived; he bestows new, everlasting life when we become believers in Jesus. Someday, the Holy Spirit will give life to our dead bodies. Our new, eternal life in Christ is something that can't be cloned or mixed up in a test tube. And it's a life worth living for.

July 26

* * *

Fight the good fight for the true faith.
1 TIMOTHY 6:12

Mike Tyson's shortest boxing match was on this day in 1986, when he defeated Marvis Frazier in just thirty seconds. Tyson had become the youngest heavyweight champion in boxing history at age twenty. He was undefeated in thirty-seven consecutive fights until he lost the championship to Buster Douglas in 1990.

Tyson served three years in prison for a rape charge from 1992 to 1995, and then he returned to boxing. In his 1997 match with Evander Holyfield, Tyson was disqualified for biting and mutilating Holyfield's ear. He was fined $2,980,000, and his license was suspended. Tyson resumed his career in 1999 but returned to jail for four months after he assaulted two people following a car accident.

Paul sometimes used the images of the athletic contests at the Grecian Games to illustrate the Christian life. In his first letter to Timothy, he urged the young pastor to "fight the good fight" (1 Timothy 6:12). The believer lives a life of ongoing conflict, both physical and spiritual. We are engaged in the most noble fight of all—the cause of Christ. Paul urged Timothy to give his best in this struggle.

In a later letter, Paul looked back over his own life and said, "I have fought the good fight. . . . I have remained faithful" (2 Timothy 4:7). Paul had lived a life of integrity and commitment to God's Word and work. He looked forward to receiving the prize the Lord had for him. As we fight our own battles for the faith, we must be careful to not disqualify our witness by doing something to disgrace the name of Christ. And we must keep on fighting. A match with God's enemies may last only thirty seconds or many rounds, but we know who will be knocked out in the end.

In what ways are you fighting the good fight for the faith?

July 27

* * *

I will repay you for the years the locusts have eaten.
JOEL 2:25, NIV

On this day in 1931, hordes of grasshoppers swept across several western states and destroyed thousands of acres of crops. Eyewitnesses said the grasshoppers were so thick they could be scooped up in shovels. Nebraska, Iowa, and North and South Dakota were the most affected areas. In one sixteen-thousand-mile area of Iowa inspected by entomologists, there was not enough vegetation remaining to feed even a single animal.

Newspaper reports at the time called the grasshopper infestation the worst in fifty years. Some farmers in Nebraska sold grasshoppers for twenty cents a pound to be used as fish food at state hatcheries. Other farmers collected grasshoppers to feed their poultry during the following winter.

In the book of Joel, God told his people to mourn over the locust plague that he had sent among them like a great destroying army (2:25). Four different types of locusts had completely devastated all their crops and destroyed not only that year's harvest, but seed for their crops for years to come. Yet God promised Israel that he would repair the damage done, and they would again have abundance.

Sometimes our life seems as if it has been hit by a swarm of locusts or grasshoppers. All our hopes and dreams have been stripped away by either consequences of our own actions or circumstances out of our control. We feel we will never be productive again. But God promises to repair damage done by "plagues" to his children. If we trust in him, he will heal relationships, restore our hope and joy, and make us fruitful again. Then we will know him in a new way and will respond as Israel did, "You will praise the LORD your God, who does these miracles for you" (Joel 2:26).

July 28

* * *

Even children are known by the way they act, whether their conduct is pure,
and whether it is right.

PROVERBS 20:11

While the ancient Assyrians and Chinese were probably among the first to use fingerprints in the signing of legal documents, the English first used fingerprints in July 1858. Sir William Herschel, chief magistrate in India, had a local businessman press his handprint on the back of a contract. The local population believed the personal contact made the contract more binding. Herschel later noticed that fingerprints could prove or disprove identity, since they are unique to the individual and permanent throughout life.

After the London police established the first fingerprint files in 1901, the use of fingerprinting as a way to identify criminals spread quickly throughout Europe and the United States. In 1924, the U.S. government set up a central agency within the FBI to manage fingerprint archives throughout the country. Today, the FBI has approximately 250 million sets of fingerprints in its files.

We all leave our fingerprints on every situation and every relationship we are involved in. Our fingerprints are our actions. Proverbs 20:11 reminds us that we can't always judge what people are like by what they say—it's our behavior and our lifestyle that reveal our true character. That's how people can identify us.

Believers' "fingerprints" should have special characteristics that infallibly identify them as children of God. We should follow God's commands. We should love each other unselfishly and have a heart for those who don't yet know God. We should be daily exhibiting characteristics such as peace, joy, self-control, and patience. As we become obedient followers of Christ, we will leave our unique mark wherever we go. And when people identify us, they will see Christ's true identity.

What kind of "fingerprints" are you leaving on people's lives?

July 29

* * *

God will wipe every tear from their eyes.
REVELATION 7:17

Lady Diana Spencer and Prince Charles, heir to the throne of Britain, were married in London on this day in 1981. The couple exchanged vows at St. Paul's Cathedral before 3,500 guests. After arriving in the Glass Coach, Diana walked down the red-carpeted aisle in her specially designed gown with a twenty-five-foot train. Prince Charles wore his naval commander dress uniform. The Archbishop of Canterbury led the ceremony, assisted by clergymen from different denominations.

The storybook wedding attracted an estimated worldwide television and radio audience of 750 million people. Hundreds of thousands of spectators lined the route from the cathedral to Buckingham Palace, the site of the reception. After the wedding, the public continued to have an insatiable desire for details of the couple's seemingly fairy-tale life. Sadly, the royal family announced in December 1992 that the prince and princess had decided to separate; they divorced in 1996.

Who can resist a fairy tale? The desire to live "happily ever after" seems to be ingrained in our nature. America's Declaration of Independence acknowledges our belief in the inalienable right to pursue happiness. If our home or job doesn't make us happy, we want something better. If we don't have a "fairy-tale" marriage, too often we go looking for a new Prince Charming or Princess.

The problem is that we expect the happy ending to happen on earth, but God never promised that. When John saw the new Jerusalem coming down from heaven, he heard a loud voice describing what life will be like when God makes his home among his people. "There will be no more death or sorrow or crying or pain. All these things are gone forever" (Revelation 21:4). Whenever we wish we had a fairy tale life, we need to hold on through the hard times and remember that our happy ending is coming—complete with a King on a white horse (Revelation 19:11-16).

July 30

* * *

Trust in the LORD and do good. Then you will live safely in the land and prosper.
PSALM 37:3

On this day in 1956, President Dwight Eisenhower approved a law passed by Congress that made "In God We Trust" the national motto of the United States. The House Judiciary Committee acknowledged the importance and frequency of another phrase: *E Pluribus Unum* ("One out of Many"). Congress has used both mottoes.

The origins of the national motto go back to Secretary of the Treasury Salmon P. Chase during the Civil War. Prompted by letters, Chase asked Congress to pass a law changing the design of the two-cent piece to include the motto "In God We Trust." Many American coins and currencies eventually used the phrase. In July 1955, legislation made the motto mandatory on all coins. Since 1966 it has been added to all paper money.

Our nation's currency may be stamped with "In God We Trust," but our heart is not. We hear God's name spoken in times of crisis, but the moral condition of America belies our national motto. Apparently, we trust in our power, intellect, and wealth rather than in the name of God. How can we dare claim God's promise of protection when our country is filled with things detestable to God and contrary to his laws?

Even if our nation does not trust in God's name, individual believers can. David gives us a picture of someone trusting God wholeheartedly: "I trust him with all my heart. He helps me, and my heart is filled with joy. I burst out in songs of thanksgiving" (Psalm 28:7). The only thing worthy of implicit trust is God, because of his character and because "all he does is just and good, and all his commandments are trustworthy" (Psalm 111:7).

July 31

* * *

The Son is the radiance of God's glory and the exact representation of his being.
HEBREWS 1:3, NIV

On this day in 1964, *Ranger 7* transmitted over four thousand high-resolution photographs of the moon's surface back to Earth. The robot craft was equipped with six television cameras, two wide-angle and four narrow-angle. An arrangement of the cameras in two separate, self-contained channels with separate power supplies, timers, and transmitters ensured success in obtaining high-quality video pictures.

Ranger 7 took the pictures during the final seventeen minutes of flight before its planned crash landing. Scientists were ecstatic because the still photographs were a thousand times clearer than any previous images of the moon taken through Earth-based telescopes.

In a similar way, the writer of Hebrews explained that Jesus gave us a clear and accurate picture of God. The Greek word for "exact representation" is *charakter*, indicating an impressed character such as a steel engraving or stamp. God had already revealed himself through his creation and through the words of prophets. But when he sent his Son, he gave us an exact representation of himself, a perfect reflection of his own glory.

Many people call Jesus a great prophet or teacher, but that is not an accurate description. When Philip asked Jesus to show him the Father, Jesus answered, "Anyone who has seen me has seen the Father!" (John 14:9). When we worship Jesus, we are worshipping God. When we imitate him, we are imitating God. Jesus shows us the divine nature and character of God. We were not around to be eyewitnesses when Jesus walked on the earth, but we have sixty-six books full of God-breathed words painting a picture of him. You can't get a higher-resolution image than that.

August 1

* * *

The king said to Joab and the commanders of the army,
"Take a census of all the tribes of Israel."

2 SAMUEL 24:2

T he first U.S. census began in 1790, shortly after George Washington
became president. Federal marshals and their assistants finished collecting the information on this day the following year. According to the Census Bureau, the government instructed the marshals to post their returns "at two of the most public places . . . to remain for the inspection of all concerned." The census counted 3.9 million people.

Today, a director who is nominated by the president and confirmed by the Senate heads the Census Bureau, which Congress created in 1902. The bureau oversees twelve regional offices plus processing and support facilities.

When God wanted to express his anger against Israel, he caused David to take a census (2 Samuel 24). Although God had earlier used a census to draft an army to conquer the Promised Land, at the time of David's census Israel was a powerful nation at peace. As soon as he completed the census, David realized his sin and repented. God punished the nation with a plague that killed seventy thousand people.

Many of us like to make lists, but we need to be careful what we number. If we take a census of our abilities and strengths or list what we have accomplished, we can become self-centered and our pride will keep us from depending on the Lord. If we take an inventory of our problems, we may become depressed. The best thing is to count our blessings and what God has done for us. Since God "performs countless miracles" (Job 9:10), we will never get to the end of that list, but our mind will be focused in the right direction.

August 2

* * *

Seek the LORD while you can find him. Call on him now while he is near.
ISAIAH 55:6

Alexander Graham Bell died on this day in 1922. Bell had moved from Scotland to the United States in 1871 to work with the deaf. At this time, businesses were growing so rapidly that the telegraph was no longer sufficient to handle the necessary communication. Bell and other inventors were working to come up with an improved telegraph when he envisioned the telephone.

In 1876, Bell became the first person to transmit audible words through electric wire when he said to his assistant, "Watson, come here. I want you." He filed his telephone patent just two hours before another inventor submitted a similar sketch. Bell continued to invent and to work with the deaf until his death at age seventy-five. Telephone switchboards in the United States and Canada were shut down for one minute as a tribute; operators silenced all thirteen million telephones in operation to honor Bell's memory.

We live in an age of grace, when God's salvation is available to everyone who calls on him in repentance. God is waiting and ready for unbelievers to confess their sinful condition and receive forgiveness and eternal life. But there will come a time when the "switchboard" will be shut down. God has set a time in the future when he will judge all those who have refused to receive his grace.

Isaiah 55:6 gives a sober warning to seek God and call on him while there is opportunity. Some people plan to accept Christ later in their life but then drift further and further away from him. They may find that the older they get, the harder it is to turn to him. We don't know when death or God's judgment on the earth will shut the door to salvation. The wise thing to do is call on him now, while the line is still open.

August 3

***

[Gamaliel said,] "If they are planning and doing these things merely on their own,
it will soon be overthrown. But if it is from God,
you will not be able to overthrow them."

ACTS 5:38-39

I n August 1937, Adolph Hitler boasted that the Third Reich would last a thousand years. Hitler had become the leader of the Nazi Party in 1921. With the 1932 elections, the Nazis became Germany's largest political party. Hitler continued to gain power through manipulation until President Paul von Hindenburg invited him to be chancellor in 1933. Hindenburg died the next year, and Hitler adopted the twin titles of chancellor and führer ("leader").

As dictator, Hitler spread his campaign of extreme German nationalism, which resulted in the murder of millions. Hitler made his famous boast at the 1937 Nationalist Socialist Party rally. Eight years later, with Allied forces crushing his regime, Hitler decided to commit suicide.

When Peter and the apostles refused to stop teaching about Jesus, the high council wanted to kill them. But the Pharisee Gamaliel reminded his colleagues of an earlier leader and movement that had been short-lived. Gamaliel pointed out that if the apostles were doing these things merely on their own, they would soon be overthrown. But if their work was from God, the council would not be able to stop them and might even end up fighting against God (Acts 5:33-39).

History has proven that the apostles' work was not based on human origins. The only authority that will last comes from God. Christ will rule the earth for a thousand years during the Millennium, but his reign is everlasting. We must choose whether we want to be allied with an eternal power or be dedicated to a short-term, earthly one. We also decide whether to invest our time, energy, and money in earthly things or in what has eternal value.

August 4

* * *

Then the LORD gave the donkey the ability to speak.
NUMBERS 22:28

On this day in 1998, Jo Ann Altsman collapsed on the floor from a heart attack. Her Vietnamese potbellied pig, Lulu, ran outside through the doggy/piggy door into the fenced yard and somehow managed to push open the gate. Witnesses later told how Lulu would wait for a car to approach, then walk onto the road and lie down in front of it. Several times she ran back to the house to check on Jo Ann.

Finally, a man stopped his car, followed Lulu to the house, and called an ambulance. Doctors told Altsman that she would probably have died if fifteen more minutes had elapsed. Medics had to stop Lulu from getting into the ambulance with her owner. Altsman later discovered that Lulu had cut her stomach getting through the pet door. The American Society for the Prevention of Cruelty to Animals honored Lulu with a Trooper Award for her lifesaving actions.

God doesn't use only people to fulfill his purposes; he uses animals and even insects, too. He sent plagues of frogs, gnats, flies, and locusts to goad the Egyptians into releasing the Israelites (Exodus 8; 10). He brought poisonous snakes among the Israelites as judgment for sin (Numbers 21:6). God commanded ravens to bring bread and meat each day to Elijah (1 Kings 17:4). He let Balaam's donkey speak to bring Balaam to his senses (Numbers 22:28).

What significance does God's use of animals hold for us? First, it testifies to his sovereign control over all the earth and everything in it. It also helps us have a proper view of ourselves and our place in God's work. We can't get puffed up if we remember that even frogs can carry out God's work. And no matter how inadequate we may feel, if he can use a gnat, then surely he can use us.

August 5

✷ ✷ ✷

For I can do everything through Christ, who gives me strength.

PHILIPPIANS 4:13

I n 1941, an early August issue of *Parade* magazine devoted three pages to "the Army's most intriguing gadget" that could do "practically everything." One officer said it could do anything except bake a cake. The military had given a list of ten priorities to American automakers for a universal military vehicle. The manufacturers came up with a vehicle, the G. P. ("general purpose"), later known as the "jeep."

The jeep could handle a forty-degree slope, drive in a thirty-foot circle, and tilt right or left on a fifty-degree angle without tipping over. It drove up rocky mountains, crossed scorching deserts, forded shallow streams, and roamed beaches. It hauled materials and ammunition, carried personnel, dodged snipers, and pulled other vehicles out of the mud. After the war, uses were found for the jeep in civilian life.

Paul said that he could do everything that was God's will for him, not through his own abilities but through the strength that Christ gave him. Whenever God has a job for us to do, he will provide the power and whatever else we need to accomplish it. Within God's plan, we are limited only by our lack of trust and our unwillingness to obey.

When we are asked to do something, we usually assess how it lines up with our natural talents and past experience. But God often pulls us out of our comfort zone. Moses went from being a shepherd with speech problems to a mighty deliverer who confronted the pharaoh of Egypt. Fearful Gideon led a vastly outnumbered army to victory in battle. God gave both men assurances that he was with them. He gives us the same assurance in his Word. Through God's power we can handle all the twists, turns, deserts, and rough terrains of our life and do not "practically everything" but everything that is his will.

August 6

***

Jonah got up and went in the opposite direction to get away from the LORD.
JONAH 1:3

On this day in 1971, Chay Blyth successfully completed what no one had ever attempted before. Blyth sailed nonstop around the world in the "wrong" direction (east to west), against the prevailing winds and currents. Blyth had left Britain the previous October on his thirty-thousand-mile voyage. A crowd of six thousand people—including the Prince of Wales, Princess Anne, and the Duke of Edinburgh—welcomed him home 292 days later.

Born in Scotland in 1940, Blyth had joined the Parachute Regiment at age eighteen and soon became the regiment's youngest platoon sergeant ever. After leaving the army, he garnered a long list of racing successes and arranged racing competitions. Because of his illustrious accomplishments in sailing, the queen of England knighted Blyth in 1997.

Living the Christian life can be extremely difficult at times. That's because we're supposed to go in the opposite direction of the world around us. When we accept Christ, we do a 180-degree turn, and from then on, we are going against the prevailing standards of our culture and our natural tendencies. If we let down our guard, we will be swept along with the flow in our original, sinful direction. We can succeed in our right course only with supernatural strength from the Holy Spirit.

It's a bad alternative to go in the opposite direction from God. Jonah tried this when he sailed in the opposite direction of Nineveh instead of going there to preach as God had instructed—with disastrous results. We have to make a choice every day whether we will travel toward God or away from him. Going along with the current of the world may sometimes seem more like smooth sailing, but in the end it leads to shipwreck.

In what areas of your life have you been moving away from God?

August 7

* * *

Now we see things imperfectly as in a cloudy mirror, but then we will see everything with perfect clarity. All that I know now is partial and incomplete, but then I will know everything completely, just as God now knows me completely.

1 CORINTHIANS 13:12

B efore this day in 1959, people were able to only speculate about what the earth looked like from outer space. That changed when NASA launched the U.S. satellite *Explorer VI.* The first crude picture transmitted by the satellite showed an area of the Pacific Ocean and its cloud cover. At the time, *Explorer VI* was crossing Mexico about seventeen thousand miles above the surface of the earth. The signals were picked up at the tracking station in South Point, Hawaii.

No matter how much time we spend in prayer and study of God's Word, we can only speculate about many of the circumstances in our lives. Paul compared our present understanding to looking into one of the bronze mirrors familiar in Corinth. We see only an imperfect, obscure reflection right now. But when we look back at our life from heaven, we'll be able to see truths openly and clearly. We will understand perfectly things that confuse us now, like the reasons behind all our hurts, disappointments, and trials.

We also won't have to speculate about what God looks like. Now we see reflections of God in his creation and in the Bible, but someday we'll see him face-to-face. Then we will have much clearer knowledge of God and know him in ways that are impossible while we live on Earth. We won't be omniscient like God, but he will enable us to understand him as he understands us now. And we won't even need a satellite.

August 8

* * *

[The Queen of Sheba said,] "How happy your people must be!"
1 Kings 10:8

In 1999 the Secret Society of Happy People designated August 8 "Admit You're Happy Day." Due to the positive response, the following year the group expanded the celebration to include the entire month of August. The society has since changed the names to "Happiness Happens Day" and "Month." The purpose is to encourage people to recognize and express happiness and to remind them that "despite global and personal chaos happiness still happens."

The Secret Society of Happy People was formed in August 1998 to "encourage the expression of happiness and discourage parade raining." The society gained international attention in December 1998 by challenging Ann Landers' discouragement of writing happy holiday newsletters. The group has been featured in major magazines, newspapers, and television programs.

People spend a lot of money, time, and effort chasing after happiness. Those who have what the world considers the necessary ingredients for happiness are often the ones who lack it. The book of Psalms says that joyful people are those who get their strength from the Lord (84:5), trust in him (84:12), are disciplined by him (94:12), "deal justly with others and always do what is right" (106:3), fear him and "delight in obeying his commands" (112:1), have integrity (119:1), and "search for him with all their hearts" (119:2).

The happiness described in the Bible is based on more than just good feelings, a positive attitude, or favorable circumstances. It comes from being in a right relationship with God and with other people. This leads to a deep, lasting joy that can't be destroyed by personal or global chaos. The only road to true happiness is summed up in Psalm 119:35: "Make me walk along the path of your commands, for that is where my happiness is found."

August 9

* * *

Jesus called out to them, "Come, follow me, and I will show you
how to fish for people!"
MATTHEW 4:19

T he 1992 Summer Olympics in Barcelona, Spain, closed on August 9. The U.S. men's basketball team, unofficially nicknamed the "Dream Team," brought home a gold medal. For the first time, professional athletes had been allowed to compete in the Olympics. The Dream Team included NBA stars Michael Jordan, Larry Bird, and Magic Johnson.

The U.S. team beat its eight opponents by an average of forty-four points, finishing up with a 117–85 win over Croatia. The Dream Team attracted attention and fans everywhere it went. Many consider it the greatest collection of talent ever assembled on any team in any sport. After the 1992 Olympics, the popularity of basketball exploded; today it challenges soccer as the world's most popular sport.

Out of all his followers, Jesus assembled his own "dream team," a group of twelve men whom he personally chose and mentored. At times they must have seemed more like a "nightmare team." They often failed to understand Jesus' teaching and behavior. Sometimes they argued among themselves, once "about which of them was the greatest" (Luke 9:46). Peter denied knowing Jesus; Judas betrayed him. Thomas doubted Jesus' resurrection.

In spite of the apostles' faults and failures, they accomplished the mission of spreading the gospel and laying the foundations for the church. Through the power of the Holy Spirit, this small team had the wisdom, strength, and courage to do amazing things. Today, the church is God's "dream team." We may not feel like all-stars, but with the Holy Spirit living in us, we can rise above our faults and shortcomings to do God's work and win souls for Christ.

August 10

✳ ✳ ✳

The wise shall inherit glory, but shame shall be the legacy of fools.
PROVERBS 3:35, NKJV

B ritish scientist James Smithson never visited the United States, but in 1829 his will stated that if his nephew, his sole heir, died childless, his fortune would go to the United States to be used for "an establishment for the increase and diffusion of knowledge." Congress accepted the legacy, and two years later the gift of eleven boxes of gold coins was shipped from England.

After almost a decade of debate, Congress passed an act on this day in 1846, creating the Smithsonian Institution as a trust to manage the bequest. Today the Smithsonian is the largest museum complex in the world, with collections numbering more than 140 million items. It is also one of the world's leading research institutions.

We Christians are also responsible for leaving a legacy—to contribute to "the increase and diffusion of knowledge" of the gospel. Paul had traveled with and mentored Timothy for many years. As Paul's ministry drew to an end, he urged Timothy to teach what he had learned to trustworthy people who would then pass it on to others (2 Timothy 2:2). Paul wanted to make sure that the ministry of the gospel for which he had labored so faithfully would continue after his death.

Some people are careful to manage their finances and arrange their will so they have something to leave to their children. What a shame it would be to focus on an earthly bequest and not leave behind what we learned on our faith journey. The most valuable thing we can pass on to others is the knowledge of God's love through Jesus Christ and the riches available to those who believe in him. There is no greater legacy.

What are you doing to make sure you leave a spiritual legacy?

August 11

* * *

The heavens will be black above them; the stars will give no light. The sun will be dark when it rises, and the moon will provide no light.

ISAIAH 13:10

On this day in 1999, millions of people went outside to get a glimpse of the last total solar eclipse of the millennium. The eclipse was most visible in the Middle East because of clear weather and the configuration of the solar system. But the event attracted scientists and curious viewers from Canada to Europe and Asia.

There are at least two solar eclipses each year, but most are partial eclipses. Total eclipses occur almost once a year, but they are often over an ocean or remote countries. The August 11, 1999, eclipse came at the peak of summer and passed over a number of heavily populated areas, making it one of the most-watched eclipses of all time.

In Isaiah, God used the image of darkened heavens to describe the political and social turmoil that would be part of his judgment for sin. The prophecy applied to Isaiah's day and also to the future period just before the Day of the Lord. Just before Christ sets up his millennial Kingdom, "darkness as black as night" will cover all the earth, but the glory of the Lord will shine over Israel. Israel, in turn, will shine out as a light to the nations and help remove the spiritual darkness over the world (Isaiah 60:2-3).

We live in a time of great spiritual darkness, when truth is often eclipsed by lies. Even though the world will continue to grow darker until God's final judgment and redemption, believers have the light of God's grace shining within them. That light should radiate out to other people and reveal his glory. When God's truth illuminates the shadows of deception, no one is left in the dark.

August 12

* * *

They shoot from the shadows at those whose hearts are right.

PSALM 11:2

Famous sharpshooter Annie Oakley was born in the month of August in 1860 in a log cabin in Darke County, Ohio. She began shooting as a child and supported her family by hunting small game after her father's death. Annie became known for her uncanny accuracy with a rifle, pistol, or shotgun. She could hit a playing card with the thin edge toward her from ninety feet away.

Annie married Frank Butler, also a marksman, and joined his vaudeville act. From 1885 until 1902, they traveled with Buffalo Bill's Wild West Show, and Annie became a sensation throughout America and Europe. Annie's act included shooting off the end of a cigarette held in her husband's mouth. In Berlin, Crown Prince William insisted she perform the trick with the cigarette in his mouth.

Believers sometimes feel like practice targets for sharpshooters. David felt that way, too. He complained that evil people were hiding in the shadows shooting arrows at those who tried to do right. There will always be those who long to see godly people destroyed. They shoot out slanderous words to ruin reputations or accusations designed to wound. Often they hit their mark.

Paul warns about the most dangerous marksman in Ephesians 6, describing the spiritual armor provided by God as a protection against that enemy. Satan continually shoots "fiery arrows" of temptation at believers. His aim is good because he knows our weak spots. He prepares his custom-made ammunition for us from an arsenal of fear, doubt, lust, greed, and anything else that would lead us into sin. The only way to stop these flaming arrows is to take up our shield of faith (v. 16). Satan may have an uncanny ability to know how to attack us, but God has a supernatural way to protect us.

August 13

* * *

[Jesus said,] "When you give to someone in need, don't let your left hand know what your right hand is doing."

MATTHEW 6:3

I nternational Left-Handers Day has been celebrated on this day since 1976. An organization called Left-Handers International selected this day because August 13, 1976, fell on Friday the thirteenth. The group saw it as a way to make fun of the superstitions directed at left-handed people for hundreds of years in many cultures, some of which still lead to prejudice today.

The goals are to raise awareness of left-handedness and the challenges of living in a right-handed world, to educate manufacturers and designers who might accommodate the comfort and safety of left-handed people in new products and buildings, to promote research into different aspects of left-handedness, and to celebrate the strengths and advantages possessed by left-handers.

Sometimes God uses what makes us "different" in a special way. When Israel cried out for deliverance from Moab, God raised up Ehud, a left-handed man. Because Ehud carried his sword on his right side instead of the left, he was able to slip in with his weapon unnoticed and kill the king (Judges 3:12-23). The fighting men of the tribe of Benjamin included seven hundred left-handed men who could "sling a rock and hit a target within a hairsbreadth without missing" (Judges 20:16). Some translations call these men "choice" or "chosen."

Whether we are right- or left-handed, God wants us to use our hands for giving to the needy. Whichever hand we use, we're not supposed to give as the Pharisees did, making a show of it so others will see our good works. Jesus taught that giving is a personal matter between us and God. We are to give so secretly that one hand doesn't know what the other one is doing. The only kind of giving that God rewards is quiet, humble, generous—and ambidextrous.

August 14

* * *

It is not kept beyond the sea, so far away that you must ask,
"Who will cross the sea to bring it to us so we can hear it and obey?"
DEUTERONOMY 30:13

O n this day in 1816, the British formally annexed the remote island Tristan da Cunha. Known as "the remotest island in the world," it is located in the South Atlantic Ocean midway between South America and southern Africa. The British annexed the island as a precautionary measure to make sure the French did not use it as a base to rescue Napoleon from exile on nearby Saint Helena.

Although a volcanic eruption forced the evacuation of the island in October 1961, the main body of 198 islanders chose to return to Tristan da Cunha in November 1963. Today, the thirty-eight-square-mile island has modern conveniences but retains an "old world" feel. It has a thriving economy and virtually no unemployment or serious crime.

Like a faraway island, sometimes we feel God's will is too remote and mysterious for us to comprehend. Moses told the Israelites that the law was very close, on their lips and in their heart so they could obey it (Deuteronomy 30:11-14). Paul quotes Moses' words after he reminds his readers that Christ has accomplished the purpose for which the law was given (Romans 10:4).

Salvation is never too remote for anyone to obtain, and neither is discovering God's will. He doesn't give detailed instructions for every specific question or situation, but his Word provides the guidance we need to make godly choices. When we study the Scriptures, the Holy Spirit reveals God's mind to us. As we obey what he shows us, he will reveal further truths to us. But we will never understand God's will if we aren't even remotely obedient.

August 15

* * *

And the angel said to me, "Write this: Blessed are those who are invited to the wedding feast of the Lamb."
REVELATION 19:9

The most famous rock festival of the sixties, the Woodstock Music and Art Fair, opened on this day in 1969 and lasted three days. Even though the three promoters who organized the event were inexperienced, they managed to sign major artists for the "Three Days of Peace and Music."

The festival was almost canceled when the towns of Woodstock and Wallkill, New York, both denied permission. A farmer named Max Yasgur eventually offered his property in Bethel. Although few advance tickets were sold, approximately four hundred thousand people showed up. Most of them demanded free entry and obtained it because of the lack of security.

In one story, Jesus compared the Kingdom of Heaven to a wedding feast. When all the preparations had been made, the king sent out the final summons, but the guests refused to come to the party. So the king had his servants go out into the streets and invite everyone they saw. The hall soon filled with guests, but when the king saw a man who had come without proper wedding clothes, he had him bound and thrown into the outer darkness (Matthew 22:1-14).

God is preparing a party for the end of the age, a wedding feast for his Son. Everyone is invited, but unlike the Woodstock festival, we can't just show up when the time comes and demand free entry. We have to accept the invitation in advance. Like the wedding feast in Jesus' story, we can only be there with proper attire. We must be clothed with the righteousness of God by accepting Christ's sacrifice on our behalf. God's "festival" will be perfect in every way—an eternity of peace and music.

August 16

* * *

Pilate said, "So you are a king?"
JOHN 18:37

O n this day in 1977, the world was saddened by the news that Elvis Presley was found dead at Graceland, his estate in Memphis, Tennessee. Elvis had begun his singing career in 1954 and, within two years, became an international sensation. His blending of musical styles and his charismatic performances ushered in a new era of American music.

Worldwide, Elvis sold more than a billion records, far more than any other artist. His concert performances often broke records, and his many awards included fourteen Grammy nominations. Every year around the anniversary of Elvis's death, fans from all over the world still flock to Memphis for a week of activities commemorating the "King" and his music.

The world doesn't always know how to use the title "king." When Jesus miraculously fed a crowd of thousands, the people wanted to forcefully make him king to lead them out of Roman bondage. He fled into the hills. Later, when he rode a donkey into Jerusalem for Passover, the crowd hailed him as king. A few days later they were demanding his crucifixion. After his trial, soldiers mocked him as king, with a robe and a crown of thorns.

Jesus told Pilate that he was not an earthly king. His Kingdom was not of this world. In order to come into his Kingdom, he had to become a servant and a sacrifice for the human race. But someday, when Jesus comes back to earth to reign, no one will ask him if he is a king. His title will be written on his robe and his thigh: "King of all kings and Lord of all lords" (Revelation 19:16). And then all the earth will be "Grace Land."

August 17

* * *

*[Jesus said,] "Bless those who curse you, and pray for those
who spitefully use you."*

LUKE 6:28, NKJV

8-17-08

The Charles M. Schulz Museum and Research Center in Santa Rosa, California, opened to the public on August 17, 2002. The nonprofit organization highlights the work of the most widely syndicated cartoonist of our time. At its peak of popularity, Schulz's *Peanuts* comic strip had a daily readership of 355 million people from 2,600 newspapers and included 75 countries and 21 languages.

Schulz created the strip in 1950, using themes and experiences from his own life. Charlie Brown is sometimes referred to as an "everyman," a sensitive child who is often the butt of jokes. Despite Charlie's failures and frustrations, he remains ever optimistic and trusting. He always runs to kick the football that the tyrannical Lucy holds for him, even though she always yanks it away at the last minute.

We can all identify with the themes of disappointment and mistreatment in the *Peanuts* comics, and so could King David. When David was leaving Jerusalem because of his son's rebellion, Shimei, a member of Saul's family, followed him, throwing stones and cursing. One of David's followers wanted to cut off Shimei's head. David responded, "If the LORD has told him to curse me, who are you to stop him? . . . And perhaps the LORD will see that I am being wronged and will bless me because of these curses today" (2 Samuel 16:10-12).

Not everyone reacts to persecution as David and Charlie Brown did. Some people become bitter, resentful, or withdrawn and never trust anyone again. Sometimes people lash out violently, with tragic consequences. There is a time for being assertive and speaking up, but we need to remember Jesus' example. When he was insulted, he left his case in God's hands (1 Peter 2:23). God is in control of our life, and we can trust him. He will never yank away a football.

How do you respond when you're disappointed or mistreated?

August 18

* * *

Each morning I bring my requests to you and wait expectantly.
PSALM 5:3

Aaron Montgomery Ward and his partner offered their first mail-order catalog on this day in 1872. It was a single eight-by-twelve-inch sheet showing a few dry goods items and instructions for ordering. By 1904, the company was mailing out three million catalogs weighing four pounds each. Beginning in 1926, the company added Montgomery Ward retail stores. The catalog ceased to exist in 1985, and the company announced in 2000 that it was closing.

Previous to 1872, Ward had been working as a traveling salesman when he developed a revolutionary concept. After listening to farmers complain about high prices and middlemen's profits, Ward conceived the idea of purchasing large quantities of merchandise directly from manufacturers for cash and selling to customers on a cash basis. He also offered a "satisfaction guaranteed" return policy.

Sometimes we treat prayer like a mail-order catalog. We follow the instructions, presenting our requests with praise and thanksgiving and asking in Jesus' name. But sometimes our order is not filled, or we get something different. We could understand if the items were out of stock, but God owns the cattle on a thousand hills and his resources are limitless. Why aren't our desires granted?

Ordering from a catalog involves *our* will only, but prayer involves *God's* will, too. He wants what is best for his children, and he's the only one who knows what that is. Sometimes the things we ask for would be detrimental to us or other people. Jesus said that our heavenly Father gives us good gifts, more than any earthly parent gives (Matthew 7:11). Prayer is a more revolutionary concept than a mail-order business: God doesn't give us what we want; he gives us what we truly need.

August 19

* * *

*I pray also that the eyes of your heart may be enlightened in order that you may
know the hope to which he has called you.*

EPHESIANS 1:18, NIV

The American Academy of Ophthalmology designates August as Cataracts Awareness Month to make people aware that cataracts are one of the most curable causes of vision loss. A cataract is the clouding of an eye's usually clear lens, which then blocks the passage of light necessary for vision. Cataracts are painless and form slowly. An estimated 20.5 million Americans aged forty and older have cataracts.

Cataracts are one of the leading causes of blindness around the world, but surgery is able to reverse the vision loss in most cases. The cloudy lens is replaced with an artificial lens to enable the eye to focus. More than a million surgeries are performed each year in the United States.

The Bible says that Satan has blinded the "spiritual eyes" of those who don't believe so that they are "unable to see the glorious light of the Good News" (2 Corinthians 4:4). Once we accept Christ as our Savior, those blinders are removed and we understand what he did for us. Yet even believers can develop cloudy vision. Paul prayed that God would give the Ephesian believers spiritual wisdom and understanding so they would grow in their knowledge of him. He asked God to flood their heart with light so they could see their wonderful future and glorious inheritance (1:17-18).

Peter said that in contrast with a growing believer, an immature Christian is spiritually blind, or at least shortsighted. As growing believers we should be leading a life of moral excellence, which can help us know more about God. If our life doesn't display traits of self-control, patient endurance, godliness, and love, then we must have forgotten that we've been cleansed from our old sins (2 Peter 1:5-9). The prescription for keeping our vision clear is obeying God and getting to know him better.

August 20

* * *

*I will make you a light to the Gentiles, and you will bring my salvation
to the ends of the earth.*

Isaiah 49:6

NASA launched the twin *Voyager* spacecraft in 1977 to explore the outer planets in our solar system. *Voyager 2* took off on August 20, followed by *Voyager 1* sixteen days later. Both spacecraft visited Saturn and Jupiter, and *Voyager 2* traveled on to Uranus and Neptune. In the spring of 1990, *Voyager 2* broadcast images looking back across the span of the entire solar system.

In August 2003, *Voyager 2* reached a distance of seventy-one astronomical units (10.6 billion kilometers) from Earth and is escaping the solar system at about 3.3 AU per year. It will take about forty thousand years for the spacecraft to approach another planetary system. *Voyager 2* carries a golden record containing pictures and sounds of Earth, along with symbolic instructions for playing the record.

Believers have an even more important and exciting mission than the *Voyager* spacecraft. Isaiah prophesied that Jesus would carry salvation to the ends of the earth. Just before Jesus went up into heaven, he told his followers that after they received the Holy Spirit, they would tell people everywhere about him—not just in Jerusalem, but "throughout Judea, in Samaria, and to the ends of the earth" (Acts 1:8).

This commission is not just for the church; it is a personal command for each one of us. We all have a role to fill in spreading the gospel to the farthest reaches of the earth. Some of us are sent out as missionaries or Bible translators. Others are given the resources to provide financial support for missions work. All of us are responsible for prayer support. All Christians should be traveling to the very ends of the earth, whether it is with our body, our money, or our prayers.

August 21

* * *

Death has crept in through our windows and has entered our mansions.
JEREMIAH 9:21

More than 1,700 people died on this day in 1986, when a cloudy mixture of toxic gas and water droplets erupted from Lake Nyos in the West African nation of Cameroon. The lethal gas crept down the valleys so quickly that it flattened vegetation and even a few trees. It completely wiped out villages, including thousands of cattle.

At first, scientists puzzled over the cause of this sudden catastrophe. People had dropped dead while sleeping or cooking, seemingly suffocated. Investigators eventually identified the gas as carbon dioxide, harmless in small amounts but lethal in high concentrations. Scientists already knew that carbon dioxide had accumulated in the bottom of the volcanic lake. It is now believed the gas was released when the lower layers of the lake were somehow moved up to the surface.

Apathy toward God is as deadly as toxic gas. The people of Judah felt smug because they had God's law, but they had refused to obey his instructions. God warned them through Jeremiah that judgment would come suddenly. Ezekiel had a following among the exiles in Babylon, but God complained that while they pretended to be sincere and listen to him, they had no intention of obeying (Ezekiel 33:31).

Today, apathy has crept into many churches. We have more Bibles, buildings, seminars, music, and resources than ever. But many people get absorbed in church activities while being indifferent to obedience. Some church leaders are more concerned with numbers and programs than in discipling members to lead godly lives. The lifestyles of many Christians are not that different from those of unbelievers. Apathy suffocates God's work and chokes spiritual growth. The only antidote is to repent and commit to obeying God's Word—before a catastrophe happens.

August 22

* * *

Hold on to what you have, so that no one will take away your crown.
REVELATION 3:11

On this day in 1911, officials at the Louvre Museum in Paris realized that the world's most famous painting had been stolen. On the previous day, employees had noticed that Leonardo da Vinci's *Mona Lisa* was not hanging in its usual spot. They assumed the museum photographer had it in his studio. When they discovered their mistake, police spent a week searching the forty-nine-acre building but found only the frame.

Twenty-seven months later, Vincenzo Perugia tried to sell the *Mona Lisa* to a gallery in Florence, Italy. Perugia said he didn't think a painting by a famous Italian should be kept in France. Perugia had been one of four men previously hired to put the Louvre's masterpieces under glass. After hiding in the Louvre overnight, he had cut the painting from its frame, unscrewed a knob from a locked door, and walked out of the museum.

Sometimes it takes us awhile to realize that the joy of our salvation has been stolen. The culprit is usually something we have allowed into our life. Compromising our standards, playing around with sin, or giving something other than God first place in our life can rob us of peace and joy. Those things can also rob us of rewards we would have received, as Jesus cautioned the church at Philadelphia in Revelation 3:11.

Thankfully, we can never be robbed of our salvation. Jesus said that he gives eternal life to his followers, and no one can take them away from him (John 10:28-29). Since Jesus is a permanent high priest who lives forever to intercede for us, "he is able, once and forever, to save those who come to God through him" (Hebrews 7:25). When we notice our joy and peace missing, we should immediately let God search our life. He is the only one who can make it a masterpiece.

What things are you allowing to steal your joy and peace?

August 23

* * *

The people of God will sing a song of joy, like the songs at the holy festivals.
ISAIAH 30:29

O n this day in 1989, two million people from the Baltic States—Estonia, Latvia, and Lithuania—formed a human chain that stretched for hundreds of miles as people held hands and called for secession. When the Soviet Union had begun to fall apart in 1988, the Singing Revolution swept across Estonia. The mass singing demonstrations reinforced solidarity and affirmed the cultural identity of a people who had been ruled by other countries for seven hundred years. At one point, a total of three hundred thousand Estonians came together to sing national songs. The bloodless revolution erupted from the massive song festivals held every five years. Estonia became an independent state by order of the Estonian parliament in 1991.

The Bible is filled with hundreds of verses about singing. The book of Psalms instructs the godly to sing with joy to praise the Lord (33:1). Hebrews says that when we praise God by proclaiming the glory of his name, we are offering a sacrifice (Hebrews 13:15). Singing and praising God is not an option in the Scriptures; it is a command for believers.

Singing praises has a powerful effect on Christians, both personally and on the church as a body. Singing praise to God uplifts our spirit as we focus on his divine character and what he has done for us. There is no room in our mind for dwelling on personal problems. Praising is a potent antidote to worry and anxiety. When we sing praises together with fellow believers, we affirm our identity as a family in Christ. The contagious nature of praise links us together to form a supernatural chain that can truly lead to revolution.

August 24

* * *

There is no greater love than to lay down one's life for one's friends.
JOHN 15:13

On this day in 1901, one of America's most dedicated and courageous nurses died. Clara Louise Maass worked as an army nurse in several locations during the Spanish-American War, including Cuba, Florida, and the Philippines. She returned to Cuba in 1900 after the war as requested by Major William Gorgas, the chief sanitation officer. There, Maass became involved in the debate over the cause of yellow fever.

In experiments to determine if the disease was caused by the bite of a mosquito or by the lack of sanitation in cities, Maass and six others volunteered to be bitten by mosquitoes. Two men died, but Maass survived. She again volunteered several months later. This time she suffered fever and severe pain and died of yellow fever at age 25.

Jesus said that the greatest expression of love is dying for someone. He then demonstrated that kind of love. There should be no debates over whether the Romans or the Jews killed Jesus. He answered that question himself: "No one can take my life from me. I sacrifice it voluntarily" (John 10:18). His willingness to die on the cross was the ultimate proof of his love for us.

Such a love demands more than gratitude on our part. Just as Christ gave up his life for us, we are expected to "give up our lives for our brothers and sisters" (1 John 3:16). We are not all called to physically lay down our life for fellow believers, but we *are* called to give up our selfish desires in order to serve one another. When some people are asked to serve at church, you'd think they'd been asked to be bitten by an infected mosquito. That's not the kind of love that Jesus, or even Clara Maass, modeled.

August 25

* * *

Only simpletons believe everything they're told!
PROVERBS 14:15

The Great Moon Hoax, a series of articles in the *New York Sun* that began on this day in 1835, described observations of life on the moon purportedly made using a new type of powerful telescope. The articles were falsely attributed to Sir John Herschel, a respected British astronomer, and were supposedly reprinted from the *Edinburgh Journal of Science*, which had ceased publication years before.

Readers became fascinated by the descriptions of vegetation, oceans, animals, and furry, winged men who looked like bats and built temples made of sapphire. Other papers began reprinting the articles. When a journal wanted to publish the series in a pamphlet, Richard Adams Locke confessed authorship. People seemed amused rather than outraged when the hoax was exposed, and the *Sun* retained its increased circulation that had skyrocketed with the series.

The greatest hoax occurred in the Garden of Eden, when Satan assured Eve that if she ate from the tree in the center of the Garden, she would become like God and know "both good and evil" (Genesis 3:5). She chose to believe what Satan said rather than obey God. Adam and Eve received separation from God and eventual death instead of the promised enlightenment. The human race still suffers from their falling for this hoax.

Many people consider Christians the most gullible people alive, believing everything they're told. But 1 Thessalonians 5:21 commands us to "test everything that is said." Paul commended the Bereans because they "searched the Scriptures day after day to see if Paul and Silas were teaching the truth" (Acts 17:11). We can't take everything we hear or read at face value; we need to check it out. Our understanding of the Bible will help determine whether we are simpletons or Bereans.

August 26

* * *

The boundary lines have fallen for me in pleasant places;
surely I have a delightful inheritance.
PSALM 16:6, NIV

P remiering in theaters in August 1939, *The Wizard of Oz* has probably been seen by more people than any other movie over multiple decades. For years it regularly aired on television as a prime-time event, and then later as an annual event on holidays. Its images (the yellow brick road), characters (Dorothy, the Wicked Witch), and dialogue ("Lions and tigers and bears! Oh my!") are remembered by people all over the world.

The movie is an adaptation of L. Frank Baum's classic children's book, *The Wonderful Wizard of Oz*, published in 1900. The film was not commercially successful at first, but it received six Academy Award nominations. It won only two, for Best Song and Best Original Score, as it was competing with the multiple-Oscar-winning movie *Gone with the Wind*.

In the story, Dorothy wanted to run away from home, but when the tornado took her to Oz, she wanted nothing more than to get back home again. Sometimes we feel like running away to some place "over the rainbow." We might be dissatisfied with our physical circumstances, a relationship, a job, or simply our identity. Our attitude at these times is the opposite of David's, who praised God for the spiritual blessings in his life, his wonderful inheritance.

God wants us to be satisfied with our lot in life. He has placed us where we are at this moment, and he will give us what we need to have contentment and fulfillment. If we are feeling dissatisfied, we can honestly share our feelings with him. God will give us a new attitude if we ask for it. We might not own ruby slippers, but we'll know that "there's no place like home."

August 27

* * *

Stay alert! Watch out for your great enemy, the devil. He prowls around like a roaring lion, looking for someone to devour.

1 PETER 5:8

This day in 1896 marked the beginning—and the end—of the shortest war in history, according to the online Guinness World Records. For years, Britain and Germany had been disputing over the small island of Zanzibar, off the coast of East Africa. The British gradually gained control, and the sultan obeyed their commands. When he died, however, his second son, Khaled, seized the throne and declared himself ruler, with German support.

Britain ordered Khaled to retire, but he refused. The British fleet began bombarding the island at 9:02 a.m. When the dust settled, the palace was in ruins with about five hundred bodies among the rubble. The war was over in thirty-eight minutes. At 9:40 a.m. Khaled surrendered and escaped to seek sanctuary at the German consulate.

Unlike Khaled, Satan doesn't know when to surrender. His doom was sealed in the Garden of Eden when God promised that Eve's offspring would strike his head (Genesis 3:15). Christ accomplished that when he voluntarily went to the Cross and broke Satan's grip on death by taking the punishment for sin for the human race. Yet Satan still prowls around looking for victims. At the end of this age, there will be war in heaven, and Satan will be cast down to earth once for all. He will still be furiously battling against God, knowing full well that he has little time left (Revelation 12:12).

God has allowed Satan to exert some control over the earth until he is finally bound at the end of the Tribulation. Satan works to keep people from believing in Christ and to prevent believers from growing in their faith. In reality, he has already been defeated, but he still causes a lot of damage. We need to remember that even though he has lost the war, Satan will never surrender.

August 28

* * *

Christ has truly set us free. Now make sure that you stay free, and don't get tied up again in slavery to the law.

GALATIANS 5:1

T he first Software Freedom Day was celebrated on this day in 2004. The event was a worldwide effort to make people aware of the virtues of Free and Open Source Software (FOSS) and to promote its widespread use. FOSS offers the right to use the software for any purpose, even commercial use. Anyone can access and examine the programs' designs, make any changes desired, and redistribute the software to others, either in its original form or with modifications.

Grassroots groups utilizing volunteers around the world organized Software Freedom Day as a global marketing campaign. Some groups set up stations in public locations to give away informational flyers and CDs with FOSS. According to organizers, thirty-three countries participated.

In his letter to the Galatians, Paul expressed concern that they were leaving the freedom they had found in Christ to return to legalistic religion. They had accepted God's free gift of salvation by faith. Now they had started to observe special days and seasons as though this would earn them extra favor from God. Paul asked them why, after they had found God, they would want to return to "the weak and useless spiritual principles of this world" (Galatians 4:9).

Many people today are trying to earn their way to heaven by being "good." Believers sometimes get caught up in thinking they can earn God's favor by diligent church attendance, prayer, or service. Salvation is a free gift that could be paid for only with the blood of Christ. Why would we try to earn his favor instead of choosing to live a life of obedience and gratitude for his freely bestowed grace?

August 29

* * *

[Jesus said,] "When you pray, don't babble on and on as people of other religions do.
They think their prayers are answered merely by repeating their words
again and again."

MATTHEW 6:7

O n August 28, 1957, at 8:54 p.m., South Carolina senator Strom
Thurmond began a one-man filibuster against a civil rights bill. He
had prepared himself with a good rest, a steak dinner, and a steam bath to get
liquids out of his body. Equipped with throat lozenges, he recited the voting
rights of every state, the Declaration of Independence, and the history of
Anglo-Saxon juries.

Minor infractions of Senate rules were overlooked so Thurmond could
keep the floor. Some senators asked questions to let him rest his voice; he was
allowed to sit while others made brief comments. Thurmond left the chamber
the next day at 9:12 p.m., after talking for twenty-four hours and eighteen
minutes. The bill passed less than two hours later, but he had set a new
record for a congressional filibuster.

There have always been people who approach prayer like a filibuster.
The Jews had a saying: "He who multiplies prayer must be heard." The self-
righteous Pharisees tended to treat prayer like a performance, reciting long,
repetitive sentences. People in other religions at the time thought they had
to babble on and on to rouse their gods to take action. Jesus condemned
these types of prayer.

At another time, Jesus used a parable to encourage persistence in prayer,
and he often spent long periods alone in prayer. Obviously, we can't pray too
much, but we do need to check the content of our prayers. God knows
exactly what we need before we ask him (Matthew 6:8). We can present our
requests with simplicity and openness. We don't need to ritually repeat
phrases or sentences, and we don't need to filibuster.

August 30

* * *

*Inside the Tent of Meeting, the LORD would speak to Moses face to face,
as one speaks to a friend.*

EXODUS 33:11

I n August 1965, Gordon Cooper became the first astronaut to make a second orbital flight when he launched as commander of *Gemini 5*. The eight-day mission proved that astronauts were able to survive in space for the time required to go from Earth to the moon and back again.

The mission also accomplished another first on August 29, the last day of the flight. Cooper and his pilot, Charles "Pete" Conrad, held a conversation by radio with astronaut Scott Carpenter. At the time, Carpenter was aboard SEALAB II, an underwater habitat off the coast of La Jolla, California, 205 feet below the surface of the Pacific Ocean. This was the first instance of an astronaut in space speaking to an aquanaut under the ocean.

As amazing as that conversation was, it pales in comparison to the thought that the God of the universe communicates with us. Before sin entered the world, God walked and talked with Adam and Eve in the Garden of Eden. In the Tabernacle, God spoke to Moses as a man talks with a friend. God and Moses spoke openly and freely with each other, as intimate friends talking face-to-face.

How is it possible for humans to communicate with God? We are flesh and blood and he is spirit. We are sinners and he is holy. We are bound by time and space, while he lives outside these constraints. God has overcome all these barriers by giving his Holy Spirit to believers. He wants us to be in communion with him constantly, not just in times of crisis. We can converse with God anytime and anywhere, even if we're in outer space or under the ocean.

August 31

✳ ✳ ✳

The LORD will protect you from all sickness.
DEUTERONOMY 7:15

N ational Partners for Immunization (NPI) has designated August as National Immunization Awareness Month. The purpose is to call attention to the importance of immunizations, which are crucial for maintaining health and preventing life-threatening illnesses for people of all ages and cultures. According to NPI, tens of thousands of people in the United States die every year from vaccine-preventable diseases or their complications. Many more suffer pain and disability.

God promised Israel many blessings if they obeyed all his commands and completely destroyed the ungodly nations they were replacing in the Promised Land. He promised to protect them from the terrible diseases they knew while enslaved in Egypt (Deuteronomy 7:15). The Israelites failed to fully obey God by not driving out all the inhabitants in the Promised Land. As a result, they became physically and spiritually contaminated and did not enjoy the perfect health God intended for them.

Obedience to God's commands can immunize us against a number of diseases. Proverbs 5:11 warns about the possible consequences of giving in to lust: "In the end you will groan in anguish when disease consumes your body." Remaining sexually pure protects us from the sexually transmitted diseases that cause so much suffering and death. Heeding the Bible's warnings against excessive use of alcohol protects against other diseases. And living our life according to God's principles and letting him renew our mind protects us from many illnesses caused by stress. Even though our bodies are susceptible to aging and many environmental factors, a shot of obedience to God's Word goes a long way toward preventing a number of diseases.

**What areas of your life need to be "immunized"
by obedience to God's commands?**

September 1

* * *

Develop your strategies, but they will not succeed. For God is with us!
ISAIAH 8:10

O n this day in 1972, Bobby Fischer became the first native-born American to be named world chess champion, when he defeated Boris Spassky of the Soviet Union in a well-publicized match. Fischer began to play chess as a child. At age sixteen, he dropped out of high school to devote himself to the game. In 1958, he won his first American championship and became the youngest grand master in history.

Fischer's victories typically resulted from surprise attacks or counter-attacks rather than from accumulating small advantages. In 1975, he refused to meet a Soviet challenger, Anatoly Karpov. The International Chess Federation stripped Fischer of his title and declared Karpov champion by default. Fischer withdrew from serious play for almost twenty years. He returned to defeat Spassky again in a privately organized match in 1992.

Strategy is found not only in chess but in spiritual warfare as well. In his second letter to the Corinthians, Paul urged them to forgive and restore a member who had been disciplined because of sin and had repented. Paul wanted to make sure that the incident did not give Satan a foothold, "so that Satan will not outsmart us. For we are familiar with his evil schemes" (2 Corinthians 2:11).

Satan uses every strategy he can devise to destroy believers' ministries and thwart their spiritual growth. Within the church he encourages bitterness, jealousy, a lack of forgiveness, and tolerance of sin. He will do anything he can to keep believers from prayer and the Word. We need to develop strategies of our own so we can be prepared when Satan tempts us to doubt God's goodness or give in to sin's pull. With God's help, we will not be defeated by Satan's schemes, whether they are surprise attacks or small advantages.

September 2

* * *

Encourage one another day after day, as long as it is still called "Today."
HEBREWS 3:13, NASB

The Julian calendar was eleven minutes and fourteen seconds longer than the solar year. By 1582, the discrepancy had accumulated to the point that the vernal equinox came ten days early, and church holidays did not fall in the appropriate seasons. Pope Gregory XIII dropped ten days from the calendar and instituted the Gregorian calendar.

The new calendar was gradually implemented throughout Europe but not adopted in Britain and the colonies until the British Calendar Act of 1751. In 1752, the month of September had only nineteen days. The day after Wednesday, September 2, became Thursday, September 14. The change led to protests and rioting in the streets, with some people demanding their eleven days back.

Too many of us live like we have all the time in the world. David asked God to remind him that his days were numbered and that his life was fleeting (Psalm 39:4). Realizing the brevity of life helps us grow in wisdom (Psalm 90:12). Psalm 144:4 compares our life on earth to a "breath of air" or a "passing shadow."

Like the people in 1752, we may wake up one day to discover it's later than we think. Knowing how brief our time on the earth is should motivate us to invest each day wisely. Hebrews 3:13 urges us to encourage one another to godliness daily. The psalmist cried, "If only you would listen to his voice today!" (Psalm 95:7). There is no better use for every day of our life than to listen and obey God's will and to minister to others. Then we will be ready for the day when calendars become obsolete, and it will be "today" forever.

How does God want you to spend this day?

September 3

* * *

I will never abandon you.
HEBREWS 13:5

Texas was the first state to pass a law addressing the problem of newborn babies being abandoned in garbage containers or other public places. House Bill 3423 went into effect in September 1999, and allowed a "parent or other person who is entitled to possess a child thirty days old or younger" to leave that child with an emergency-care provider. The law exempts the abandoner from prosecution, provided the child's health was not endangered.

As of November 2004, forty-six states had passed laws to lessen or remove the threat of prosecution against parents who bring infants to designated safe havens. Proponents see this as a way to save lives by helping parents in a crisis situation. Critics point out that many laws do not provide for a change of mind or do not require parents to identify themselves, sign a document to relinquish parental rights, or give family medical history.

The fear of abandonment is a universal human fear compounded by the lack of commitment in our society today. Parents abandon their children, and adults abandon their elderly parents. Husbands and wives leave their spouse and children when things seem too hard. Sometimes we may feel that God wants to abandon us when we've failed miserably or fallen into the same old sin we've asked forgiveness for so many times. But we have the same promise that God gave Joshua: "I will not fail you or abandon you" (Joshua 1:5).

Since we live with such a wonderful assurance, we can be a safe haven for other people. By reaching out to someone in crisis or those who have been rejected by the world, we can show God's love and faithfulness. Through us, they may come to know the Father who never abandons his children.

September 4

God bought you with a high price.
1 CORINTHIANS 6:20

 remiering on NBC in November 1956, *The Price Is Right* ran until its cancellation in 1965. On this day in 1972, the show returned to television on CBS and is still going strong today. The producers completely overhauled the game show, but the goal has never changed—for participants to guess the suggested retail price of various merchandise and prizes.

The Price Is Right is the country's highest-rated daytime game show and the longest running game show in the history of television. Host Bob Barker, who is now also executive producer, has won fifteen Emmy Awards, more than any other performer. On April 26, 2002, he broke Johnny Carson's record for continuous performances on the same network television show.

There is no way we could ever guess the price of our salvation. We know that God bought us with a high price, but how can we fully understand what it cost him? Even if we could gain some understanding of the physical pain of Jesus' crucifixion, that represents only the beginning of the price he paid. Jesus' greatest suffering must have come from the fact that even though he had never sinned, God made him to be sin for us (2 Corinthians 5:21).

Discipleship comes at a high price as well. Jesus warns that we should not choose to follow him until we count the cost (Luke 14:28). Becoming his disciple involves great sacrifice. We must be willing to give up everything we own (Luke 14:33). That can seem like too great a demand if we overestimate the value of our earthly possessions. But we will hold nothing back when we remember what our salvation cost God. Then the price seems about right.

September 5

* * *

There is a special rest still waiting for the people of God.
HEBREWS 4:9

L abor Day was first celebrated on this day in 1882 in New York City. Approximately ten thousand workers organized a parade sponsored by the Knights of Labor. The idea of a holiday to honor workers and give them a day of rest quickly spread, and in 1894 Congress passed a bill making Labor Day a national holiday. While most countries honor workers on May Day, Labor Day is observed on the first Monday in September in the United States, Canada, and Puerto Rico.

The significance of Labor Day changed over the years, especially as the influence of unions diminished. Many people now consider it a time to cele-brate the end of summer and enjoy family gatherings. Some also attend Labor Day parades or political rallies.

God took a day of rest after his six days of creating, not because he was tired but because his work was finished. He commanded the Israelites to observe the Sabbath day of rest as a sign of his covenant with them (Exodus 31:12-13). When Jesus ascended to heaven after his resurrection, he sat down at God's right hand to show that his work of redemption was finished. Now believers can rest from the work of trying to earn our salvation.

However, as long as we are on earth, God has appointed work for each of us to do. Our work is bringing new people into his Kingdom and building up the body of Christ. Hebrews 4:1-11 describes the special rest in store for believers someday. First Corinthians 3:8 says we will each be rewarded for our hard work. God has his own special Labor Day planned for the future to honor his workers and give them his eternal rest.

September 6

* * *

Search for the LORD and for his strength; continually seek him.
1 CHRONICLES 16:11

G oogle, Inc., opened for business on September 7, 1998, in Menlo Park, California, with a staff of three working out of a friend's garage. Google.com was already receiving ten thousand search queries a day. The press began to publicize the new Web site, and in December, *PC Magazine* named Google one of the top ten Web sites and search engines for 1998.

Google is a play on the word *googol*, which was popularized in the book *Mathematics and the Imagination*, by Edward Kasner and James Newman. Kasner's nephew Milton Sirotta coined the term *googol* to denote the number represented by the numeral one followed by one hundred zeros. Google uses the term to express its mission to organize selections of material from the seemingly infinite amount of information on the Web.

There are a great number of people in the world, but God far surpasses Google in keeping up with everything that goes on. He told Zechariah that the seven lamps in his vision represented "the eyes of the LORD that search all around the world" (Zechariah 4:10). God describes himself as a shepherd searching for his scattered sheep (Ezekiel 34:11) and as the One who searches all hearts (Jeremiah 17:10).

Many people go through their life searching for something they can't identify. Once we become children of God, we know we have found what we were looking for. But we search the Scriptures to learn more about him, and we search for wisdom like hidden treasure (Proverbs 2:4). We look for ways to serve him and evidence of his hand in our life. In the meantime, his eyes are searching the earth "in order to strengthen those whose hearts are fully committed to him" (2 Chronicles 16:9). And God's eyes are more powerful than a googol of search engines.

September 7

* * *

Preach the word! Be ready in season and out of season.
2 TIMOTHY 4:2, NKJV

September 7 is sometimes called "Neither Snow Nor Rain Day" (or "Neither Rain Nor Snow Day"). This day is the anniversary of the opening of the New York Post Office Building in 1914. The building included this famous inscription: "Neither snow nor rain nor heat nor gloom of night stays these couriers from the swift completion of their rounds."

Most people mistakenly believe this is the motto of the United States Postal Service. Although the postal service does not have a motto, this would be an appropriate one, considering the hardships and dangers faced by the early mail carriers. Today, the postal service delivers hundreds of millions of messages each day to over 141 million homes and businesses.

Paul instructed Timothy to always be prepared to proclaim the Word of God, whether the weather was favorable or not. The wording Paul uses in the Greek conveys a sense of urgency. Timothy needed to be ready and willing to give out the Word under any circumstances. He was to patiently correct, rebuke, and encourage people, because a time is coming when people will no longer listen to sound teaching (2 Timothy 4:2-3).

Like Timothy, we are expected to be prepared to carry out God's will at any time, whether it is convenient for us or not. These days, we love time-management courses and tools, but the things we've written down in our day planner may not be the appointments that God has planned for us. God calls us to show his love and share his truth with those he brings into our life, whenever and wherever that may be. Like a faithful mail carrier, we should be ready at all times to deliver the most important message of all—regardless of the "weather."

September 8

* * *

You should clothe yourselves instead with the beauty that comes from within.
1 PETER 3:4

T he Miss America pageant can be traced back to a beauty contest on this day in 1921. The Businessmen's League of Atlantic City had developed a plan to entice vacationers to the popular beach resort after Labor Day. A committee asked newspapers as far west as Pittsburgh and as far south as Washington, D.C., to sponsor local beauty contests. East Coast advertisements promised a beachfront bathing suit parade of "thousands of the most beautiful girls in the land."

On September 8, a crowd of one hundred thousand people assembled on the boardwalk, but there were only a handful of contestants. Sixteen-year-old Margaret Gorman of Washington, D.C., was crowned and wrapped in an American flag. As years passed, the contest expanded in 1935 to include talent competition, and scholarship grants in 1945. The pageant became more focused on achievement and community service, and the platform program that was added in 1989 required each contestant to name a personally meaningful social issue she would enthusiastically support as Miss America.

Long ago, Isaiah pointed out that we are temporary and that our beauty "fades as quickly as the flowers in a field" (Isaiah 40:6). Peter advised women to not be concerned with the outward beauty that depends on hairstyles, jewelry, or fancy clothes. He told them to concentrate on developing the internal beauty that never fades—a quiet, gentle spirit. This is the kind of beauty that is precious to God (1 Peter 3:3-4).

It's hard not to base our self-esteem on how we look, while living in a world obsessed with outward appearance. Women and men often feel they don't measure up to society's standards. If we could only understand how beautiful we are in God's sight, how he looks past our physical imperfections and sees people worth dying for. When we accept our Father as the judge of *our* "pageant," we will grow in true beauty—the enduring kind that shines from the inside out.

September 9

* * *

Let him turn to the LORD, and he will have mercy on him, and to our God,
for he will freely pardon.
ISAIAH 55:7, NIV

S oon after the Watergate scandal in 1973, it became obvious that
President Richard Nixon would face criminal charges for his
involvement. When the House Judiciary Committee passed three articles of
impeachment, Nixon resigned. On August 9, 1974, Vice President Ford took
the oath of office.

A month after he took office, Ford pardoned Nixon "for all offenses
against the United States" that he had committed "or may have committed"
while serving in office. This action protected Nixon from any criminal prosecution. In October, Ford voluntarily appeared before a subcommittee of the
House of Representatives to explain his reasoning. Ford cited his concern
over "the immediate future of this great country" as the basis for his decision.

Isaiah urged the wicked to change their ways and turn to the Lord, who
would have mercy and generously forgive them. David cried out for pardon for
his many sins, "for the honor of your name, O LORD" (Psalm 25:11). We don't
receive forgiveness on the basis of any merit we have but because of God's
character, which incorporates mercy along with judgment of sin. He promises
a full pardon when we come to him through repentance and faith in Christ.

Too often we live more like criminals than pardoned people. Satan
encourages us to keep dredging up our past sins so that we are weighed down
with guilt. Then we can't enjoy the freedom of one who has been freed from
the threat of prosecution. But God's pardon is clear and irrevocable: "So now
there is no condemnation for those who belong to Christ Jesus" (Romans 8:1).
You can't be more pardoned than that.

September 10

* * *

Let us come boldly to the throne of our gracious God.
HEBREWS 4:16

The television series *Star Trek* premiered in early September 1966. The show lasted only three seasons but turned into a phenomenon never seen before in the history of television. The series led to movies with the original cast and to several spin-off series. In syndication, the original series still attracts devoted fans in the millions and is seen in over one hundred countries throughout the world.

Star Trek was set in the twenty-third century and featured the adventures of the *Starship Enterprise* as it explored the galaxy. Captain James T. Kirk commanded a diverse crew on a five-year mission "to explore strange new worlds, to seek out new life and new civilizations—to boldly go where no man has gone before."

The fourth chapter of Hebrews explains that since Jesus is our High Priest, we can boldly approach God's throne. The Greek word translated "boldly" implies confidence and freedom of speech. We don't have to approach God through Old Testament sacrifices or works. We have free access to God's presence if we come on the basis of Christ's sacrifice and a relationship with him.

We can be confident that our High Priest understands our weaknesses and will give us mercy and grace. Since Jesus took on human form, he faced all the same temptations that we face, but he never sinned (Hebrews 4:15). Jesus has walked everywhere we have walked. He went to the grave where so many had gone before. But then he rose from death and went where no one had gone before. Jesus went to the right hand of God, where he intercedes for us. Now we have a mission to seek out and explore our new life, and someday we will join Jesus and explore a strange—and wonderful—new world.

What is keeping you from boldly approaching God's throne?

September 11

* * *

You have been a shelter for me, a strong tower from the enemy.
PSALM 61:3, NKJV

O n this day in 2001, billions of television viewers saw hijacked commercial jetliners crashing into the towers of the World Trade Center in New York City and the Pentagon near Washington, D.C. Tragically, approximately 2,800 people lost their life as a result of the plot masterminded by Osama bin Laden and his al Qaeda organization.

Many political leaders of other nations rushed to offer sympathy and assistance to America. But shockingly, within hours cameras showed Palestinians cheering the terrorists' success. In China, Internet discussions applauded the blow against "American arrogance." Some people in other countries felt sympathy for the terrorists rather than for the victims.

Americans felt shock at the hatred demonstrated by the terrorists' acts and by the antipathy toward the United States expressed afterward. We forget that although God is sovereign and ultimately in control, "The world around us is under the control of the evil one" (1 John 5:19). Satan delights in spreading evil such as the hatred that led to men giving up their own life to murder thousands of people who were just going about their job.

Believers sometimes forget how much hatred Satan feels for us. He can't have our soul, so he works furiously to destroy our life, working much like a terrorist. Just as some of the 9/11 hijackers were trained in our country's flight schools, Satan often uses our own abilities and gifts to tempt us to stray from God. Terrorists work to infiltrate the society they are targeting; Satan tries to infiltrate our church, our home, and our mind. Satan desires our downfall, but our security in Christ is a strong tower of refuge—a tower that can never be destroyed.

September 12

* * *

Let us offer through Jesus a continual sacrifice of praise to God, proclaiming our allegiance to his name.

HEBREWS 13:15

T he pledge to the flag of the United States first appeared in the children's magazine *The Youth's Companion* in September 1892. Although controversy later arose as to its authorship, historians now accredit it to Francis Bellamy, an editor at the periodical. He proposed a patriotic ceremony for schoolchildren to celebrate the four-hundredth anniversary of Christopher Columbus's arrival in North America. This would include saluting the flag and reciting the new pledge in unison.

Students across the nation recited the Pledge of Allegiance for the first time on October 21, 1892. "The flag of the United States of America" replaced "my flag" in 1924. Congress officially recognized the pledge in 1942. The words "under God" were added in 1954 at President Eisenhower's urging.

Being loyal to our country is important, but it shouldn't form the basis of our life. Sadly, many people offer their primary allegiance to someone or something other than the God who created them and died for them. He is the One who deserves our full loyalty and the One who has the right to demand it. Yet he gives us free choice as to where we place our devotion.

If we bear Christ's name, then we have pledged our allegiance to him and are bound by an unbreakable covenant. His interests and purposes are now our own; his enemies are ours as well. We can't divide our loyalty. "Friendship with the world makes [us] an enemy of God" (James 4:4). Our allegiance lies with God's Kingdom, where there is truly "liberty and justice for all."

September 13

* * *

We have peace with God through our Lord Jesus Christ, through whom we have gained access by faith into this grace in which we now stand.

ROMANS 5:1-2, NIV

In September 2000, the city of LaGrange, Georgia, became the first city in the world to offer free Internet access for all its residents and businesses. LaGrange, located sixty miles southwest of Atlanta, gained international attention when it offered its twenty-seven thousand citizens free access through their cable television. The city provides all the necessary hardware, software, and access at no cost to the public.

City leaders cited their desire to create a wired community capable of competing in a high-tech world. The World Teleport Association of New York recognized LaGrange with the "Intelligent City of the Year" award for 2000. *Government Technology* magazine also honored the city with the "Government Technology Leadership" award.

Jesus' death and resurrection provides free access to God for every man, woman, and child in the world. He opens the way for us to connect directly with God, with no need to approach him through sacrifices, the law, a priest, a church, or any ritual. Out of his great love and mercy, God provides everything necessary for us to become his children and receive forgiveness and the promise of eternal life with him.

We were all born "wired" for a relationship with our heavenly Father. There is a void within us that can be filled only by knowing God personally. We can search for meaning and fulfillment in many different places, but we were created to love and worship God and to enjoy fellowship with him. Our deepest longings will never be satisfied until we put our faith in Jesus Christ and finally make that connection with God.

September 14

* * *

I am not surprised! Even Satan disguises himself as an angel of light.

2 CORINTHIANS 11:14

T he first lighthouse in North America was lit just before sunset on this day in 1716. Boston Light was located on Little Brewster Island to mark the entrance to the harbor at Boston, Massachusetts. Previously, shipwrecks on the area's treacherous rocks had resulted in many deaths. Sometimes "wreckers," who lit signal fires in the wrong places, lured other ships aground to be plundered.

British forces demolished Boston Light during the Revolutionary War. Later, in 1783, John Hancock, governor of Massachusetts, ordered its rebuilding. On April 16, 1998, Boston Light became the last lighthouse in the United States to be automated. Special congressional funding allows coast guard staff to remain on the island, making it a living museum of lighthouse history. Its light operates twenty-four hours a day.

Many lights "beacon" to us today, and a significant number of them try to lure us away from faith in Christ. Even Satan can disguise himself as an angel of light. Sometimes it's hard to distinguish the light of truth from all the others. If we're not careful, we can follow the wrong signal light and make a wreck of our life.

Trials and tragedies can make our life seem like a stormy sea with high waves crashing. At these times, the newest Christian best seller and the latest gimmicky plan for spiritual growth don't mean very much. We need to follow the light that "beacons" us to God's Word, back to basic truths: God loves me, Jesus died for me, my life is in his hands, my future is secure. The light of God's love is steadfast, and it is the only one that will guide us safely into the harbor of home.

September 15

* * *

Two people are better off than one, for they can help each other succeed.

ECCLESIASTES 4:9

O n this day in 1949, *The Lone Ranger* premiered on television. The first episode told the story of six Texas Rangers, ambushed and attacked by outlaws. Only one of them, John Reid, managed to crawl to safety. A Native American he had once helped nursed him back to health. Tonto vowed to stay with him as Reid donned a mask and rode off to fight injustice in the Old West.

The Lone Ranger became ABC's biggest hit in its early years. Parents liked the show because of the lack of overt killing and the hero's perfect grammar. The Lone Ranger never killed anyone himself, but sometimes his enemies killed each other or themselves.

John Reid might have been the lone survivor of his band of Texas Rangers, but he was never alone. In Ecclesiastes 4:9-12, Solomon gives the benefits of having a companion over being alone. If one person falls, the other can help him or her get up. One person standing alone can be easily attacked and overcome, but two people "can stand back-to-back and conquer." Solomon adds that three are even better than two.

God didn't create us to go through life alone. If we aren't involved in close friendships, we are missing out on part of his plan for us. Christians should be enjoying rich fellowship more than anyone. In spite of our differences, we love and serve the same Savior. It may seem easier and safer to hold people at arm's distance, but we were made to be in relationships that offer mutual help and encouragement. Satan can attack us more easily if we are trying to stand alone. It doesn't matter if we're the Lone Ranger or the faithful sidekick, as long as we're riding together.

How much time and effort are you investing in your friendships?

September 16

* * *

We capture their rebellious thoughts and teach them to obey Christ.
2 CORINTHIANS 10:5

National Prisoner of War/Missing in Action Day honors the commitment and sacrifices made by America's POWs and those still missing and unaccounted for from our nation's wars. The day is typically observed in Pentagon services on the third Friday in September, but the date has been moved in the past because of conflicts with religious observances. Local planners make decisions on exact dates of observances.

The first POW/MIA commemoration was held on July 18, 1979, at the National Cathedral in Washington, D.C. An air force squadron flew the Missing Man formation. The Veterans Administration issued a poster with only the letters "POW/MIA." In 1982, a black-and-white drawing of a POW in captivity was added to highlight President Reagan's commitment to achieve the fullest possible accounting for those still missing.

Paul uses military terms to illustrate the Christian's war against sin and Satan in 2 Corinthians 10:3-6. Using God's powerful weapons of the Word and prayer, we are to "knock down the strongholds of human reasoning," destroy false arguments, and remove every obstacle that keeps people from knowing God. We are to take captive their rebellious thoughts and help them learn to obey Christ.

We are also responsible for capturing our own thoughts and attitudes that don't belong in the mind of a believer. Satan subtly introduces thoughts into our mind; sometimes it's hard to detect which ones come from the enemy and which ones come from other sources. Like sentries, we are to evaluate every thought to see if it lines up with God's Word and his will. If it doesn't pass the test, we are to take that thought captive. If we fail to take inappropriate thoughts as prisoners of war, then our witness and service will be affected, and we may become "missing in action."

September 17

* * *

The tongue can bring death or life.
PROVERBS 18:21

On this day in 1998, Jack Kevorkian helped Thomas Youk, a man with Lou Gehrig's disease, die by lethal injection. Although Kevorkian admits to helping over 130 people die, this was the first time he had directly administered the lethal dose. In 1999, Kevorkian was convicted in Michigan of second-degree murder. He is eligible for parole in 2007.

As a pathology resident, Kevorkian had presented a paper that launched his crusade advocating medical experiments on consenting death-row inmates. He later praised Nazi doctors for their experiments in concentration camps. Kevorkian called for the establishment of centers for death-on-demand, again using consenting adults for research. In 1982, he retired from his pathology practice and devoted himself to helping terminally ill patients end their life. Kevorkian first gained worldwide attention in 1990 by helping a woman in the early stages of Alzheimer's disease kill herself with a machine he had developed.

Kevorkian, nicknamed "Dr. Death," used the same medical training and knowledge that allowed him to practice medicine to help people end their life. In a similar way, James said that both blessing and cursing can come from the same mouth. People can use their mouth to praise God, then use it to curse someone who was made in God's image (James 3:9-10).

The tongue is a powerful instrument, and we decide if we will use it to heal or to harm. We can choose words that encourage and build others up or carelessly say things that hurt, maybe even destroy others. As believers, we have words about the gospel that can lead to eternal life. Failure to share can contribute to someone's death. A Christian using words that wound or kill is as unthinkable as a doctor purposely ending life.

September 18

* * *

He saved us, not because of the righteous things we had done,
but because of his mercy.

TITUS 3:5

I nventor Dean Kamen introduced his Segway Human Transporter in December 2001. Kamen predicted that the scooter—with built-in gyroscopes, computer chips, and tilt sensors—would make getting around in the city so easy that cars would become unnecessary. In 2002, almost half the states changed their laws so that people could legally ride the Segway on sidewalks and bicycle paths.

In late September 2003, the company announced a recall of six thousand Human Transporter devices to upgrade the software. Customers had notified the company of three falls, one involving a head injury that required stitches. Apparently, when the batteries were low, some Segway scooters tipped forward, allowing the rider to fall. This could happen if the rider sped up suddenly, encountered an obstacle, or kept riding after receiving a low-battery alert.

Many people are scooting along through life, riding on their "goodness" to get them to heaven. They reason that as long as their good deeds outweigh their bad ones, they must be okay with God. Even within the church there are many who rely on their church attendance, knowledge of the Bible, and service to others to maintain their standing with God. This reflects our human idea of justice, but it's not biblical.

God won't let anyone into heaven because of good behavior. He will only accept those who are reborn. Paul's letter to Titus makes it clear that we are saved only by God's mercy and grace (3:5-7). God does it all: He washes away our sins, gives us a new birth and new life, pours his Spirit upon us, and declares us righteous. Only the power of God can allow us to make that segue. Anyone depending on human effort to get to heaven is destined for a fall.

September 19

* * *

I press on to reach the end of the race and receive the heavenly prize for which God,
through Christ Jesus, is calling us.

PHILIPPIANS 3:14

The outnumbered Greeks defeated the previously invincible Persians on the plain at Marathon in September 490 B.C. Miltiades, the Athenian general, realized that although the Persians had lost seven ships, the fleet could sail to attack the undefended city of Athens. According to tradition, he sent Phidippides to Athens to take news of the victory and to warn of the approaching Persian ships.

Phidippides raced the approximately twenty-six miles to Athens, delivered his message, then dropped dead from exhaustion after fighting in the battle all day and completing his run. When the Persian fleet arrived at Athens, they found the soldiers ready to protect their city, so the Persians sailed home in defeat.

The process of sanctification is like a marathon. We might wish it were a hundred-yard dash or a sprint, but becoming transformed into the image of Jesus Christ is no simple footrace. Paul explained that he stayed focused on one thing: He didn't dwell on his past but always looked forward to what lay ahead, pressing on toward doing God's will and becoming like Christ Jesus.

We live in an age when people like things to be quick and easy. People prefer instant gratification over perseverance. But becoming like Jesus takes more than a few seminars or Bible courses. It requires a lifetime of following him. Sometimes we feel as though we will drop dead from exhaustion from our spiritual battles. Sometimes it seems that we're slipping backward instead of moving forward. But God will give us the strength to follow the examples of Phidippides and Paul to continue pressing on.

September 20

* * *

Let your "Yes" be yes, and your "No," no, or you will be condemned.
JAMES 5:12, NIV

In late September 1998, President Bill Clinton's August 17 grand jury testimony was released to the public on television and the Internet. This was the first time he admitted to an inappropriate relationship with former White House intern Monica Lewinsky after almost seven months of denying the allegations.

For four hours, prosecutors questioned the president about the exact nature of his affair with Lewinsky and tried to establish whether he had formerly lied under oath. Clinton tried to protect himself from his own previous statements as he argued and quibbled over the precise definitions of certain words. At one point Clinton said, "It depends upon what the meaning of the word '*is*' is. If '*is*' means 'is and never has been' that's one thing—if it means 'there is none,' that was a completely true statement."

James warns his readers to use a simple "yes" or "no" instead of taking an oath by heaven or earth or something else. At the time he was writing, there were two problems with oaths: There was such an excessive amount of oath-taking that it had become commonplace and was no longer respected. Also, a distinction was made between binding and nonbinding oaths, especially among the Jewish people. Only oaths that directly invoked God's name were considered binding. Some people became skillful at making oaths that were not binding.

Today, many people are skillful at "spinning" their words. Exaggerations, half-truths, and omissions are often not considered lying. God expects believers to be so honest that others accept their word as truth even without an oath. Since he witnesses every word we speak, our "yes" should always be "yes," our "no" always "no," and our "is" should be "is."

September 21

* * *

You will experience God's peace, which exceeds anything we can understand.
PHILIPPIANS 4:7

In 2001, the United Nations General Assembly passed a resolution designating September 21 of each year as the International Day of Peace. The idea is to have the entire world observe a day of global cease-fire and nonviolence. Observances include a twenty-four-hour vigil for peace and nonviolence organized in houses of worship, neighborhoods, and communities all over the world. A suggested "peace pledge" encourages dialogue about peace within communities and between nations.

The United Nations hopes to unite our global community and shift people's consciousness. The goal of the International Day of Peace is to show people that if we can create one day of peace, we can work together to create a culture of peace, one day at a time.

The most important kind of peace to achieve is peace with God. We were all born into sin, which makes us enemies of God. Jesus Christ died to take away that sin so we can become reconciled to God. When we accept Christ's sacrifice, we are no longer God's enemy. We still live in a world that reflects the ongoing war in the spiritual realm between God and the forces of Satan, but we have peace with God because the Prince of Peace is living in our heart.

We also have access to the peace *of* God. Paul gives the secret of achieving this: Worry about nothing, pray about everything, tell God all our needs, and thank him for everything that he has done (Philippians 4:6). When we do this, God's peace will guard our heart and mind no matter what outward troubles plague us. We will have inner peace and tranquility regardless of our circumstances—a peace that is beyond human understanding.

September 22

* * *

[Jesus said,] "If you try to hang on to your life, you will lose it. But if you give up your life for my sake, you will save it."

LUKE 9:24

American hero Nathan Hale died on this day in 1776. Hale graduated from Yale, taught school for a year, and then joined in the American Revolution. After distinguishing himself in battle, he joined a small group called the Rangers, who were known for their daring participation in dangerous missions. Hale volunteered to obtain information on the British position, at General Washington's request.

Hale successfully crossed the British lines and secured the vital information, but as he attempted to return to his regiment on September 21, the British captured him. He was sentenced to be hanged the next day without a trial. Twenty-one-year-old Hale calmly made a speech before his execution. According to tradition, his last words were "I only regret that I have but one life to lose for my country."

Despite some people's belief in reincarnation, we all have been given only one life. We choose how we use that life. Some people give their life to a career, fame, or money. Others devote their life to pursuing pleasure and self-fulfillment. Believers are called to use their life for doing God's will.

We will all eventually lose our life in some way. Some people live a long, full life and die of natural causes. Others give their life in service for their country or in saving another person. God decides how our life will end, but we choose whether we spend it honoring him. Jesus said that the only way to find true life is to lose our life in serving him. Then, when we come to the end of our life, our only regret will be that we had but one life to lose for our Savior.

September 23

* * *

*In your struggle against sin, you have not yet resisted
to the point of shedding your blood.*
HEBREWS 12:4, NIV

O
n this day in 1779, John Paul Jones uttered a battle cry still remembered today. When the American Revolution broke out, Jones was commissioned into the new Continental Navy. He eventually took command of the *Bonhomme Richard* and began sailing around the British Isles, accompanied by four small ships. On September 23, the little squadron met a British convoy in the North Sea.

The leading ship of the British force was larger and better equipped than the *Bonhomme Richard,* so Jones brought his ship alongside it so close that their rigging became entangled. Early in the battle, Jones answered the British demand to surrender with his famous words, "I have not yet begun to fight!" The British surrendered three-and-a-half hours after the grueling battle began.

The verses in Hebrews 12:1-4 urge us to not become weary and give up in our fight against sin, both the sin within us that tries to gain control of our will and the external sin in the world that wars against the people of God. Remembering all that Jesus endured for us encourages us to endure. No matter how difficult our trials seem, we have not given our life in the fight against sin, as he did.

Sometimes we feel like giving up and surrendering in our struggles—and we should. We should surrender our fight to God. Once we come to the end of our human strength, then he can fill us with his power. When we realize we have no resources of our own for our spiritual battles, then we will pick up the spiritual weapons God has provided. And just when it looks like we're going down with the ship, we can turn to Satan and say, "I have not yet begun to fight!"

September 24

* * *

[Jesus said,] "I tell you the truth, anyone who doesn't receive the Kingdom of God like a child will never enter it."

LUKE 18:17

Kiwanis International has sponsored Kiwanis Kids' Day on the fourth Saturday of September since 1949. Kiwanis clubs design events that demonstrate to the community that children are important and appreciated. Local clubs plan all types of kid-focused activities from picnics and sporting events to turtle races.

Kiwanis International began in 1915 in Detroit as an organization of service- and community-oriented individuals who desire to support children and young adults around the world. Today, Kiwanis includes more than six-hundred-thousand members in ninety-four countries, guided by the service slogan "Serving the Children of the World." In 2004, Kiwanis clubs sponsored one-hundred-fifty-thousand community service projects focused on addressing the needs of children.

Jesus thought children were important, too. When some parents brought their little children for Jesus to touch and bless, his disciples scolded the parents for bothering him. But Jesus reproached the disciples: "Don't stop them! For the Kingdom of God belongs to those who are like these children" (Luke 18:16).

Jesus used the picture of a little child to illustrate the attitude needed to become a child of God. Like children, we come not in pride and self-sufficiency, but in humility and total dependence on him. We come with no agenda of our own but implicitly trusting him to save us. It's important for us to bring children to the Lord and help them believe in him; it's also vital for us as adults to make sure we hold on to our childlike faith and trust.

September 25

* * *

You say, "I am allowed to do anything"—but not everything is good for you.
1 CORINTHIANS 6:12

B anned Books Week is observed during the last week of September each year with the overall theme "Celebrating the Freedom to Read." According to the American Library Association, one of the cosponsors of the annual event, Banned Books Week "celebrates the freedom to choose or the freedom to express one's opinion even if that opinion might be considered unorthodox or unpopular and stresses the importance of ensuring the availability of those unorthodox or unpopular viewpoints to all who wish to read them."

During Banned Books Week, librarians, teachers, and booksellers highlight books that have been challenged in the past in libraries and schools. Many of the titles are part of school curricula but were questioned by parents concerned about their appropriateness for their children.

Paul reminded the Galatian believers of the freedom that they had been called to live in through Jesus Christ. They had been set free from the rules and regulations of the Mosaic law. But he warned them to not use that freedom as an excuse to indulge their "sinful nature" (Galatians 5:13). Peter echoes that idea, reminding us that even though we are free, we are still to be slaves to God. We are not to use our freedom as "an excuse to do evil" (1 Peter 2:16).

Freedom brings great responsibility, especially in the spiritual realm. If we don't voluntarily submit to God's limits and restrictions, we will become enslaved to our old sinful nature again. We can lose our freedom by not making wise choices. Even though we're free from the law and from legalism, it does matter how we live our life. Everything we do and say, and read, should line up with God's guidelines. That's the only freedom truly worth celebrating.

September 26

* * *

*[Jesus said,] "What do you benefit if you gain the whole world
but lose your own soul?"*
MARK 8:36

The longest winning streak in the history of sports came to an end on this day in 1983. After American yachts had succeeded in defending the America's Cup without a loss since the first challenge in 1870, the Australian yacht *Australia II* won the trophy. Four years later, the Americans regained the cup and held it until 1995, when New Zealand won the competition.

The America's Cup is the oldest and best-known trophy in international sailing competition. It was first offered in 1851 as the Hundred Guinea Cup by the Royal Yacht Squadron of Great Britain as the prize for a race around the Isle of Wight. A schooner from New York City won the trophy, which then became known as the America's Cup. The winners later donated the cup to the New York Yacht Club for a perpetual international competition.

We all have a picture of how a Christian's life should look: a strong family with a caring spouse and godly children, good health, meaningful work to provide for our physical needs, and a loving church family with opportunities for ministry. Then one day our children rebel; our marriage breaks up; we lose our job, our ministry, or our health; our church splits. How do we react when it seems our winning streak has come to an end?

Jesus said that gaining everything in the world is worthless if we lose eternal life. Winning all the trophies in the world can't compare to knowing God. We will all experience some kind of loss during our life, either because of our own choices or because of circumstances beyond our control. At these times, it helps to remember what we can never lose and how much we still have to gain.

September 27

* * *

*[The woman at the well said,] "Come and see a man who told me everything
I ever did! Could he possibly be the Messiah?"*
JOHN 4:29

Rest Ministries sponsors National Invisible Chronic Illness Awareness Week (NICIAW) in late September to educate the public worldwide about the effects of living with a disease that is not readily apparent. Rest Ministries is an organization offering support for people living with chronic pain or illness.

The organization estimates that more than one in three Americans live with a chronic condition, with the majority being invisible. This includes the millions who currently live with cancer or suffer side effects from treatment. Living with an invisible illness can cause severe emotional strain from others' not understanding or doubting the validity of the condition.

Jesus was able to perceive people's invisible chronic illnesses, such as that of the woman in the crowd who touched his robe and was healed (Mark 5:24-34). He also saw people's chronic spiritual condition. When the Samaritan woman said that she didn't have a husband, Jesus told her that she had had five husbands and was living with a man who was not her husband. Jesus was able to pinpoint people's needs because of his omniscience; he gave them healing and forgiveness because of his compassion and mercy.

Our Savior plainly sees all the hidden pains in our life and longs to give us comfort and strength if we will share those burdens with him. He also wants us to show compassion for those around us. Everyone we meet has some type of invisible pain. It may be a physical condition or an emotional wound, a disappointment, or a heartache. We can be more compassionate with others if we remember the One who sees and heals our chronic condition of sin.

What invisible wounds do you need to bring before God?

September 28

* * *

I am suffering and in pain. Rescue me, O God, by your saving power.
PSALM 69:29

I n September 1982, seven people in the Chicago area died from taking Extra-Strength Tylenol capsules contaminated with cyanide.
Someone had pulled bottles of the painkiller from store shelves and injected
sixty-five milligrams of potassium cyanide into the capsules; that's ten thousand times the amount needed to kill a human. Victims included a twelve-
year-old girl and a young mother who had just given birth to her fourth child.
Police never caught the "Tylenol Murderer."

Authorities feared copycat crimes as 270 cases of product tampering were
reported in the months following the Chicago deaths. In 1983, Congress
approved the "Tylenol Bill," which made malicious tampering with consumer
products a federal offense. The Food and Drug Administration developed
new guidelines for tamper-resistant packaging and sealing of products.

Hurting people who are looking for relief from psychological pain sur-
round us. The painkillers offered by the world often hurt more than heal
and sometimes lead to death. People try to dull their pain by turning to
money, possessions, work, hobbies, friendship, sex, alcohol, drugs, or false
religions that bear the word *spiritual* but lack the power of God. We can
show hurting people that true relief from pain is found only in a close relationship with God.

Even believers can get caught up in wrong ways to deal with the pain of
life's trials and disappointments. A relationship or an activity that starts out
as wholesome may end up poisoning our life if it causes us to stray from God.
When it replaces him as our first priority, it can kill blessings that we could
have enjoyed. We can be prepared to deal with emotional pain by having
God's Word memorized in our head and heart. That way, our source of pain
relief can never be tampered with.

September 29

* * *

*If you think you are wise by this world's standards,
you need to become a fool to be truly wise.*

1 CORINTHIANS 3:18

S even people met at a home in Brooklyn, New York, in late September 1960, to form American Mensa. Today, the national headquarters is located in Arlington, Texas. As of March 2004, American Mensa had 52,398 members. Internationally, Mensa boasts one hundred thousand members representing more than one hundred countries.

Mensa originally formed in Great Britain in 1946. The international society has one qualification for membership: a score in the top two percent of the general population on a standardized intelligence test. The organization has three purposes: to identify and foster human intelligence for the benefit of humanity; to encourage research into the nature, characteristics, and uses of intelligence; and to provide a stimulating intellectual and social environment for members.

People have admired and sought wisdom ever since Adam and Eve ate the forbidden fruit hoping to gain knowledge of good and evil. Paul says that God made all the scholars and philosophers look foolish by making sure that the world would never find him through human wisdom. The gospel seemed foolish to the Jews because they wanted signs from heaven as proof. It seemed foolish to the Gentiles because it did not agree with their own wisdom. But believers see that God's "foolish" plan is far wiser than any human plan (1 Corinthians 1:20-25).

To test ourselves for God's wisdom, we look at *qualities* instead of *qualifications*. The wisdom from heaven is pure, peace loving, always gentle, sincere, impartial, full of mercy and good deeds, and willing to yield to others (James 3:13-18). In some circumstances, these qualities appear foolish to the world, but the criterion for God's society of the wise is an obedient attitude. Now that's an intelligent goal to have.

September 30

* * *

Be careful to live properly among your unbelieving neighbors.
1 PETER 2:12

World Bible Translation Day is celebrated each year on this day. Congress proclaimed the first Bible Translation Day in 1966 at the request of several universities. September 30 also marks the death of St. Jerome, the first translator of the Old and New Testaments. This day gives Bible translators throughout the world an opportunity to highlight the importance of translation as a basic tool in global evangelism.

Out of the estimated 6,819 languages spoken today, approximately 2,700 do not have even one Bible verse translated into their language. Wycliffe Bible Translators has helped complete over 611 Scripture translations since it was founded in 1942. The organization hopes to help begin translation work among every remaining group during this generation.

There can be no more valuable ministry to invest our resources in than providing God's Word to people who have never had Scriptures written in their native language. At the same time, all believers are responsible for a different type of translation. Our life is to be a translation of God's Word that can be read by those around us who might never open a Bible.

Peter tells women married to unbelievers that their godly life will speak better to their husbands than any words. The men will be won over by watching their wives' "pure and reverent" lifestyle (1 Peter 3:1-2). Peter also says that all believers should be careful how we live so that our unbelieving neighbors will see our honorable behavior and believe in God (1 Peter 2:12). All our actions should reflect God's love, forgiveness, mercy, grace, and holiness. When people watch us, they should see a living translation of the gospel of Christ.

How is your life "translating" the gospel?

October 1

* * *

I had to feed you with milk, not with solid food,
because you weren't ready for anything stronger.

1 CORINTHIANS 3:2

In 1977, the North American Vegetarian Society (NAVS) designated October 1 as World Vegetarian Day. NAVS is a nonprofit, educational organization committed to promoting the vegetarian way of life. It has organized and sponsored annual vegetarian conferences, including two worldwide events.

NAVS publishes a quarterly newsmagazine called *Vegetarian Voice*, sponsors regional and national conferences, distributes books and educational materials through the mail and at local and national events, and answers questions from the public concerning the vegetarian lifestyle.

A vegetarian diet may be healthy, but in the spiritual life it doesn't pay to avoid the "meat" of the Word. Paul scolded the Corinthians because he had to treat them like "infants in the Christian life." They had new life in Christ but were not spiritually mature enough for "solid food," or teaching about sanctification. Their sinful nature and the world still controlled them (1 Corinthians 3:1-3). The writer of Hebrews complained that the readers of the letter ought to be teachers, but instead they needed someone to teach them the basic truths of God's Word. The author compared them to infants unable to eat solid food (5:12-14).

If we want to grow in our faith, we can't feed just on a diet of a few basic spiritual principles. We have to take in the harder doctrines and learn how to handle the whole truth. Some Christians never go beyond their favorite passages of the Bible, which are familiar to them and easy to understand. They're believers, but their life is worldly and lacks power. Parts of the Bible do seem mysterious and hard to interpret, but God's Holy Spirit will give us the understanding we need. A balanced diet of the Word is necessary for a life of wisdom, discernment, and godliness.

October 2

* * *

*[Jesus said,] "God is Spirit, so those who worship him must worship
in spirit and in truth."*

JOHN 4:24

O n this day in 1959, *The Twilight Zone* premiered on television. The
program spanned five seasons, with a one-year gap between the third
and fourth seasons. Many consider *The Twilight Zone*, created and hosted by
Rod Serling, one of the best dramas in the history of television. An anthol-
ogy of science fiction/fantasy parables, each show explored some aspect of
human nature using metaphor rather than conventional drama.

During the first season, each episode began with these familiar words:
"There is a fifth dimension, beyond that which is known to man. It is a
dimension as vast as space and as timeless as infinity. . . . It is an area which
we call the Twilight Zone."

Human beings are born with a spiritual dimension that goes beyond the
physical senses. In this dimension, we follow either God's Spirit of truth or
Satan's spirit of deception (1 John 4:6). If we want to enter the Kingdom of
God, we must have a spiritual birth (John 3:5) and experience growth as
God's Spirit teaches us spiritual truth (1 Corinthians 2:12-13). True worship
of God happens within this spiritual dimension (John 4:24).

If we want to have a full understanding of human behavior, we have to
take the spiritual dimension into account. Even programs for physical healing
are more effective when the spiritual component is included. We need to
remember to nourish our spiritual side every day. It's too easy to focus on our
physical self and forget that someday we will receive a "spiritual body"
(1 Corinthians 15:46). Once we get our new, permanent body, we will learn
the real meaning of "timeless as infinity."

How will you nurture your spiritual dimension today?

October 3

* * *

[God said,] "If you refuse to do what is right, then watch out! Sin is crouching at the door, eager to control you. But you must subdue it and be its master."
GENESIS 4:7

S iegfried and Roy had performed together in Las Vegas for more than thirty years when a tragic accident brought their show to an end on this day in 2003. The duo's well-known act combined illusion with tiger stunts. During a Friday night performance at the MGM Mirage Hotel and Casino, a seven-year-old white tiger attacked Roy Horn.

About midway through the show, the tiger lunged at Horn, bit him on the neck, and dragged him behind a curtain. Emergency personnel treated the fifty-nine-year-old magician and trainer for massive blood loss and rushed him to a medical center for emergency surgery.

Sometimes we think we can tame our sinful nature in our own strength by sheer willpower. It may seem like we're successful for a time, but eventually we find out how wrong we were. An old sin we thought we had conquered rears its head again. Some temptation becomes an overpowering desire. Sinful thoughts and attitudes fill our mind and pull us away from wholehearted devotion to God. We thought we had jealousy, lust, and greed on a leash, but suddenly they end up dragging us away into full-blown sin.

When Cain became jealous and angry, God warned him to watch out because he was vulnerable to sin. God compared sin to an animal crouching, waiting to pounce on Cain (Genesis 4:7). In Gethsemane Jesus urged Peter to keep watch and pray so "[he would] not give in to temptation" (Matthew 26:41). We need to keep a prayerful vigilance over our thoughts, attitudes, and actions. The only way to keep sin from overpowering us is to let God's Holy Spirit master us instead.

October 4

* * *

*[God said,] "The seventh day is a Sabbath day of rest dedicated to
the LORD your God."*

EXODUS 20:10

One of the world's most recognized advertising symbols debuted in October 1989. A pink bunny wearing sunglasses and blue sandals and beating a drum kept going and going and going—powered by an Energizer battery. The Energizer Bunny became famous in parodies of popular television commercials.

Since his debut, he has appeared in over a hundred television commercials and has made surprise appearances on television shows, at community events, and online. The Energizer Bunny campaign has received a number of television advertising awards. *Advertising Age* magazine named the Energizer Bunny in its list of the Top 5 Advertising Icons of the 20th Century.

God created us so that we need to periodically "recharge our batteries." He gave the Israelites instructions to work for six days and then rest on the seventh. Observing a Sabbath rest honored God and allowed them "to be refreshed" (Exodus 23:12). We don't live under the old law, but the principle still holds value for us. Having a special day to focus on worship and communion with the Lord rather than on work renews our spirit and prepares us for further service.

Christians can also refresh one another. Paul wrote to Philemon that he had gained much joy and comfort from Philemon's love. He commended Philemon for his kindness, which had "often refreshed the hearts of God's people" (Philemon 7). Believers can help each other recharge by prayer support, words of love and encouragement, and gestures of kindness and practical help. Then we will experience the two-way power surge mentioned in Proverbs 11:25: "Those who refresh others will themselves be refreshed." Maybe then we can keep going and going and going . . .

October 5

* * *

But you, Timothy, are a man of God; so run from all these evil things.
1 TIMOTHY 6:11

O n this day in 1877, Chief Joseph of the Nez Percé tribe uttered words that still move people today. Earlier in the year, the government had ordered the tribe to relocate to a small reservation in Idaho. Chief Joseph reluctantly agreed, but while preparations were being made, some young warriors killed a group of white settlers and prospectors. Chief Joseph decided to lead his band of two hundred warriors and their families to Canada.

For more than three months, Chief Joseph led the Nez Percé on a courageous retreat of fourteen hundred miles, pursued by army troops who outnumbered them ten to one. The Nez Percé skillfully outmaneuvered the troops and defeated the soldiers and Indian auxiliaries in four major battles and several skirmishes. On October 5, Chief Joseph formally surrendered as his band was surrounded, within forty miles of the Canadian border. His eloquent speech ended with these words: "From where the sun now stands, I will fight no more forever."

There are some things we all need to run away from. Paul advised Timothy to run away from the love of money and all the evils that come from greed. In his second letter, he instructed him to "run from anything that stimulates youthful lusts" (2 Timothy 2:22). At the same time, Timothy was to pursue a godly lifestyle, "along with faith, love, perseverance, and gentleness" (1 Timothy 6:11).

Sadly, some people spend a lifetime running away from God. All the while he pursues them, offering them every opportunity to accept his love and forgiveness if they will surrender to him. Even believers sometimes avoid God. Stubbornness, selfishness, fear, or lack of trust can make us run in the opposite direction of God's will. We will not know complete fulfillment until we surrender to our Father, saying, "Because of where I stand with the Son, 'I will fight no more forever.'"

October 6

* * *

[God told Moses,] "I, the LORD your God, am a jealous God who will not tolerate your affection for any other gods."

DEUTERONOMY 5:9

I n October 1890, the Mormon church officially ended its sanction of polygamy. Plural marriage had become a doctrine in the Mormon church in 1852. This practice was highly controversial, and after extensive debate the U.S. Congress outlawed polygamy in 1862. Even so, Brigham Young and his successor, John Taylor, insisted that polygamy was a mandate of God and could not be legislated.

In September 1890, Wilford Woodruff, the new church president, had written a manifesto that he claimed was a revelation from God, advising members to obey the law regarding legal marriages. In early October, the General Conference of the Mormon church accepted Woodruff's manifesto.

Polytheism has been around longer than polygamy. God's first commandment makes his thoughts clear: "You must not have any other god but me." The second commandment prohibits making idols to worship (Exodus 20:3-5). Yet people have always tried to worship more than one god. When Paul preached in Athens, he saw idols and shrines everywhere. The people even had one inscribed "To an Unknown God" in case they had missed some deity (Acts 17:23).

God punished Israel whenever the Israelites turned away from him to worship idols or when they tried to combine worship of him with other religions. The church is in the same danger today. Our idols are less visible than Israel's—ours are money, fame, pleasure. It's easy to go through the motions of serving God even when our heart is not fully committed to him. But God is jealous for our love and wants all our affection for himself. Nothing less than first place in our life will do. Christ does not want to share his bride with anyone.

October 7

* * *

The human heart is the most deceitful of all things, and desperately wicked.
Who really knows how bad it is?

JEREMIAH 17:9

O n this day in 1959, the Russian unmanned spacecraft *Luna 3* photographed the dark side of the moon for the first time. After passing the moon, *Luna 3* turned back and took twenty-nine photographs of the far side of the moon. The pictures were taken over a forty-minute span, developed onboard the craft, and relayed back to Earth on October 18.

The photographs covered 70 percent of the moon's far side. Despite the low resolution, many features were recognizable. The pictures provided the first view of this part of the moon's surface. The dark side of the moon can never be viewed from Earth, because the moon revolves and rotates in such a way that the same part is always facing Earth.

Some people believe that we are born inherently good and learn evil, but the Bible gives us a picture of the dark side of human nature. In the days of Noah, God saw that people's thoughts were "consistently and totally evil. . . . It broke his heart" (Genesis 6:5-6). After the Flood, God said the human race is "bent toward evil from childhood" (Genesis 8:21). No matter how hard we try to be good, we are born with a heart inclined toward evil.

We can't appreciate God's goodness until we face our badness. And we can't be found until we admit we are lost. Adam and Eve's choice to disobey broke God's heart; we have also disobeyed and broken God's heart. God's response was to die for us. Even after we are born again, we struggle with our old sinful nature. We need God's truth to shine on our dark side and show us where we need forgiveness and help. The sight of our dark side may not be pretty, but we need to take a good look at it from time to time.

What part of your dark side does God
want you to honestly examine and deal with?

October 8

Do not put out the Spirit's fire.

1 THESSALONIANS 5:19, NIV

The National Fire Protection Association has sponsored Fire Prevention Week since 1922. It is the longest-running public health and safety observance on record. President Woodrow Wilson declared the first National Fire Prevention Day in 1920. Two years later, it was changed to the week in which October 9 falls.

Fire Prevention Week was established in commemoration of the Great Chicago Fire in 1871, which began on October 8 but did most of its damage on October 9. The fire killed over 250 people, left 100,000 homeless, destroyed over 17,400 buildings, and burned more than 2,000 acres. Recent research has confirmed that the fire began in the O'Leary barn, but the exact cause remains unknown, even though the popular legend of a cow starting the fire by kicking over a lantern persists.

The image of fire is used throughout the Bible. God appeared to the Israelites at night as a pillar of fire during their exodus from Egypt. He spoke to them from fire on a mountain, prescribed offerings by fire, and used fire to destroy rebellious people and cities. The book of Revelation shows that fire will be part of God's final judgment on sin, as well (20:9-10, 14-15).

The New Testament uses the metaphor of fire to warn believers against burning with anger or passion or letting uncontrolled words start fires. There is one type of fire that we are *not* to put out: In 1 Thessalonians 5:19, Paul warns against putting out the Holy Spirit's fire, which had appeared as flames resting on the believers at Pentecost. Sin or disobedience can lessen or even extinguish the Spirit's working in our life. The warmth of the Spirit's encouragement and the burning of his conviction are fires we don't want to prevent. And the fuel that keeps the Holy Spirit's fire burning, giving us power, is obedience to God's will.

October 9

* * *

Dear children, remain in fellowship with Christ.
1 JOHN 2:28

On this day in 1992, eyewitnesses saw a large fireball streaking over the eastern United States, first appearing over West Virginia. Several people videotaping a football game in Peekskill, New York, captured pictures of the meteor. The fireball had a greenish color and a flight time that lasted more than forty seconds.

As the fireball exploded into many pieces, one fragment fell to the earth and hit a parked car owned by Michelle Knapp of suburban Peekskill. Knapp heard the crash and ran out to find a warm, twenty-seven-pound meteorite underneath her 1980 Chevrolet Malibu. The meteorite had cut through the lid of the trunk and sliced a path a few inches away from the gas tank. The car later sold for tens of thousands of dollars.

Some people think that a true believer can't fall, like a meteorite, into serious sin, but the Bible gives us examples of people who started out following God and then experienced a downfall, with tragic consequences. David was called a man after God's own heart, yet he fell into adultery and murder. Solomon started his reign focused on following God's will, but he allowed his heart to be led astray.

When we become Christians, we gravitate toward Jesus. We delight in learning about him and obeying his commands. But after a while, we may give in to sin's pull and go off into a different orbit. Jesus described his relationship with believers as a vine and branches (John 15:5). In order to grow and flourish, we have to stay close to him and receive our life from him. If we're not careful to stay attached to our Lord, we may lose his power in our life. Then we're headed for a crash and burn.

October 10

* * *

[Jesus said,] "Do to others whatever you would like them to do to you.
This is the essence of all that is taught in the law and the prophets."
MATTHEW 7:12

T he National Crime Prevention Council (NCPC) has designated October as National Crime Prevention Month. Communities plan activities to highlight crime prevention and provide information on issues including child safety, home security, neighborhood watches, senior safety, and safe Internet surfing. NCPC estimates that every year more than twenty-five million Americans are victims of crime.

NCPC is a private, nonprofit organization that serves as the nation's resource for crime prevention by offering technical assistance and training, developing and implementing programs, publishing consumer education materials, and disseminating information to thousands of individuals and organizations. The NCPC is responsible for the familiar "Take A Bite Out Of Crime" public-service campaign, featuring McGruff, the Crime Dog.

God gave the Ten Commandments to the Israelites as a type of crime prevention program. The last six commandments deal with how to treat other people: "You must not murder . . . commit adultery . . . steal . . . testify falsely against your neighbor . . . [or] covet your neighbor's [possessions]" (Exodus 20:13-17).

Jesus gave an even higher principle for our treatment of others. Many teachings and religions had put the Golden Rule in a negative form: "Don't do to others what you don't want done to you." Jesus expressed it in a positive form: We are to treat others as we want to be treated. This involves more than just refraining from hurtful actions; it calls us to actively do good to others, looking out for their best interests and safety. We can do this only if we have the Holy Spirit living in us and helping us live a righteous life. Then the Golden Rule does more than "Take A Bite Out Of Crime."

October 11

* * *

You are all children of God through faith in Christ Jesus.
GALATIANS 3:26

I n October 2002, the European Union recognized feta cheese as a Greek branded product and gave it Protected Designation of Origin (PDO) status. This meant that only cheese made in Greece could be called "feta." A battle over feta had been going on for thirteen years because Denmark, France, and Germany also produce cheeses called "feta."

According to the Greeks, feta is the oldest cheese type in the world. The soft cheese is made of sheep milk or a blend of sheep and goat milk in a proportion of up to 70:30 percent. Under the European Union's ruling, cheeses made in imitation of feta in other countries must be marketed under a different name within five years.

Some people call themselves Christians just because they are not affiliated with any other religion or because they consider themselves moral people. Others think they are part of God's family because they were baptized into a church or because they belong to a certain denomination or adhere to some doctrine. Even terrorists committing evil acts often claim to be followers of God carrying out his will. Many people believe that we are all God's children simply because we were all created by him. That's not what the Bible teaches.

God created each one of us, but we were not born as his children. John 1:12 explains that only those who believe in Jesus and accept him as Lord and Savior are given the "right to become children of God." We have to respond to Jesus in faith in order to experience the new birth and gain the privilege of becoming God's child. Until then, we are only an imitation and can't rightfully be called by his name.

October 12

* * *

*Let's not get tired of doing what is good. At just the right time we will reap a harvest
of blessing if we don't give up.*

GALATIANS 6:9

On this day in 1492, some very weary sailors rejoiced at sighting land. The previous month, Christopher Columbus had set sail with three ships looking for a short route to the Indies. During the voyage, there were a number of false sightings, which led to dashed hopes as the days went by. After three weeks of sailing, which was the longest anyone had ever sailed in one direction out of sight of land, Columbus had to convince the men to carry on.

By October 10, resentment among the sailors had grown almost into a mutiny. Columbus persuaded the crew to sail on for three more days, promising they would turn back if no land was sighted. Two days later, at two o'clock in the morning, a lookout spotted an island in the distance that Columbus named San Salvador.

We all feel like giving up sometimes. After years of witnessing and praying for someone to come to Christ, we get discouraged. After struggling with a difficult relationship for a long time, we're tempted to call it quits. Sometimes we just get weary of trying to do the right thing and not seeing any return for our efforts. The Bible encourages us to not give up.

Turning back is not an option in the Christian life. When many of Jesus' disciples deserted him, he asked the twelve if they wanted to leave too. Peter asked, "Lord, to whom would we go?" (John 6:68). There is nothing behind us worth returning to. Ahead of us is God's promise that if we don't give up, we'll reap a harvest of blessings at just the right time. If we keep doing what's right and trusting God for the outcome, any day now we may sight just what we're looking for.

October 13

* * *

From Judah will come the cornerstone.

ZECHARIAH 10:4

President George Washington laid the cornerstone of the White House on this day in 1792. Washington and Charles L'Enfant, the French-born planner of the capital city, had chosen the site. Congress selected a design submitted by James Hoban, an Irish immigrant architect, who modeled his plan after Leister House in Dublin. Hoban's design beat out several proposals, including the one Thomas Jefferson submitted.

In November 1800, President John Adams and his wife, Abigail, moved into the "Presidential Palace." People began to call the mansion the White House around 1809 because of the sharp contrast between its white-gray sandstone and the nearby red brick buildings. President Theodore Roosevelt officially adopted the term in 1902. During the War of 1812, British troops burned the White House, but it was rebuilt and reoccupied in 1817.

God prophesied through Isaiah that he would place a foundation stone in Jerusalem, "a precious cornerstone that is safe to build on" (Isaiah 28:16). Zechariah specified that this cornerstone would come from the tribe of Judah. Hundreds of years later, Jesus identified himself as this stone that had been rejected by the builders, or Israel, but had become the cornerstone (Matthew 21:42).

In Ephesians 2:20-21, Paul explains that all believers are part of the holy temple that God is building. This temple is built on the foundation of the apostles and prophets, and Christ Jesus is the cornerstone. In ancient buildings, the cornerstone was laid as a guide to line up the rest of the structure. We need to make sure that our life lines up with Christ and his teachings. There is no other cornerstone that is safe to build on.

What cornerstone are you building on?

October 14

* * *

He heals the brokenhearted and bandages their wounds.
PSALM 147:3

O n this day in 1912, Theodore Roosevelt was shot while campaigning in Milwaukee, Wisconsin, just three weeks before the presidential election. The crazed assailant fired at short range, aiming directly at Roosevelt's heart. The .32-caliber bullet was slowed by a glasses case and the folded fifty-page speech in his coat pocket. Roosevelt did not realize he had been hit until he touched his chest and saw the blood.

In spite of the protests of those around him, Roosevelt insisted on completing his scheduled speech, which some sources say lasted ninety minutes, with the bullet lodged in his chest. Blood stained his white vest as he spoke to a packed auditorium. After the meeting ended, Roosevelt was taken to the hospital and treated.

Not many of us would give a speech with a bullet lodged in our chest, but there are many people walking around wounded. Some people carry deep wounds from their childhood, when they suffered abuse or hurtful words from their parents or other significant people in their life. Others have injuries received as adults, when spouses or friends betrayed them. Some people have been wounded by the world's rejection or the trials in their life.

God doesn't want his children to live that way. He doesn't always prevent our hurts, but he always wants to heal them. Healing requires total honesty with God, as David displayed in a psalm: "I am poor and needy, and my heart is full of pain" (109:22). God may lead us to open our wounds to trusted counselors or fellow believers so we can receive their prayers, comfort, and advice. Too often we learn to ignore or hide our hurts from others, but God doesn't want us to live our life as though we have a bullet lodged in our chest.

October 15

Praise the LORD, the God of Israel, who lives from everlasting to everlasting.

PSALM 41:13

T he man who announced the death of God was born on this day in 1844. Friedrich Nietzsche was a German philosopher who analyzed the values and root motives underlying traditional Western philosophy, morality, and religion. The son of a Lutheran minister, he repeatedly criticized Christianity. In *Thus Spake Zarathustra*, he proclaimed: "God is dead." Nietzsche believed that religion had lost its meaning and power and was no longer a foundation for moral values.

Nietzsche suffered physical and mental problems; he never fully recovered from a major breakdown in 1889. But his writings deeply influenced generations of philosophers, theologians, psychologists, and writers. Adolf Hitler admired Nietzsche for his disdain of democracy and his ideal of the "superman." The Nazis edited Nietzsche's writings to fit their propaganda.

Many people think that Jesus is dead, but they're wrong, too. A few days after his crucifixion and burial, he was visiting his followers, even appearing to five hundred people at one time. We can't see Jesus on earth anymore, but he is the One who is sustaining the universe by his power (Hebrews 1:3). If Jesus were dead, there would be no spark of life anywhere in the universe.

The news we should be proclaiming is that *people* are dead. Spiritually speaking, we are dead from the time of our birth because of our sin. Just as God raised Christ from the dead, he gives us life when we accept his gift of salvation, made possible by Christ's death on our behalf (Ephesians 2:5). We can live forever because of God's mercy and love. Someday people will be announcing our death, but like Nietzsche, they will be dead wrong.

October 16

* * *

My words are plain to anyone with understanding, clear to those with knowledge.
PROVERBS 8:9

I n honor of the birth of Noah Webster on this day in 1758, October 16 is designated as Dictionary Day. Webster was a teacher, journalist, and lawyer who began his campaign to provide a distinctively American education for children by publishing *The American Spelling Book* in 1783. The famous "Blue-Backed Speller" has never been out of print; its total sales may have exceeded one hundred million.

Webster published his famed two-volume *An American Dictionary of the English Language* in 1828, when he was seventy years old. The dictionary contained thirty to forty thousand new definitions. Webster's spelling book and dictionary reflected his belief that spelling, grammar, and usage should be based on the living, spoken language instead of artificial rules.

Today we are surrounded by words as never before. Radio and television talk shows blare day and night. A staggering number of newspapers, magazines, and books bombard us. Chat rooms on the Internet are always open. But many of the words we hear are empty or twisted, not like the wise words mentioned in Proverbs 18:20 that "satisfy like a good meal."

Only God's words give wisdom and life; only God's words are eternal. The meaning and usage of words change, but the message of the Bible does not. God has given us his Holy Spirit to interpret his words and teach us how to apply them to our life. As we continue to study the Scriptures, God increases our understanding and makes his will clear. A good dictionary is a valuable tool, but prayer and the Holy Spirit are essential if we want God's words to define and give meaning to our life.

October 17

* * *

[Jesus said,] "Blessed are the poor in spirit, for theirs is the kingdom of heaven."
MATTHEW 5:3, NASB

I n 1993, the United Nations General Assembly declared October 17 the International Day for the Eradication of Poverty. The goal of the observance each year is to increase public awareness of the need to eliminate poverty and destitution in all nations, especially in developing countries, and to remind people around the world that sustained and intensive effort is essential to attain the U.N.'s millennium development goal of cutting in half the number of people living in poverty by the year 2015.

The Bible has a lot to say about poverty, especially in the book of Proverbs. There are verses that deal with possible causes of poverty, the results of poverty, and how Christians should react to the poor. But there is one type of poverty we should all desire: In the Sermon on the Mount, Jesus said that God blesses those who are poor in spirit and "realize their need for him" (Matthew 5:3). Before we come to God, we must understand that we have nothing to offer him; our salvation is totally dependent on him.

The opposite of this inner poverty is pride and arrogance. Our culture admires those of us who have strong self-confidence and encourages us to base our worth on our achievements, abilities, or place in society. Even godly people can become prideful after enjoying success, either worldly or spiritual. Sometimes it takes failure to bring us back to a proper attitude toward God. When David asked forgiveness for his adultery with Bathsheba, he prayed, "The sacrifice you desire is a broken spirit" (Psalm 51:17). He knew God wouldn't reject a broken and repentant heart. Being poor in spirit doesn't mean we have low self-esteem. It means we esteem God correctly.

October 18

* * *

God created human beings in his own image.
Genesis 1:27

October 18 is Persons Day in Canada, commemorating the 1929 ruling that declared women to be persons. Canadian law was based on English common law, which had previously considered women persons only in "matters of pains and penalties" but not in "matters of rights and privileges." Five women from Alberta brought a constitutional challenge to the law.

The group's leader was Emily Murphy, whose actions as a magistrate had been challenged on the grounds that she was not a "person" under the law. The Supreme Court of Canada's initial ruling recognized women as human beings but declared that they were not persons within the meaning of the British North America Act of 1867. The decision was appealed, and eight years later the Judicial Committee of the Privy Council in England affirmed that women were indeed persons.

It seems ridiculous to us that a court had to debate for years whether women are actually "persons." We feel ashamed that at one time slaves were seen as property rather than persons under the law. Yet many people today don't consider unborn children to be persons, so they justify ending their life. Other groups of people are also sometimes treated as though they are less than persons, such as the mentally ill, the disabled, the homeless, or people with AIDS.

God created every person on earth in his own image. He didn't send Jesus to die for a certain group of people; he died for the whole world. That gives each one of us an inherent value that is priceless no matter who we are. Any person created by God is worthy of our respect. God loves each one of us unconditionally. The *very least* we can do is treat other people as persons.

October 19

* * *

How sweet your words taste to me; they are sweeter than honey.

PSALM 119:103

S weetest Day originated in Cleveland, Ohio, around 1930 and is now observed on the third Saturday in October. Herbert Birch Kingston, a candy company employee, wanted to do something nice for the sick, shut-ins, and orphans of his city. With help from friends, he began distributing candy and small gifts to those who tended to be forgotten. On the first observance of Sweetest Day, film star Ann Pennington provided boxes of candy for 2,200 newspaper boys in Cleveland to show gratitude for their services.

Sweetest Day gradually spread to other areas of the nation, but it is still mainly a regional celebration concentrated in the Northeast and the Great Lakes regions. Sweetest Day has expanded into a day to express romantic love and to show appreciation to one's friends.

Christians should be known as the sweetest people on earth. We are loved by a God who is "so rich in kindness and grace" that he paid for our freedom and forgiveness of sin with his own Son's blood. Now he showers his kindness on us, along with all kinds of spiritual blessings (Ephesians 1:7-8). Kindness is part of the fruit that the Holy Spirit works to produce in our life (Galatians 5:22).

Too many people have the opposite view of Christians, seeing us as sour, self-righteous, and condemning. Sometimes it's necessary to take a stand against sin, and we may have to share some truths that are hard to hear, but we can do these things in a spirit of loving-kindness. Jesus set the example by showing love and kindness to people while confronting their sinful actions. Now we can share the wonderful news of the redemption made possible by God's kindness, and those words are sweeter than candy.

October 20

* * *

[Angels said,] "Jesus has been taken from you into heaven, but someday he will return from heaven in the same way you saw him go!"

ACTS 1:11

G eneral Douglas MacArthur kept a promise on this day in 1944. On December 8, 1941, MacArthur was commander of the U.S. army forces in the Far East when the Japanese attacked the Philippines. MacArthur withdrew his isolated forces to Bataan Peninsula, where they resisted courageously. Four months later, President Roosevelt ordered MacArthur to take command of the Allied Forces in the Southwest Pacific. Reluctant to leave his men in the Philippines, MacArthur promised, "I shall return."

Over the next two years, MacArthur's forces liberated most of New Guinea, New Britain, the Solomons, and the Admiralty Islands. On October 20, 1944, MacArthur's forces invaded Leyte Island, a Philippine island under Japanese control. Wading ashore, MacArthur said, "I have returned."

Jesus promised that at the right time he will come back to get his followers so we can live with him forever (John 14:3). Paul often reminded his readers of Christ's return, for which they were "eagerly" waiting (1 Corinthians 1:7). Jesus' return will complete our sanctification process. We will no longer have to deal with the power or presence of sin. We will receive rewards for our service and meet our Savior face-to-face.

Our attachment to this world often keeps us from living in anticipation of Jesus' return as we should. What difference would it make if we lived our life looking forward to this glorious event? According to 1 Peter 1:14, it would keep us from slipping back into our "old ways of living." We would have more patience to endure trials and would keep God's Kingdom as our first priority. The best way to start each day is to remember that, any day now, Jesus will keep his promise to return and we will be truly liberated.

What would you do differently if you knew Jesus was returning today?

October 21

* * *

Love each other with genuine affection, and take delight in honoring each other.
ROMANS 12:10

In October 1970, Dr. Norman E. Borlaug was awarded the Nobel Peace Prize for his work in world agriculture. Borlaug spent years in Mexico developing new wheat varieties and improving crop management practices, which transformed Mexico's agricultural production as well as that of many other nations. His new strains of wheat and rice led to increased yields, which allowed many developing countries to become agriculturally self-sufficient.

Borlaug's work is credited with helping lay the foundation for the "Green Revolution," technological advances that promised to alleviate world hunger. After winning the Nobel Peace Prize, Borlaug envisioned a prize to honor those who have made significant and measurable contributions to improving the world's food supply. In 1986, he established the World Food Prize, making possible the wide recognition of others in his field.

There's no place for superstars in the body of Christ, either. The apostle Paul led many to Christ and planted a number of churches, but he never acted like a celebrity. His letters to the churches often praised other believers who had encouraged him or labored diligently in God's work. Paul corrected the Corinthians for the divisions caused by their tendency to put individual leaders, including himself, on pedestals (1 Corinthians 3:4-5). He reminded them that all believers work together as a team with the same purpose (1 Corinthians 3:8).

Being a part of God's team means we seek his approval rather than the limelight. If we do receive awards or special attention, we give the glory to God and share the honor with our fellow workers. Much like agricultural scientists, we are trying to feed a hungry world. We won't be very effective if we're also trying to feed our ego.

October 22

* * *

Now go; I will help you speak and will teach you what to say.
EXODUS 4:12, NIV

D r. Ralph C. Smedley established the first Toastmasters club on this day in 1924, in Santa Ana, California. His goal was to help people communicate more effectively in public speaking. More clubs formed, and in 1932, Toastmasters International was incorporated. Over three million people worldwide have completed Toastmasters training. More than a thousand corporations, universities, government agencies, and community groups currently use the training.

A Toastmasters club typically includes twenty to thirty people who meet for an hour each week. Members present impromptu speeches on assigned topics or prepared speeches. Each speaker then receives constructive feedback from an evaluator, who points out strengths and gives suggestions for improvement.

When God told Moses to take a message to the pharaoh of Egypt, Moses protested that he had never been good with words. God said that he was the one who made each mouth and that he would instruct Moses in what to say (Exodus 4:10-12). Similarly, Jesus urged his disciples not to worry in advance about how to answer charges against them: "I will give you the right words and such wisdom that none of your opponents will be able to reply or refute you!" (Luke 21:15).

Fear of speaking in public is one of the most common of all fears. Fear of witnessing about Christ is one of the most common fears among believers. We may try to excuse ourselves by claiming that we are not good at talking to others about our faith, but that doesn't exempt us from the responsibility. The Jewish leaders were amazed by Peter and John's bold words. They could see that the apostles were ordinary, uneducated men, but they also recognized the apostles as men who had been with Jesus (Acts 4:13). If we've been with Jesus, we, too, have words to say about him.

October 23

* * *

At that moment the curtain in the sanctuary of the Temple was torn in two, from top to bottom. The earth shook, rocks split apart, and tombs opened.

MATTHEW 27:51-52

The Concorde's last commercial flight was on this day in 2003. In October 1969, the Concorde had completed its first supersonic flight with a maximum cruising speed of 1,354 miles per hour. It began offering commercial flights in 1976. In 2003, British Airways and Air France announced the plane's retirement as a result of decreasing customer revenue and increasing maintenance costs.

Charles (Chuck) Yeager was the first pilot to break the sound barrier on October 14, 1947. The former World War II fighter pilot and flight instructor was selected to test-fly the secret experimental X-1 aircraft, which reached a speed of 670 miles per hour. Until then, no one knew whether a pilot could successfully control a plane through the battering effects of the shock waves produced at such speeds.

When Jesus died on the cross, he broke the sin barrier that separated people from God. The prescribed sacrifices were not enough to break through the barrier: They had to be offered over and over. The law was not enough: People were unable to follow it faithfully. Only the voluntary sacrifice of Jesus was enough to remove the barrier.

An aircraft traveling at the speed of sound produces shock waves followed by an explosive sound, or sonic boom. At the moment Jesus released his spirit at the crucifixion, there was an earthquake strong enough to split rocks and open tombs. In the Temple, the heavy, thick veil that separated the Holy of Holies from the Holy Place was ripped from top to bottom, signifying the removal of the barrier of sin for those who accept Jesus' sacrifice. Jesus made it possible for us to enter God's presence any time and any place, and we can get there faster than the speed of sound.

October 24

* * *

For the word of God is alive and powerful.
HEBREWS 4:12

he National Book Foundation has designated October as National Book Month. Although the foundation promotes authors and books year-round, major events are planned around the country during October to coincide with the announcement of the finalists for the National Book Awards. The awards recognize books of exceptional merit written by Americans.

The National Book Awards had been around for almost forty years when, in 1989, the board of directors decided to expand the organization's scope beyond literary recognition. The board established the National Book Foundation to raise cultural appreciation of great writing in America. National Book Award authors participate in unique outreach programs that encourage communities to read and write together.

The Bible is no ordinary book. Paul writes to Timothy, "All Scripture is inspired by God," literally "God-breathed" (2 Timothy 3:16). The sixty-six books reflect the personalities and cultural and historical settings of the forty different writers, but the Holy Spirit chose the words. Just as God breathed life into the man he made from the ground, he breathed life into his Book. The Bible reveals God and his plan for the world. It is as relevant today as it was centuries ago. It still has the power to transform lives.

Since the Bible is like no other book, we need to treat it like no other. We don't stop at reading Scripture; we meditate on it until the same Holy Spirit that originally breathed the words breathes understanding into our mind. Then we allow God to show us how to apply it to our daily life. Whether the passage is fascinating history, beautiful poetry, or a list of names, it has some personal application for us. God is the only Author who has a living Book.

October 25

✳ ✳ ✳

*I know the one in whom I trust, and I am sure that he is able to guard
what I have entrusted to him until the day of his return.*

2 TIMOTHY 1:12

I n October 1950, the popular radio show *You Bet Your Life* first aired
on television. In the first part of the program, host Groucho Marx
"interviewed" two contestants by asking questions about their life. He managed to find a joke in almost every answer they gave, especially to trick questions such as, "Have you stopped beating your wife?"

After the interviews came the quiz-show portion, when contestants
answered trivia questions. They could win extra money by saying the secret
word, an ordinary word suspended above the stage on a duck that dropped
down when the word was spoken. The show was nominated for five Emmys
but never won.

Many people are betting their life without realizing it. Those who never
give a thought to spiritual things are taking a chance that there is no God.
Others are counting on a philosophy or a religion other than Christianity to
make them right with God. They are betting that Jesus is not who he claimed
to be or who the Bible says he is.

We don't have to gamble with our life. Hebrews 11:1 defines faith as
"confidence that what we hope for will actually happen; it gives us assurance
about things we cannot see." Two of the Greek words in this verse mean
"assurance" and "proof." Near the end of Paul's life, while he was imprisoned,
he declared his unwavering trust in the God to whom he had entrusted his
life. He knew his Savior, so he knew his destiny was safe. Faith in Christ is
not a gamble; it's the only sure thing.

October 26

[Job said,] "I will never admit you are in the right."
JOB 27:5, NIV

n October 1992, the Vatican admitted that it had erred the past 359 years for formally condemning Galileo for scriptural heresy. Galileo's work supported the findings of Copernicus that Earth moves around the sun. In 1633, the Roman Inquisition forced Galileo to swear that he "abjured, cursed, and detested the errors of his work." The sixty-nine-year-old Galileo spent the last eight years of his life under house arrest.

In 1979, Pope John Paul II appointed a commission of historic, scientific, and theological scholars. After thirteen years of inquiry, the commission returned a "not guilty" finding for Galileo. Pope John Paul II himself appeared at a meeting of the Pontifical Academy of Sciences to help set the record straight.

Some people, too, have a hard time admitting when they've made a mistake. This stubbornness often strains or damages relationships. Sometimes people get to the end of their life before they realize how much they missed just because their pride kept them from acknowledging that they were wrong. We would be healthier, happier, and wiser if we faced up to our mistakes, admitted our guilt, and offered apologies to those we've wronged.

Then there are times when we find ourselves in Galileo's predicament. People often react indignantly to hearing God's truth. If we say that Jesus is the only way to God, we may be accused of intolerance. When we point out that the Bible says God hates homosexuality, we may be called a "homophobe." If we point out that sex outside of marriage is wrong, we may be labeled narrow-minded and judgmental. Other people's response doesn't change our responsibility to speak God's truth. We may be persecuted for the truth, but some day God will appear himself to set the record straight.

October 27

* * *

[The grace of God] teaches us to say "No" to ungodliness and worldly passions.
TITUS 2:12, NIV

O ctober 28 is Ochi Day in Greece, a national holiday. In October 1940, Italy planned to invade Greece and requested passage into the country. General Ioannis Metaxas responded simply, "Ochi!" ("No" in Greek). Greece not only refused to open its borders but heavily outnumbered Greek forces drove Mussolini's forces back deep into Albania. But Germany came to Italy's aid, and by the following April, German forces defeated the defenders and occupied Greece.

Many historians believe that if Metaxas had not said "No!" World War II would have lasted much longer. If Greece had surrendered without resistance, Hitler could have invaded Russia in the spring rather than waiting until winter; the results of waiting were disastrous for Hitler. Ochi Day commemorates the anniversary of Metaxas' answer with military parades and special services in many Greek Orthodox churches.

Some people have a hard time saying no, but it's a word that God expects his children to use. Once we accept his gift of salvation, we are instructed to turn away from "godless living and sinful pleasures" (Titus 2:12). It's easier to deny things that are obviously evil, but sometimes we get in trouble when we fail to resist thoughts, actions, or relationships that seem harmless enough yet are not within God's will for us. Small compromises can lead to an invasion of sin in our life.

Anytime we say no to sin, we are saying yes to God. He wants to give us the wisdom, strength, and guidance to help us live a righteous life that brings glory to him. By relying on God's Holy Spirit to help us say "ochi" to sin, our changed life can demonstrate his power and point others to the Savior. In this case, a negative answer guarantees positive results.

October 28

* * *

Jesus said, "Come to me, all of you who are weary and carry heavy burdens,
and I will give you rest."

MATTHEW 11:28

T he monument of Liberty Enlightening the World, known as the Statue of Liberty, was unveiled on this day in 1886 in New York Harbor. President Grover Cleveland dedicated the monument amid a swirl of confetti. Its sculptor, Frederic Auguste Bartholdi, also attended the ceremony.

Work began on the statue in France in 1875, with funds contributed by French citizens. In 1885, workers disassembled the statue and shipped it to New York City as a gift to commemorate the friendship between France and the United States. The pedestal of the monument is inscribed with the well-known lines written by Emma Lazarus: "Give me your tired, your poor, your huddled masses yearning to breathe free."

For many immigrants coming to America to escape tyranny, persecution, or oppression, the first glimpse of their new home was the Statue of Liberty. For people coming to Christ to escape the tyranny and oppression of sin, the first glimpse of our new home is the cross. The cross commemorates Jesus' sacrifice, which made friendship between God and humans possible—the ultimate liberty.

Jesus issues an invitation similar to the one on the Statue of Liberty's pedestal. He calls for people who are weary to come to him. They may be tired of sin and its consequences, tired of the world, or tired of trying to be in control of their own life. They may be carrying heavy burdens of the demands of legalism or a false religion, or a load of guilt from their past. Jesus promises us freedom and rest for our soul when we become yoked together with him (Matthew 11:29-30).

What is keeping you from experiencing the rest promised by Jesus?

October 29

* * *

They shall still bear fruit in old age; they shall be fresh and flourishing.
PSALM 92:14, NKJV

John Glenn made history on this day in 1998 when he became the oldest person to travel in space. Glenn had been a Marine Corps pilot who served in World War II and the Korean War. In 1959, NASA selected him to be part of its first group of astronauts. Glenn became the first American to orbit the earth in 1962.

Glenn resigned from the astronaut program in 1964 to pursue a career in private business. He also worked as a consultant for NASA and served four terms as a senator from Ohio. During the late 1990s, Glenn lobbied NASA for the chance to travel in space again. NASA accepted his offer to take part in detailed experiments concerning the aging process. At age seventy-seven, John Glenn served as payload specialist on the space shuttle *Discovery*.

Caleb was one of the two men who spied out Canaan and brought back a good report. The Israelites believed the other ten men, who had brought bad reports, so they were afraid to claim the Promised Land. Forty-five years later, when God finally allowed their descendants to claim it, Caleb said to Joshua, "Today I am eighty-five years old. I am as strong now as I was when Moses sent me on that journey, and I can still travel and fight as well as I could then" (Joshua 14:10-11). Caleb was ready to claim his inheritance in the hill country where the formidable Anakites lived.

We can't stop our bodies from physically aging, but our spirits are ageless. We can maintain a vibrant ministry and be used by God in our later years if we follow Caleb's formula. The Scriptures mention it several times: "He wholeheartedly followed the LORD" (Joshua 14:14). Then no matter what our age, God will be able to use us—whether routing out enemies from the Promised Land or traveling in space.

October 30

He was pierced for our rebellion, crushed for our sins.

ISAIAH 53:5

On this day in 1998, a law went into effect that made identity theft a federal crime. Identity theft is one of the fastest-growing crimes in America. A person's identity is stolen when someone obtains another's Social Security number, credit-card number, or other identifying information. The perpetrator then uses the stolen information to empty out bank accounts, to charge purchases to credit cards, or to open new charge accounts. The victim sometimes doesn't know of the identity fraud until he or she receives suspicious bills or discovers drained bank accounts.

Victims of this crime often spend months or years trying to restore their good name and credit record. Meanwhile, their job may be affected, they may be refused loans, or they may even get arrested for crimes they did not commit. In 1998, Congress passed the Identity Theft and Assumption Deterrence Act to help protect against this potentially devastating crime.

There is one instance of someone taking our identity that should drive us to our knees in gratitude and praise. Isaiah 53 describes how Jesus took on our identity when he went to the Cross. "It was our weaknesses he carried; it was our sorrows that weighed him down" (Isaiah 53:4). Since the forgiveness of sin required the shedding of blood, Jesus took on a physical body in order to die in our place. Although he was still God and was sinless, he took our identity and "the LORD laid on him the sins of us all" (Isaiah 53:6). When Jesus was crucified, he was assuming our punishment.

Jesus' sacrifice makes an astounding transaction possible. He offers *us* the chance to assume *his* identity. When we identify with Christ's death and resurrection, God sees us as he sees his Son—"holy and blameless" and "without a single fault" (Colossians 1:22). Jesus didn't take our identity to make us victims but to allow us to become victors.

October 31

* * *

[The people said,] "What authority and power this man's words possess! Even evil spirits obey him, and they flee at his command!"

LUKE 4:36

Halloween's origins go back to the festival of Samhain, celebrated by the Celts in ancient Britain and Ireland on the evening before All Saints Day. They believed the souls of the dead returned to visit their earthly homes on November 1. The Celts built bonfires to offer sacrifices, relight hearth fires, and scare away evil spirits. The people sometimes wore masks to keep from being recognized by ghosts.

The Romans conquered the Celts in A.D. 43 and combined Samhain with their two autumn festivals. Although the church later made November 1 a holy day, people retained some old pagan customs. Early American colonists were mostly forbidden to celebrate Halloween, but large numbers of immigrants from Ireland and Scotland brought Halloween customs with them, and it became a popular holiday by the mid-nineteenth century.

When it comes to evil spirits, we can make one of two serious mistakes: Some people dismiss the existence of supernatural beings as legends left over from a time of ignorance and superstition. Then there are people who go to the other extreme and see evidence of demons in things better attributed to nature, psychology, or consequences of their own actions.

The Bible shows many examples of evil spirits at work in the world and in people. In Ephesians 2:2, Paul identifies Satan as "the commander of the powers in the unseen world." The Gospels demonstrate that Jesus had control over Satan and his demons, or fallen angels. Paul explains that we need the armor provided by God because we are fighting against "evil rulers and authorities of the unseen world" and "evil spirits in the heavenly places" (Ephesians 6:12). Halloween may be considered a children's holiday, but evil spirits are real and we need the armor of God every day.

November 1

* * *

Whenever we have the opportunity, we should do good to everyone—
especially to those in the family of faith.

GALATIANS 6:10

Many churches celebrate All Saints' Day on November 1 to praise God for all his saints, known and unknown. The holiday's origins probably go back to fourth-century commemorations of martyrs who had died in groups or whose names were unknown. These celebrations eventually came to include all saints, not just martyrs. Pope Gregory IV ordered the first churchwide observance of All Saints' Day in A.D. 837.

During the Reformation, Protestant churches reinterpreted the feast of All Saints' as a celebration of the unity of the church, reflecting the biblical meaning of *saints* as "all believers." All Saints' Day is celebrated on November 1 in Western churches. Eastern churches observe the day on the first Sunday after Pentecost.

Even though we understand the meaning of the word *saint*, we rarely apply that label to ourselves or fellow Christians. We may explain an imperfection by saying, "I'm certainly no saint." More often, we make that comment about someone else. All saints are imperfect people who share the same faith in Jesus Christ and the same power of God's Holy Spirit living in them.

It's possible to become so zealous for reaching the unsaved that we forget we have a special duty to other saints. Jesus says the world will know we are his followers by the love we have for one another (John 13:35). Paul commended the members of the Colossian church for their "faith in Christ Jesus" and their "love for all of God's people" (Colossians 1:4). We are instructed to do good to everyone, but especially to other believers (Galatians 6:10). When we treat one another this way, we're sharing the gospel in a powerful way. We do need to be working to bring the lost to Christ, but we shouldn't neglect our relationships with fellow saints. Within the family of God, every day is rightfully All Saints' Day.

November 2

* * *

Everyone must submit to governing authorities.
ROMANS 13:1

I n 1845, Congress selected the first Tuesday after the first Monday in November as Election Day. During the 1800s, most rural citizens had to travel a considerable distance to the county seat to vote. November was chosen as the most convenient time to travel since the fall harvest was over and the weather was still mild enough to permit travel over unimproved roads.

Monday was not suitable because many people would need to begin the journey on Sunday, interfering with church services. Lawmakers wanted to keep Election Day from falling on November 1 because All Saints' Day is a Holy Day of Obligation for Roman Catholics. Also, merchants at that time typically balanced their books from the preceding month on the first.

Although Romans 13 makes it clear that all governmental authorities are ultimately established by God, that doesn't diminish our responsibility and privilege in the democratic process. Our duty is to thoughtfully and prayerfully cast our vote for leaders who we believe will govern in a fair and godly manner. In his sovereignty, God determines the final outcome of elections.

After Election Day comes the hard part. The Bible instructs us in no uncertain terms to submit to our leaders. At the time Paul wrote these instructions, the church at Rome was suffering horrible persecution under Emperor Nero. Yet Paul said that when we rebel against governmental authority, we rebel against what God has instituted, and we will be punished (Romans 13:2). A submissive attitude to leadership serves as a testimony to outsiders, as long as that submission does not include violating any of God's laws and commands. We may not admire all our leaders, but we can pray for them and show respect for the position of authority God has allowed them to have.

November 3

* * *

*[Jesus said,] "Make them holy by your truth; teach them your word,
which is truth."*

JOHN 17:17

O n this day in 1948, the *Chicago Daily Tribune* published a mistake in big, bold letters. In the weeks before the 1948 presidential election, early Gallup polls predicted incumbent Harry Truman's defeat by Thomas Dewey. The Democrats were badly split, and Truman had little money backing him. So Truman went directly to the people, traveling thousands of miles in his "whistle stop" campaign. Still, when Truman went to bed on November 2, he was losing the election.

Meanwhile at the *Tribune*, returns were coming in slowly, the printing deadline was approaching, and inexperienced workers were filling in for regular staff members out on strike. After delivery of their early edition bearing the headline "Dewey Defeats Truman," it became obvious that Truman would win after all. Although workers retrieved thousands of the papers, many more papers with the wrong headline remained with the customers. On his way to Washington, D.C., later that day, Truman posed for his photo with a paper bearing the erroneous headline.

It's hard to know what to believe sometimes. Rumors and speculation are often presented as truth. The "facts" in textbooks change over time. Newspapers and magazines often distort events to fit their political bias. The Internet spreads hoaxes and urban legends day and night. Long ago, Pilate asked Jesus, "What is truth?" (John 18:38). Jesus had answered the question earlier in the evening when he prayed for the disciples and for all who would ever believe in him, asking God to "teach them your word, which is truth" (John 17:17).

We should always carefully consider the source of any information. Can we trust the origin? No book, newspaper, magazine, television program, or person is infallible. The Word of God is the only source 100 percent reliable for pure, unadulterated truth. If something contradicts the Bible, we can be sure that it's as wrong as the first headline on the November 3, 1948, edition of the *Chicago Daily Tribune*.

November 4

* * *

Open my eyes that I may see wonderful things in your law.
PSALM 119:18, NIV

I n November 1922, archaeologist Howard Carter discovered the virtually intact tomb of a largely unknown pharaoh named Tutankhamen. Carter had been digging in the Valley of the Kings for years, even though experts had declared the site to be exhausted. After five years of finding nothing, Carter's sponsor, Lord Carnarvon, was losing hope. He reluctantly agreed to one more season of digging and then returned to England.

Four days later, Carter and his crew discovered steps leading to the entrance of a tomb. After waiting two weeks for Lord Carnarvon to return, they began further excavation. When the party finally reached the inner door of the tomb, Carter made a small hole in the door and, with the aid of a candle, looked in. Lord Carnarvon asked him, "Do you see anything?" "Yes," Carter responded, "wonderful things." Carter had gotten a glimpse of the great collection of treasures inside the tomb.

God's Word contains a never-ending store of riches that far surpasses any earthly treasure—ancient or modern. Through this book of God-breathed Scripture, the Creator of the universe communicates with us. He offers conviction and comfort, instruction and encouragement. He reveals his character and his plans. The Bible enlightens and empowers us. It's one of the tools that God uses to transform us into the image of Jesus Christ.

Just as people unknowingly walked over King Tut's tomb for thousands of years, we often overlook one of the greatest treasures in our possession. Many people declare the Bible to be "exhausted"—a book of history and myths with no relevance for today. But when we look into God's Word and the Holy Spirit sheds light on what it contains, we find ourselves saying, "I see 'wonderful things.'"

November 5

* * *

I have hidden your word in my heart, that I might not sin against you.
PSALM 119:11

I n November 1908, The Gideons International began placing Bibles in hotel rooms. Three traveling men in Janesville, Wisconsin, had formed the organization in 1899 for the purpose of promoting the gospel. Since then the Gideons have placed more than five hundred million Bibles and New Testaments with Psalms in hotels, motels, hospitals, nursing homes, prisons, shelters, and schools.

Today The Gideons International places and distributes Scripture in 179 countries in eighty-two languages. The organization has programs geared toward the homeless, students, nurses, military and law-enforcement personnel, firefighters, and others. Every seven days, The Gideons International distributes more than one million copies of God's Word at no cost. The work is supported entirely by donations.

But the very best location to place the Scriptures is inside us. The psalmist wrote that he had hidden God's Word in his heart so that he could avoid sinning. This requires more than just reading the Scriptures. The Bible will keep us from sinning only if we internalize it and then determine to obey it.

As the Living Word, Jesus gave a visible picture of God and demonstrated a life pleasing to him. We are likewise called to live our life in a way that points others to God. This requires a thorough knowledge of the Scriptures—studying, memorizing, and meditating until the Word influences our every thought and action. Sharing the written Word is vitally important work, but we must also saturate our mind and heart with the Scriptures so that others can read *us*.

How are you hiding God's Word in your heart?

November 6

* * *

[Jesus said,] "It is like a person building a house who digs deep and lays the
foundation on solid rock."
LUKE 6:48

I n October 2001, President George W. Bush called for the establishment of an Office of Homeland Security. In early November the following year, Congress passed the Homeland Security Act of 2002, expanding
the office into a new executive department. The legislation transferred several government agencies to the new department. Former Pennsylvania governor Tom Ridge served as the first Secretary of Homeland Security.

The Office of Homeland Security works to ensure the nation's safety by
overseeing efforts to prepare for, detect, prevent, respond to, and recover
from terrorist activity. It helps with intelligence gathering and distributes
information to appropriate agencies. It designs and implements national
strategies, including the color-coded Homeland Security Advisory System
that informs the public of the current level of threat.

Government agencies are essential, but the ultimate "homeland security"
comes from obeying God. In Luke 6, Jesus compared the person who obeys
God to someone who lays a foundation for a house on solid rock. The person
who hears God but doesn't obey him is like someone building a house with
no foundation. When a flood comes, the house with no foundation crumbles,
while the house built on rock stands strong (6:48-49). Our home will be
secure only if we obey God's commandments.

God gives specific guidelines for a secure home in Ephesians 5:21–6:4. A
wife is to submit to her husband as the leader of the family. A husband is to
sacrificially love his wife as Christ loved the church. Children are to obey
their parents, while their parents are to bring them up in the discipline and
instruction of the Lord. Following God's plan for a Christ-centered family,
where everyone treats one another with love and respect, guarantees the
security of our home—and keeps the threat level low.

November 7

* * *

We, too, wait with eager hope for the day when God will give us our full rights as his adopted children, including the new bodies he has promised us.

ROMANS 8:23

Massachusetts was the first state to proclaim National Adoption Week, in 1976. Additional states began to declare a special week to focus on adoption until National Adoption Month was instituted in 1990. Each November the president proclaims National Adoption Awareness Month to draw attention to the increasing number of children in our child-welfare system waiting to be adopted into stable, loving families.

Throughout the country, individuals, families, communities, businesses, and organizations celebrate National Adoption Awareness Month to honor adoption as a positive way to build families. Special activities and campaigns highlight the needs of children waiting for permanent homes. The celebration now includes National Adoption Day, on which many local adoption ceremonies are performed simultaneously.

Spiritually speaking, all believers are adopted children. *To be adopted* means "to be chosen." The first chapter of Ephesians tells us that God chose us "even before he made the world" (1:4). In love he planned for us to be adopted as his children "by bringing us to himself through Jesus Christ" (1:5). The Holy Spirit is our adoption certificate, proving that we have become a part of God's family—as loving and permanent a family as we can get.

However, the process is not yet complete. God wants all his adopted children to look like him. When we leave our earthly bodies someday and receive our new eternal ones, then the transformation will be complete. In the meantime, all the circumstances of our life are transforming us into God's image. Even though we're adopted, our goal is to have a striking family resemblance to our Father.

November 8

Give discernment to me, your servant.
PSALM 119:125

On this day in 1895, German physicist Wilhelm Conrad Röentgen made an accidental discovery that turned out to be a phenomenal advance for medicine and physics. Röentgen was investigating emissions called "cathode rays" when he noticed a glow that couldn't be explained by the weak cathode rays. When he developed a photographic plate that had been in a desk drawer during the experiment, he found an image of a key from the desktop.

Röentgen named his discovery "X-rays," since X stands for the unknown in science. Röentgen's later research confirmed that X-rays pass through different materials in different degrees. His findings earned him the 1901 Nobel Prize in physics. Today, X-rays, also called "Röentgen rays," are used in medical diagnoses and treatment, dental exams, industrial inspections of materials, and many other applications.

Some people seem to have "X-ray vision." They're able to look past the surface of things and see things as they really are. When God told Solomon to ask for anything he desired, the young king requested a discerning heart. God promised to give Solomon more insight and wisdom than anyone else on earth. Israel held their king in awe because of his wise rulings; people of all nations came to listen to him. The Queen of Sheba came to test Solomon with hard questions and found that nothing was too hard for him to explain.

The depth of understanding we call "discernment" may seem like a mysterious, unknown force, but it is a gift available to all believers. Proverbs 8:12 tells us that wisdom knows "where to discover knowledge and discernment." We will never be as wise as Solomon, but if we pursue discernment by seeking God's wisdom, we can move past the superficial and see things we couldn't see before.

How are you pursuing discernment?

November 9

* * *

*By his death, Jesus opened a new and life-giving way through the curtain
into the Most Holy Place.*

HEBREWS 10:20

On this day in 1989, German citizens began dismantling whole sections of the Berlin Wall, opening up access to West Berlin. The twenty-eight-mile long wall had been constructed in 1961 to separate Soviet–controlled East Berlin from Allied–controlled West Berlin. It was a response to the escape of more than two million East Germans to West Berlin. It's estimated that at least eighty people had been killed trying to cross the barrier of concrete walls topped with barbed wire and guarded by watchtowers, gun placements, and land mines.

As Communism began to erode in Eastern Europe and the Soviet Union, East German authorities faced increasing pressure to take down the barrier. After citizens initiated the process, East Germany eventually participated in the removal of the Berlin Wall and reunited with West Germany in 1990 as one nation.

Like the Berlin Wall, when sin entered the world through Adam and Eve's disobedience, a barrier went up between God and every human being who would ever live. Even though the Israelites built a Tabernacle and, later, a Temple in Jerusalem so that God could live among them, a thick curtain separated the people from his presence. Only the high priest could pass through the curtain to where God's glory dwelt, only once a year on the Day of Atonement, and only under specific conditions.

When Jesus willingly gave his life on the cross, he broke down sin's power over us. At the very moment he drew his last breath, the curtain in the Temple ripped in half from top to bottom. Christ's perfect sacrifice opened up access to God and provided a way for sinful men and women to be united with their heavenly Father. The barrier has been removed from the Most Holy Place, and we are free to enter.

November 10

* * *

You will seek Me and find Me when you search for Me with all your heart.
JEREMIAH 29:13, NASB

O n this day in 1871, Henry Morton Stanley found the person he had been searching for. In the late 1800s, missionary and physician David Livingstone was exploring the interior of Africa. When several years elapsed without any word from him, the *New York Herald* commissioned Stanley to find Livingstone. Stanley reached Africa in January 1871, organized his caravan, and began his search on March 21.

On November 10, Stanley met Livingstone at the village of Ujiji on Lake Tanganyika. He greeted the explorer with his famous line: "Dr. Livingstone, I presume?" After being reassured of Livingstone's welfare, Stanley became interested in Livingstone's goal of finding a source of the Nile River south of the known source. Stanley postponed plans to rush home with news of his success and stayed with Livingstone until March 1872. When Livingstone died the next year, Stanley carried on his friend's work.

Many people think that God likes to play a cosmic game of hide-and-seek. In reality, the creation all around us testifies to his presence and power (Romans 1:19-20). His written Word gives directions for finding him. The life of Jesus points the way to God, and the blood of Jesus paves the way for us to reach him. The book of Proverbs promises that those who search will find him (8:17).

Even believers sometimes feel that God is hiding in darkest Africa. Unconfessed sin may have created a barrier that obscures his face. He may have temporarily withdrawn the sense of his presence to help our faith mature, or we may have simply grown insensitive to the Holy Spirit. In any case, the prescription and the promise are both in Jeremiah 29:13. We are to search for God with our whole heart, not just a part of it. And when we "find" him, we will want to stay and help carry on his work.

November 11

* * *

Endure suffering along with me, as a good soldier of Christ Jesus.
2 TIMOTHY 2:3

In 1919, President Woodrow Wilson proclaimed November 11 as Armistice Day to remind Americans of the tragedies of war and to commemorate the end of World War I the previous year. In 1938 it became a legal federal holiday. Congress changed the name to Veterans Day in 1954 to honor all men and women who have served in the United States armed forces and to remember those killed in battle.

November 11 is called Remembrance Day in Canada. Great Britain celebrates the Sunday closest to November 11 as Remembrance Sunday. In the United States, Veterans Day is observed with parades, speeches, and flowers placed on military graves. Special ceremonies are held in Washington, D.C.

Believers are called to serve in a different type of armed force. David praised the God who trained his hands for war and his fingers for battle (Psalm 144:1). Paul sometimes refers to other believers as fellow soldiers (Philippians 2:25). For God's soldiers, the Bible is our combat manual. It identifies our enemy, describes the weapons that have been issued to us, and gives us our marching orders.

In 2 Timothy, Paul passed along final instructions to a younger soldier he had trained. Paul knew that soon he would be "discharged" from the Lord's army he had served in so faithfully. He urged Timothy to endure suffering like a good soldier (2:3). He reminded Timothy that someone serving as a soldier does not get involved in civilian affairs, but instead concentrates on pleasing his commanding officer (2:4). Sometimes we may feel like going AWOL, but if we take our commission as seriously as Paul did, we can look forward to an honorable discharge someday.

November 12

* * *

Do not participate in the unfruitful deeds of darkness,
but instead even expose them.
EPHESIANS 5:11, NASB

In early November 1965, a major grid-system breakdown caused the entire northeast area of the United States and large parts of Canada to go dark. The power failure affected an area of eighty thousand square miles. In New York City, ten thousand commuters were trapped in subway cars. Traffic stopped, and many people found themselves stuck in elevators. Despite the confusion, the city remained peaceful. Neighbors shared candles and flashlights, and citizens helped firefighters rescue the trapped subway passengers.

Twelve years later, New York again experienced a blackout. This time some neighborhoods erupted into violence. Thousands roamed the streets, shattering store windows to steal clothes, furniture, and televisions. One car dealership reported fifty cars stolen. More than a thousand fires burned in the city, while firefighters also answered seventeen hundred false alarms. Police made almost four thousand arrests.

When Adam and Eve disobeyed God, they tried to hide from him behind trees. Ever since then, people have tried to hide their sins from the One who sees everything. Isaiah predicts sorrow for those who "do their evil deeds in the dark" and say, "The LORD can't see us. . . . He doesn't know what's going on" (Isaiah 29:15). John says that when Jesus came into the world, "people loved the darkness more than the light" because their actions were evil and they were afraid of being exposed (John 3:19-20).

Paul urges believers to not participate in dark deeds but to live decent lives, since we belong to the day (Romans 13:13). Sometimes we behave one way in church on Sundays but another way when no one is looking. No matter how sneaky we are, there is always Someone watching, and he promises to someday bring everything to light—even our "darkest secrets" and "private motives" (1 Corinthians 4:5).

November 13 *11-11-06*

* * *

I will not forget you! See, I have engraved you on the palms of my hands.
ISAIAH 49:15-16, NIV

he Vietnam Veterans Memorial, in Washington, D.C., was dedicated on this day in 1982 to commemorate U.S. military personnel
who had died or were declared missing in action during the Vietnam War.
The V-shaped wall of polished black granite stretches 493 feet in length and
is engraved with more than 58,000 names. In 1984, designers added a bronze
statue titled *Three Servicemen* to add visual representation to the names
engraved on the wall. Erected in 1993, a bronze sculpture of three service-
women honors the more than eleven thousand women who also served in
Vietnam.

In November 1921, the body of a soldier killed in France during World
War I was interred at a site later called the "Tomb of the Unknown Soldier"
in Arlington National Cemetery. A massive marble tomb placed on the grave
in 1932 bears the inscription, "Here rests in honored glory an American soldier known but to God."

Some people honor relatives and friends with tributes and elaborate
memorial services after they die. Others pass from the earth unnoticed, as
though no one ever knew their name. Regardless of how the world marks our
death, God is well aware of every breath we take, including our last. Psalm
116:15 assures us, "The LORD cares deeply when his loved ones die." Each
life and death are important to him.

We never have to worry about being forgotten by God. When the Israelites felt that God had forsaken them, he assured them of his tender concern
by telling them he had written their name on the palms of his hands. How
could he forget them? Even when the world makes us feel anonymous or our
troubles make us question God's care, we will never be an "unknown"—in
life *or* in death.

November 14

* * *

He who calls you is faithful.

1 Thessalonians 5:24

T he Continental Congress authorized two battalions of marines in November 1775 to fight in the American Revolution. In 1798, the U.S. Congress reactivated the Marine Corps as a separate military force combining land and air elements. Today's Marine Corps is larger than most of the world's armies and flies more aircraft than most of the world's air forces.

The marines are specially trained and organized, ready to go to any part of the world to serve as America's crisis response force. Besides combat missions, the Marine Corps assists in peacekeeping, civilian evacuation, counterterrorism, and humanitarian aid. Marines have been the first to fight in nearly every major war of the United States. In 1880, the Corps adopted the motto *Semper Fidelis* ("Always Faithful").

A well-known ad proclaimed that the marines were looking for a few good men. God is also looking for faithful men—and women—to be his companions (Psalm 101:6). The Bible promises that a faithful person will be richly blessed, but warns that faithless people will be fully repaid for their ways (Proverbs 14:14; 28:20, NIV).

As long as we are in our earthly state, we will struggle with staying faithful to the God we love. Our hearts are easily led astray. In contrast, God is faithful in everything he does. Paul told Timothy, "If we are unfaithful, he remains faithful, for he cannot deny who he is" (2 Timothy 2:13). God's faithfulness doesn't depend on our behavior; it's a part of his character. Even when our hearts are far from him, God remains *Semper Fidelis*.

November 15

* * *

He calmed the storm to a whisper and stilled the waves.
PSALM 107:29

In November 1870, the Army Signal Service's new Division of Telegrams and Reports for the Benefit of Commerce began operations as the nation's weather service. The newly created service made its first official meteorological forecast: "High winds at Chicago and Milwaukee . . . and along the Lakes." Later that month, the first cautionary storm signal was issued for Great Lakes shipping.

Today the National Oceanic and Atmospheric Administration (NOAA) operates the National Weather Service as a part of the U.S. Department of Commerce. The agency is responsible for issuing weather forecasts, advisories, watches, and warnings on a daily basis. Predictions are enhanced by NEXRAD, a nationwide network of Doppler radars that detect precipitation and atmospheric movement. Trained volunteers called Skywarn spotters also assist by relaying severe weather to their local weather service office.

When the Pharisees and Sadducees asked Jesus for a sign from heaven, he scolded them for knowing "how to interpret the weather signs in the sky" but not the "signs of the times" (Matthew 16:3). God has mapped out the future of the earth for us in the book of Revelation. No one can predict when Christ will return, but we do know the signs that will usher in the events of those final times.

Jesus gave us an idea of what to expect during his last evening with the disciples before his death: In this world we will have trouble. We will be misunderstood and persecuted for following him. But because he has overcome the world, we can be overcomers too. We don't need modern, sophisticated equipment to give us the forecast for the rest of our life: "continuing periodic storms, but the Son will keep on shining."

November 16

* * *

Your eyes are too pure to look on evil; you cannot tolerate wrong.
HABAKKUK 1:13, NIV

The United Nations has designated November 16 as International Day of Tolerance to focus on what it sees as one of the most important human virtues. U.N. Secretary-General Kofi Annan defined tolerance as "an active and positive engagement with human diversity" and "therefore a key principle of democracy in our multiethnic and multicultural societies." He explained that tolerance is not the same as "passivity, complacency, or indifference."

The United Nations considers education the key to preventing intolerance and instilling a respect for the dignity and rights of others. The organization points out how intolerance is sometimes manifested in extreme violence, which causes widespread suffering and even death. At the individual level, insensitive attitudes lead to prejudice, hatred, and discrimination. Secretary-General Annan says that for these reasons, tolerance will continue to be at the center of the U.N.'s agenda.

In Romans 2:1-4, Paul warns believers against condemning others and so bringing condemnation on themselves. He equates this with showing contempt for the riches of God's kindness, tolerance, and patience, which lead people to repentance. Prejudice, discrimination, and hatred of others have no place in a believer's attitudes or actions.

On the other hand, we should have a hatred of sin, as God does. Jesus expressed the seriousness of compromising with sin when he said that if our hand or foot causes us to sin, we should cut it off. If our eye makes us sin, we should get rid of it (Matthew 18:8-9). God makes no compromise with sin and neither can we. We should always be respectful and sensitive to the rights and dignity of others who are different from us, but when it comes to sin we must have zero tolerance.

What sin have you been tolerating in your thoughts, attitudes, or behavior?

November 17

* * *

I go to prepare a place for you. And if I go and prepare a place for you, I will come again and receive you to Myself; that where I am, there you may be also.

JOHN 14:2-3, NKJV

On this day in 1800, the U.S. Congress held its first session in the Capitol Building in Washington, D.C. Twenty-six years earlier, the First Continental Congress had met at Carpenter's Hall in Philadelphia. Over the following years, the group gathered at several different locations, including a private home, courthouses, and taverns in Maryland, Pennsylvania, New Jersey, and New York.

Three years after the Continental Congress ratified the U.S. Constitution in 1788, workers began construction on the building that would permanently house Congress. The process took thirty-four years, under the supervision of six presidents and six architects. Finally, on November 17, 1800, Congress met in the north wing of the Capitol Building, the only section completed.

With the mobility in today's society, most people can identify with those early, transient days of Congress. Many families experience frequent job-related moves. But even the few people who spend their entire life in the same house are still not in their permanent home. As believers we are "foreigners and nomads here on earth" (Hebrews 11:13). Our time here is just a brief moment compared with eternity. Yet it's so easy to forget that and invest all our energy and resources on this earthly life.

Right now Jesus is preparing our permanent home, a place in our Father's house that will be perfectly suited to us for eternity. God says that what he has prepared for us is so wonderful our mind can't imagine it (1 Corinthians 2:9). If we understood what awaits us, we would be homesick for the future and less concerned with our temporary home here.

November 18

***

*God chose things the world considers foolish in order to shame those
who think they are wise. And he chose things that are powerless to shame those
who are powerful.*

1 Corinthians 1:27

On this day in 1928, the cartoon *Steamboat Willie* introduced a character that would become an American icon recognized around the world. Walt Disney and animator Ib Iwerks had originally produced two silent cartoons for Mickey Mouse. But after the enthusiastic response to the first "talkie" movie, the pair introduced a cartoon that synchronized action with songs, music, and sound effects. Mickey Mouse was an instant success.

Today, Mickey's image brings in $4.5 billion in sales each year for merchandise, including toys, watches, clothing, telephones, and home decor. Every day he is photographed with thousands of tourists at theme parks in California, Florida, France, and Japan. Who would have thought a cartoon character inspired by a mouse in Walt Disney's office would reach such heights of fame?

God has a history of exalting lowly characters. Moses was changed from being a murderer with a speech problem to a mighty deliverer and leader. The young shepherd boy, David, rose to become a great and powerful king of Israel. God chose a stable in the least of the cities of Judah to become the birthplace of his precious Son. Jesus chose fishermen to challenge the authorities of the world and to establish his church.

God is still in the business of transforming the plain and simple. He offers ordinary, imperfect people the opportunity to become his adopted children if we will acknowledge our helplessness and our need for him. In return, we receive spiritual riches beyond belief and the promise of sharing in Christ's glory someday. Who would have thought that obscure sinners like us would rise to become heirs of the Creator of the universe?

November 19

* * *

Obviously, I'm not trying to win the approval of people, but of God.
If pleasing people were my goal, I would not be Christ's servant.
GALATIANS 1:10

On this day in 1863, the ceremony dedicating the Gettysburg National Cemetery featured famous orator Edward Everett as the main speaker. His two-hour speech covered topics that ranged from ancient Greek heroes to a detailed account of the Battle of Gettysburg. Then President Lincoln spoke for two minutes. Most of the audience missed his speech, being distracted by a photographer.

Major newspapers applauded Everett's address and ignored or criticized Lincoln's remarks. A *Chicago Times* editorial said, "The cheek of every American must tingle with shame as he reads the silly, flat, and dishwatery utterances of the man who has to be pointed out to intelligent foreigners as the President of the United States." Soon, however, public opinion changed radically. Fifty years later, the chancellor of Oxford University declared Lincoln's Gettysburg Address "a pure well of English undefiled."

We all know how fickle human opinion is. Yet we struggle with a desire to gain approval from others. As believers, our responsibility is to do what pleases our heavenly Father, not what pleases those around us. Seeking popularity can become a form of idolatry, if that's what we base our behavior on. When we make pleasing God our first priority, we demonstrate our trust in him.

Paul uses the illustration of a soldier who wants to please his commanding officer (2 Timothy 2:4). Sometimes this means taking a stand that results in harsh criticism or even persecution. God may choose to vindicate us in the world's opinion or he may not. Either way, we can rest in the assurance that God is the only righteous Judge of our thoughts, motives, and actions. We are ultimately accountable to him, and his opinion is the one that truly matters.

November 20

* * *

*Put on every piece of God's armor so you will be able to resist
the enemy in the time of evil.*

EPHESIANS 6:13

B ritain introduced the use of tanks in warfare in September 1916, but
the effort failed because they were used in piecemeal fashion without
effective strategy. In November 1917, however, three hundred British tanks
crushed German defenses along a six-mile front during the Battle of Cambrai.
Engineers made improvements, and in the first campaign of World War II,
German tanks conquered Poland in less than a month.

The military still uses tanks today, especially in desert warfare. They are
effective in attacking other armored vehicles, infantry, and ground targets
and in firing on aircraft. The basic design has remained unchanged, although
additional features have been added, such as computer systems for navigation
and armor that explodes outward when hit. Modern fire-control systems
enable a moving tank to hit small targets a mile away.

In the sixth chapter of Ephesians, Paul describes the armor that God has
provided for believers' protection in our ongoing warfare with our enemy. We
are told to buckle up the belt of truth, strap on the body armor of God's righteousness, slip our feet into the peace that comes from the gospel, and hold
up the shield of faith (6:10-17). This armor is already prepared for us, but we
must choose to put it on.

Twice the passage emphasizes the importance of putting on *all* the pieces
of our armor for maximum effectiveness. Once we have all our protective
armor in place, we are ready to take up our weapons—the sword of God's
written Word and continuous prayer.

Supernatural battle requires supernatural weapons. It's only by using all
the weapons God has provided for us that we can follow the admonition to
"be strong in the Lord and in his mighty power" (Ephesians 6:10).

November 21

* * *

Do all that you can to live in peace with everyone.
ROMANS 12:18

T oday is World Hello Day. Anyone can participate in observing this holiday simply by saying "hello" to ten people. The holiday was initiated in response to the conflict between Egypt and Israel in the fall of 1973. The purpose is to demonstrate the importance of personal communication for preserving peace.

Since 1973, people in 180 countries have observed World Hello Day. People all over the world are encouraged to warmly greet at least ten people, preferably with a smile. Thirty-one winners of the Nobel Peace Prize have voiced support for World Hello Day as a means of promoting peace and harmony.

Strife and conflict are inevitable in a world under the curse of sin. Still, the God of peace calls his children to be peacemakers on earth. He urges us to "work at living in peace with everyone" (Hebrews 12:14). This doesn't mean that we should compromise the truth just to preserve peace. But we can minimize most conflict with others by staying in a close relationship with God and keeping accountable to him.

Jesus' death made reconciliation with God possible. The fruit of the Holy Spirit working in our life includes peace. This God-given peace will spill over into our relationships with others as we live a life of integrity and treat others with respect. It won't always be possible to avoid conflict in a world where not everyone knows the Prince of Peace. But we can live peaceably with others, for the most part, if we treat them as people valued and loved by the same heavenly Father we serve.

November 22

* * *

You heard my cry for mercy and answered my call for help.
PSALM 31:22

In November 1906, delegates to the International Radio Telegraphic Convention in Berlin adopted the SOS distress signal to be universally recognized as a call for help from disabled ships at sea. The International Morse code signal of three dots, three dashes, three dots (...———...) was chosen because it was convenient to send by wireless. Contrary to popular belief, the letter equivalents did not stand for any words.

Morse code officially went out of use on February 1, 1999, when a satellite system replaced it. The Global Maritime Distress and Safety System is now mandatory for most ships and has the ability to pinpoint the location of a craft signaling for help.

When Jonah tried to run away from God rather than obey God's command to go to Nineveh, he found himself in great distress at sea. From inside the fish that had swallowed him, Jonah prayed, "I cried out to the LORD in my great trouble, and he answered me" (Jonah 2:2). The Lord answered Jonah's distress call by having the fish spit him out on land and by offering Jonah another chance to be obedient.

Sometimes we find ourselves adrift in life, in distress, or even disabled. We may react by running to human help or depending on our intellect to figure a way out. Yet God has provided a way for us to call for the help we need, anywhere and anytime. Since God is omniscient, he already knows our situation even before we cry out to him. Through prayer we can call for help from the only One who can rescue us, the One who can pinpoint where we are even when the seas of life get choppy.

Who is the first one you call when you're in distress?

November 23

* * *

[Jesus said,] "Don't store up treasures here on earth."
MATTHEW 6:19

O n this day in 1780, the HMS *Hussar* sank in the East River in New York. The *Hussar* had left Charles Town loaded with gold and silver to pay British forces serving in the colonies. On the way she took on the treasure of a French frigate, an American ship, a British treasure ship, and another British frigate that carried stolen treasure from two American ships as well as her own cargo of gold, silver, and precious gems.

As the *Hussar* made her way up the East River, the severely overloaded ship smashed into Pot Rock, a jagged ledge stretching out several feet underwater. It is estimated that the *Hussar* sank with a fortune that today would be worth from $800 million to $1.5 billion. Over the years many attempts have been made to recover the treasure. None have succeeded.

Jesus told a parable about a rich farmer who planned to build bigger barns to store his wealth. "But God said to him, 'You fool! You will die this very night. Then who will get everything you worked for?'" (Luke 12:20). We live in a materialistic culture that places a high priority on wealth. It's easy to forget that our worth doesn't come from our possessions.

Our true goal is to store up treasure in heaven. These are the kind of riches that last forever: a life lived in obedience to God, time spent in intercessory prayer, souls influenced by our witness for Christ. Our life here can end at any moment. When that happens, it won't matter how much earthly wealth we've gathered, only how rich we are toward God. We'll leave behind all our material possessions, which may as well be at the bottom of a river, along with the vast fortune of the HMS *Hussar*.

November 24

* * *

Jesus replied, "I tell you the truth, unless you are born again,
you cannot see the Kingdom of God."
JOHN 3:3

T oday is my birthday. I certainly won't be the only one to celebrate. It's estimated that eleven thousand babies are born each day in the United States alone. Estimates of the birthrate for the entire world go as high as 383,000 daily. On any given day of the year, there are thousands of people receiving cards and gifts, enjoying dinners and parties with friends, and blowing out candles on a cake.

While I annually celebrate my physical birth, I also acknowledge a much more important anniversary—my spiritual birthday. Jesus told a teacher of the law that in order to be part of God's Kingdom, we must go through a second birth. Confused, Nicodemus asked how an old man could be born again, since he was unable to enter his mother's womb (John 3:4).

Jesus then explained that this second birth is of the Spirit, not another physical birth. When we accept Jesus as our Savior and Lord, God places his Spirit within us. We are then born again as children of God, and we become part of his family. That moment in time marks the beginning of our new, eternal life and transforms us into a brand-new creation.

Everyone who has ever lived has a birthday on which he or she was given the gift of life. Believers have a second, greater birthday—the day they chose to receive the gift of eternal life. So when I'm eating cake and opening birthday presents on November 24, I'm most grateful for the gift I received on January 10, 1980, when I was reborn.

November 25

* * *

*All glory to God, who is able, through his mighty power at work within us,
to accomplish infinitely more than we might ask or think.*

EPHESIANS 3:20

On this day in 1867, Swedish chemist and inventor Alfred Bernhard Nobel patented his new invention called "dynamite." For years nitroglycerin had been used for heavy construction work. Unfortunately, it was so volatile that it often exploded unexpectedly, blowing up factories and killing people. Working in his family's business, Nobel accidentally discovered that mixing the nitroglycerine with kieselguhr, a diatomaceous earth, allowed the explosive to be handled safely until detonated.

Nobel's leanings toward pacifism had long made him uncomfortable with his family's business. He eventually became seriously concerned about the potential of his invention. When he died, Alfred left his estate to fund annual Nobel Prize awards to be given in fields of science and literature and in the area of promoting international peace.

Alfred Nobel derived the name of his invention from the Greek word *dynamis*, translated "power." This is the word used most often in the New Testament to refer to God's infinite power. Paul prayed that the Christians at Ephesus might "understand the incredible greatness of God's power" (Ephesians 1:19). He prayed that the believers at Colosse would be "strengthened with all his glorious power" (Colossians 1:11).

God's limitless power is at work around us, in us, and on us. He is working in the world around us to achieve his purposes. He has put his power within us to enable us to live victoriously and carry out the work he has planned for us to do. The power of God's Holy Spirit is working on us to transform us into the image of Jesus Christ.

November 26

***

*Be thankful in all circumstances, for this is God's will for you
who belong to Christ Jesus.*

1 THESSALONIANS 5:18

T his day in 1789 marked the first time our country observed a holiday
by presidential proclamation. Special days for prayer had been spo-
radically observed by the early colonists and during the Revolutionary War.
In 1789, both houses of Congress asked President Washington to recommend
"a day of public thanksgiving and prayer, to be observed by acknowledging
with grateful hearts the many and signal favors of Almighty God."

The United States had no regular national Thanksgiving Day, although
some states celebrated it yearly. Finally, in 1863, President Lincoln proclaimed the last Thursday in November as "a day of thanksgiving and praise
to our beneficent Father." Succeeding presidents issued similar proclamations
until 1939, when President Roosevelt named Thanksgiving as the fourth
Thursday in November to help businesses by extending the Christmas shop-
ping season.

It's easy to express thanksgiving to God when we're experiencing his
abundant blessings. When we're struggling with trials and difficulties, however, our natural tendency is the opposite of gratitude. Yet God instructs us to
be thankful in *all* circumstances. This seems like a strange command, since
we live in a culture that encourages us to act according to how we feel. How
can we be expected to give thanks to God when we're not in the mood?

In the Old Testament, God laid down specific guidelines for the Israelites
to bring thank offerings. In the New Testament, believers are instructed to
give thanks in everything. Besides honoring and pleasing God, being thankful is beneficial for us. We are promised his peace in our heart and mind
when we tell him our needs along with giving thanks for what he has done
(Philippians 4:6-7). Setting aside time for thanksgiving every day is being
obedient to God's proclamation.

November 27

* * *

Let your conversation be always full of grace, seasoned with salt.
COLOSSIANS 4:6, NIV

I n 2003, Dr. Loren Ekroth created a new holiday for the last week in November. For more than twenty-five years, Dr. Ekroth had taught effective communication skills in seminars and workshops for individuals and businesses. After observing that the talk at family gatherings often stayed on the superficial level, he developed a set of guidelines for more meaningful conversations, especially in groups coming together for holiday celebrations. Dr. Ekroth designated the last week in November as Better Conversation Week. He now offers a Better Conversation Kit to help generations of family members interact on a deeper level.

The Bible is filled with specific admonitions about the words we use. Two of the Ten Commandments forbid using God's name in vain and lying about other people. Many passages instruct us to guard against using our mouth for gossip, slander, useless arguing, obscenity, or even excess words. We are warned against listening to deceptive, seductive, or empty words. It is clear that we are accountable for every word that comes from our mouth (Matthew 12:36).

God also gives us a clear picture of what our words *should* be like. We are to use our mouth to express praise and thanksgiving to him. We are to use helpful, not hurtful, words with one another, sharing spiritual truths. We are to be slow to speak (James 1:19) but quick to encourage and build one another up (1 Thessalonians 5:11). There is even a proper time for believers to correct and rebuke one another, as long as we speak the truth in love and gentleness. Unfortunately, our culture admires obscene humor and clever put-downs. But we are called to a higher level, as summed up in Colossians 4:6. That kind of grace-filled conversation is not better conversation—it's the best.

November 28

* * *

Through everything God made, they can clearly see his invisible qualities—
his eternal power and divine nature. So they have no excuse for not knowing God.

ROMANS 1:20

O n this day in 1922, Americans saw the first demonstration of skywriting. Skywriting originated in England during World War I, when Major John C. Savage used smoke from airplanes to send military signals. In May 1922, he introduced skywriting as an advertising tool by hiring Captain Cyril Turner to write a newspaper's name over England. On November 28 of that year, Savage demonstrated this advertising method in the United States to George W. Hill, head of the American Tobacco Company.

Savage had Captain Turner write the message, "Hello, USA. Call Vanderbilt 7200" over Times Square. When Hill arrived at the Vanderbilt Hotel for his appointment with Savage, he was persuaded by forty-seven-thousand phone calls in less than three hours. Skywriting enjoyed a heyday from the 1930s until the 1950s, when television made it possible for advertisers to target messages at specific audiences.

It would be hard to ignore a message written in huge white letters across a blue sky above our heads. Yet many people go through life ignoring the message that God has given us in the wonders of creation above us, below us, and around us. The psalmist declared, "The heavens proclaim his righteousness; every nation sees his glory" (Psalm 97:6).

The first chapter of Romans explains that although God is invisible, his presence and power are plainly seen in what he has created. Such an intricate, carefully planned world could only be the handiwork of an all-powerful Creator. We don't have any excuse for not believing in God when we are surrounded by such clear evidence. To deny the existence of a loving Creator is to ignore the writing in the sky.

November 29

* * *

What joy for the nation whose God is the LORD.
PSALM 33:12

S inger Kate Smith introduced the song "God Bless America" on her radio program in November 1938. Irving Berlin had composed the song in 1918, when he was an army sergeant stationed in upstate New York. He originally intended it for a comedy musical revue, but the song didn't fit the show. Twenty years later, with another war on the horizon, Berlin revised the song to reflect the current world situation. Kate Smith sang it on her program, and "God Bless America" became an instant hit.

As a Russian immigrant, Berlin wanted to give something back to the country he considered so special. He established the God Bless America Fund to allocate all royalties from that song and a number of other compositions to New York Boy Scouts and Girl Scouts. Berlin considered "God Bless America" his most important composition.

It's easier to sing "God Bless America" than to fulfill the conditions required for his blessing. God told Solomon, "If my people who are called by my name will humble themselves and pray and seek my face and turn from their wicked ways, I will hear from heaven and will forgive their sins and restore their land" (2 Chronicles 7:14).

It's also easier to bemoan the condition of our society than to do what's required to bring about change. God has given believers the responsibility to be instruments of renewal. Rather than looking around at what's wrong with our country, we are told to look within ourselves and repent of any sin before praying for our land. That doesn't mean we don't speak up and work to eradicate evil, but we can't neglect our part in moving God to heal our country. Only then will America be truly blessed.

November 30

* * *

Anyone who claims to know all the answers doesn't really know very much.
1 CORINTHIANS 8:2

Ken Jennings' record-setting reign as champion on the game show *Jeopardy!* ended on this day in 2004. Jennings' run began with the episode aired on June 2, 2004, and totaled 182 calendar days. His seventy-four game winning streak ended when he lost to Nancy Zerg. Host Alex Trebek called Zerg a "giant killer" when she defeated the long-standing winner. Zerg lost the following day, finishing in third place with two dollars.

Jennings' earnings totaled over $2.5 million, the largest amount ever won on a television game show. His *Jeopardy!* appearances gave him celebrity status. The show's ratings rose 62 percent during his reign. *Jeopardy!* officials estimated that Jennings answered about 2,700 questions correctly.

Jeopardy! is a unique game show in that the contestants are given the answers and have to come up with the questions. In our world today, everybody is looking for answers, but they often don't ask the right questions. In Matthew 16:15, Jesus asked his disciples the most important question of all time: "Who do you say I am?" Peter gave the correct answer: "You are the Messiah, the Son of the living God" (16:16).

Many people have all sorts of specific questions about God or the Bible that they feel must be answered before they can believe. Sometimes they use these issues to avoid answering the all-important question of who Jesus is. Before we can understand spiritual things, we must first accept Jesus as the Son of God and Lord of our life. Once we settle that question, some of our other questions don't seem as important or may even become irrelevant.

How would you answer Jesus' question?

December 1

* * *

Everything I plan will come to pass, for I do whatever I wish.
ISAIAH 46:10

I n early December 1942, scientists in Chicago, Illinois, produced the first artificial nuclear chain reaction. Physicist Enrico Fermi and his team at the University of Chicago began work in a makeshift lab underneath the stands of the university's football stadium on November 16. Team members worked around the clock to build a lattice of fifty-seven layers of uranium metal and uranium oxide embedded in graphite blocks. A wooden structure supported the graphite pile.

Fermi's achievement of the world's first controlled, self-sustaining nuclear chain reaction was a part of the secret Manhattan Project to develop nuclear weapons. Fermi later worked on the atomic bomb project at Los Alamos, New Mexico. After World War II, he pioneered in research involving high-energy particles.

When Adam and Eve disobeyed God in the Garden of Eden, their decision started a chain reaction that ended in broken fellowship with God and eviction from their perfect home to a hostile environment. But nothing takes God by surprise, and he started a chain of events to bring about reconciliation. It began with God making a covering for Adam and Eve's nakedness, continued through his creation of the nation of Israel and the miraculous birth of a Savior, and culminated with Jesus' death to pay for our sins.

The chain reaction from that first sin continues as the world rushes toward the time when the Antichrist will gain power and when God will pour out judgment on those who reject him. God has ultimate power over world events despite the mistaken idea that we determine our own destiny. We can take courage in his sovereignty and trust that no matter where we are in the chain of world events, he is controlling it.

December 2

* * *

[Jesus said,] "Those who exalt themselves will be humbled, and those who humble themselves will be exalted."

MATTHEW 23:12

Napoléon Bonaparte crowned himself on this day in 1804. Napoléon and his colleagues had seized power in 1799 and established a new regime in France. The regime gave Napoléon almost dictatorial powers as first consul. With the support of the people, revisions to the constitution in 1802 made him consul for life. In 1804, he transformed the life consulate into a hereditary empire.

Napoléon wanted to be consecrated by the pope so that his coronation would equal the grandeur of Charlemagne's and so that his reign would be more legitimate in the eyes of the rest of Europe. Pope Pius VII reluctantly agreed, and the ceremony took place in Paris on this day in1804. At the last minute, Napoléon took the crown from the pope's hands and set it on his own head, crowning himself emperor.

In our world today, many people are trying to "crown" themselves. We have all sorts of books, courses, and seminars on building up our self-esteem, doing self-promotion, and becoming a leader. There aren't many materials on how to become humble. Yet God says those who humble themselves will be the ones exalted in his Kingdom.

James assures us that if we humble ourselves before the Lord, he will lift us up in honor (4:10). To be humble before God means that we recognize that any good within us and any worth we possess come from him. If we properly exalt God for who he is, then we will have an attitude of humility. God will exalt us in this life by making us his children and in the future by bringing us into our full inheritance. We won't have any problem staying humble if we remember that someday we will receive a "crown of life" from God (James 1:12).

December 3

* * *

I will give you a new heart.
Ezekiel 36:26

D octors performed the first human heart transplant operation on this day in 1967 in South Africa. Dr. Christiaan Barnard led a team of twenty surgeons as they replaced the diseased heart of fifty-five-year-old Louis Washkansky with a heart taken from a twenty-five-year-old victim of a car accident.

The operation was successful, but Washkansky died eighteen days later from double pneumonia contracted when drugs given to prevent rejection of the new heart destroyed his body's immune system. Development of better antirejection drugs meant that by the late 1970s many heart transplant patients lived up to five years with their new heart. Today, thousands of heart transplant operations are performed each year.

All of us are born with spiritual heart disease. Our heart is fickle, self-centered, and attuned to sin instead of to God. When we become his child, God performs a heart transplant. He removes our "stony, stubborn" heart and replaces it with a "tender, responsive" heart (Ezekiel 36:26). Our new heart makes it possible for us to respond to God and obey him.

Even after our transplant, we can still experience heart trouble because of our lifestyle and mental diet. If we become too friendly with the world, our heart may grow cold toward God. We may respond to trials or God's discipline by hardening our heart toward him. If we fail to be consistent in our walk, we may develop an irregular heartbeat. Our heart can become sickened or even broken by sorrows, but God is able to heal any heart condition if we let him examine our heart and then apply his healing Word. If we remain open to his touch, we can maintain a healthy heart that beats only for him.

What heart conditions do you need God to heal?

December 4

* * *

Knowledge puffs up, but love builds up.
1 CORINTHIANS 8:1, NIV

On this day in 2003, a Goodyear blimp crashed while trying to land at its base airport near Los Angeles. A video of the accident showed the blimp's nose implanted in the ground with a semitruck underneath. Fortunately, the cabin of the blimp did not sustain much damage, and most of the inflated part remained intact. The occupants were not seriously hurt.

Over the years, Goodyear built more than three hundred helium-filled blimps, many of which provided the U.S. Navy with aerial surveillance during World War II. The blimps looked for rising submarines and then radioed their positions to ships. The Navy discontinued the program in 1962 because of the availability of modern technology. Today, Goodyear operates three blimps that travel more than one hundred thousand miles each year as the tire and rubber company's "Aerial Ambassadors."

In 1 Corinthians 8, Paul wrote that while knowledge makes us feel important, literally "puffs up," love is what strengthens the church. Paul was addressing the concerns of his readers about whether it was acceptable for them to eat meat that had been offered to idols in a pagan temple and then sold in the meat market. The Corinthian believers were offending each other with their strong opinions about the issue. Paul instructed the Corinthian believers that conduct should be guided by more than knowledge; it should take into account fellow believers' conscience.

The Bible teaches that we are to seek wisdom, understanding, and knowledge. Proverbs 2:10 says that when we gain wisdom, knowledge will fill us with joy. But knowledge becomes a problem when it makes us unteachable, arrogant, and so stubborn that we don't respect others' opinions. Knowledge becomes a stumbling block if it's not balanced with love. As long as we're filled with love for God and others, then our knowledge won't cause us to be puffed up like a blimp.

December 5

* * *

Study this Book of Instruction continually.
JOSHUA 1:8

S tudents at the College of William and Mary in Williamsburg, Virginia, established the nation's oldest and largest academic honor society on this day in 1776. Five students founded Phi Beta Kappa to encourage scholarship in the liberal arts and sciences. Meetings emphasized literary exercises, primarily debate and composition, and sometimes members simply shared good fellowship. In 1779, the society granted charters to Harvard and Yale.

Today, there are 270 chapters at campuses around the United States. The living membership totals more than five hundred thousand, with fifteen thousand new members elected each year. Members often continue their active affiliation with the society after graduation through Phi Beta Kappa associations. There are more than fifty active associations formed by members to promote friendship and learning in their communities.

All believers are lifelong students. The Greek word for *disciple* literally means "learner." Being a follower of Christ means we are dedicated to serious study of the Bible. Our goal is to gain the "academic honors" mentioned in 2 Timothy 2:15—to be a "good worker" who knows Scripture well and "correctly explains the word of truth."

Our purpose is not simply to accumulate facts and knowledge. It's nice to know the details of each one of Paul's missionary trips or to be able to recite the kings of Judah, but those facts likely won't change our life. Before Joshua led the Israelites into Canaan, God instructed him to meditate on the Book of the Law "day and night" so he would "be sure to obey everything written in it." Only then would he be successful conquering the Promised Land (Joshua 1:8). Bible knowledge won't do us any good if we don't obey it and apply it to our life. On the other hand, we can't apply something we don't know, and knowing God's Word will take the rest of our life.

December 6

* * *

If you keep yourself pure, you will be a special utensil for honorable use.
2 TIMOTHY 2:21

The U.S. government created the Environmental Protection Agency (EPA) in December 1970 as a response to the collection of confusing and often ineffective environmental protection laws enacted by individual communities and states. A number of federal programs dealing with pollution problems merged under single management by the EPA. The government initially charged the EPA with administering the Clean Air Act, the Federal Environmental Pesticide Control Act, and the Clean Water Act.

The EPA establishes and enforces environmental protection standards, conducts research on the effects of pollution, provides grants and assistance to cities and states for preventing pollution, and helps develop policies that are recommended to the president.

But there's one kind of pollution the Environmental Protection Agency doesn't address—mind pollution. Even believers doing their best to grow and serve God can have serious problems with impure thoughts. Some people live with a heavy load of guilt over thoughts they know are not pleasing to God. Others rationalize that thoughts and daydreams aren't really harmful. If we don't deal with our tendency to entertain unclean thoughts, chances are the tendency will become an ingrained habit and eventually affect our attitudes and then our actions. The consequences can be deadly.

Philippians 4:8 gives the antidote: "Fix your thoughts on what is true, and honorable, and right, and pure, and lovely, and admirable. Think about things that are excellent and worthy of praise." Our thought life is determined to a large extent by what we feed our mind. If we take in impure images and material from the culture around us, our thought life will reflect that impurity. If we choose to think about things that fit God's guidelines, our mind will reflect honorable things. His Word is the protection we need to ensure clean thoughts.

December 7

* * *

Get ready; be prepared!
EZEKIEL 38:7

On this day in 1941, Japan launched a surprise aerial attack on the U.S. naval base at Pearl Harbor on Oahu Island, Hawaii. The Japanese had carefully planned the attack for a Sunday morning, when the anchored ships in the harbor were not fully manned and the aircraft were lined up on the airfields, making them more vulnerable to attack. When an Army private noticed the large flight of planes on a radar screen, his superiors instructed him to ignore them because the base was expecting a shipment of B-17s.

The raid severely crippled the Pacific Fleet battleships, destroyed around two hundred aircraft, left more than three thousand dead, and pushed America into World War II. The unpreparedness of the military and the severity of the disaster sparked criticism from the public, but investigations showed that while officials had known that an attack by Japan was possible, they had no way of knowing the time or place.

Satan's attacks against believers are also carefully planned and come without warning. He knows our weak areas, and that's where he concentrates his bombardment of temptations. Satan also knows *when* we are most vulnerable. It may be during times of trial, when we are already discouraged, or periods of prosperity and peace, when we have grown complacent. Strangely, we are often most vulnerable after we've experienced a spiritual victory.

The New Testament frequently advises us to "be alert" or "be on guard." Satan never passes up an opportunity to attack us. All the spiritual training in the world won't do any good unless we're prepared to use it. The armor prepared by God is useless until we put it on. God has provided what we need for victory, but it's our job to expect and be ready for attacks from our enemy. It's not a matter of *if*, but when and where.

December 8

* * *

What joy for those whose disobedience is forgiven, whose sin is put out of sight!
PSALM 32:1

S ports programming changed forever in early December 1963 with the introduction of the instant replay. CBS director Tony Verna had been frustrated at the lulls between plays in football games and the fact that the television audience missed much of what the live audience saw. He eventually discovered a method of marking videotape in a way that allowed fast and accurate rewinding.

Verna decided to test his "video replay" at an Army-Navy game and arranged for a 1,200-pound videotape machine to be transported from New York to Philadelphia. He had trouble with static and previously taped material appearing on the monitor. Finally, in the fourth quarter Verna was able to replay a touchdown. To prevent the viewers from being confused, the announcer said, "This is not live! Ladies and gentlemen, Army did not score again!"

Our brains come equipped with an instant-replay feature. We can replay a scene, a conversation, or a decision over and over in our mind for days, weeks, even years. This tendency can be beneficial for us if we handle it properly. The Bible urges us to "examine our ways" so we can see when we've strayed from God and return to him (Lamentations 3:40). By prayerfully rehearsing our actions and decisions, we can spot our weak areas and react in a more Christlike way the next time we face similar circumstances.

Unfortunately, Satan uses our "instant replay" against us. By rehashing the details of our past failures and sins, we become stuck in guilt and regret. Psalm 32:1 says that once we confess and repent of our sins, they are literally taken away so that God no longer considers them. God doesn't use instant replay of our sins that he has forgiven, and neither should we. Sometimes we need to fast-forward the tape.

What events in your life do you tend to replay over and over?

December 9

*They are darkened in their understanding and separated from the life of God
because of the ignorance that is in them due to the hardening of their hearts.*
EPHESIANS 4:18, NIV

ongress established Arizona's Petrified Forest National Monument as a national park on this day in 1962. The scenic park covers an area of 146 square miles in the northeastern part of the state. It contains one of the world's largest and most colorful concentrations of petrified wood in several "forest" areas, the remains of ancient tropical groves.

Other attractions in the park include displays of plant and animal fossils, including some of dinosaurs; archaeological sites; historic structures, such as the ruins of ancient Native American pueblos; the Rainbow Forest Museum; and the Painted Desert, a badlands area of colorful hills where Pilot Rock, the park's highest point, is located.

Petrified wood is an accurate picture of the type of people described in Ephesians 4:18-19. The origin of the Greek word translated "hardened" originally meant a stone harder than marble. The word was later a medical term referring to callous hardening. It eventually came to denote becoming so hardened that even the ability to feel is lost. Paul uses the word here to describe Gentiles and in Romans 11:25 to describe unbelieving Jews. Hearts were petrified by sin, and the people no longer felt a sense of shame.

These verses help us understand why an unbeliever may not be responding when we share the gospel. Only God can change a hardened heart. Sometimes the best way to reach people is to pray that God will soften their heart so they can understand the truth. At the same time, we should watch our own life for any signs of the gradual process of hardening toward sin. Our goal is to become sanctified, not petrified.

December 10

* * *

He gave up his divine privileges.
PHILIPPIANS 2:7

O n this day in 1936, King Edward VIII became the only British sovereign to voluntarily resign the crown. Edward wanted to marry Mrs. Wallis Simpson, an American who was in the process of obtaining her second divorce. The royal family refused to accept her, and the marriage was firmly opposed by the Church of England, of which Edward was the head.

The king submitted his abdication on December 10, 1936. On a radio broadcast the next day, the former king explained, "I have found it impossible to carry on the heavy burden of responsibility and to discharge my duties as king as I would wish to do without the help and support of the woman I love." Edward and Mrs. Simpson were married on June 3, 1937, when her divorce was final.

The throne of England is nothing compared to what Jesus Christ gave up for us, as described in Philippians 2:6-8. Although Jesus was God, he temporarily set aside his divine rights to be born as a human being. He humbled himself in obedience to God the Father by dying a criminal's death on a cross. Jesus willingly accepted not only the frailties and limitations of a human body but also unjust persecution and a horrible death.

Paul writes that believers must have the same attitude that Christ had (Philippians 2:5). Being Christ's follower means that we lay aside our rights, put other people before ourselves, and look out for their interests, too. Nothing could be more contrary to our human nature. We can only have this attitude with the power of the Holy Spirit. It helps to remember how much Jesus gave up and that he did it all for the love of us.

December 11

* * *

It is good for me that I was afflicted, that I may learn Your statutes.
PSALM 119:71, NASB

O n this day in 1919, the town of Enterprise, Alabama, erected the first known monument to an insect. The classic statue of a woman holding a large boll weevil over her head is in the middle of the town. The boll weevil is a tiny insect that destroys the seedpods of cotton plants. It entered the United States from Mexico during the 1890s and reached southeastern Alabama in 1915.

Although the boll weevil devastated the cotton fields around Enterprise, it forced farmers to end their dependence on cotton and instead pursue diversified crops and manufacturing. Many local farmers switched to different crops, such as peanuts, which returned vital nutrients to the soil depleted by cotton cultivation and also proved to be a successful cash crop.

It's often the things that devastate us that open up new possibilities for us beyond our dreams. When Joseph's jealous brothers sold him into slavery, he was devastated. He was devastated again when false accusations by his master's wife sent him to prison. But years later, when he rose to become the second most powerful man in Egypt, he understood that "God intended it all for good." He told his brothers, "He brought me to this position so I could save the lives of many people" (Genesis 50:20).

God may use devastating events to prepare us for some great work. Other times he uses such events to teach us to know him better and encourage us to become more obedient to him. In Psalm 119:71, the psalmist understands that his affliction has been good because it taught him to obey God. We can't expect to see the benefits while we are going through some devastating circumstance. But we can trust that God can bring good out of any evil—even a weevil.

December 12

* * *

Let me reveal to you a wonderful secret. We will not all die,
but we will all be transformed!

1 CORINTHIANS 15:51

The television series *Extreme Makeover* premiered with a one-hour special in December 2002. The program differs from similar shows by going beyond the typical makeover issues of hair, makeup, and clothing and addresses the entire body. Participants meet with a group of experts called the "Extreme Team," which includes cosmetic dentists, dermatologists, plastic surgeons, nutritionists, and fitness trainers.

Out of the thousands of applicants, two are chosen each week to undergo a series of procedures. These may include eye surgery, plastic surgery, cosmetic dentistry, and reconstructive surgery. The individuals then undergo a workout and diet regime with fitness trainers and visit fashion, hair, and makeup stylists. At the end of each show, the participants make a dramatic entrance and display their new look to family and friends.

With each new believer, God starts working on the ultimate extreme makeover. He gives a new heart and a new spirit. He begins pruning away sinful tendencies and instilling qualities of love, peace, gentleness, patience, and joy. God accomplishes the makeover through the Holy Spirit living in each believer and with the power of his Word. God expects believers to take an active part in the process through growing in obedience and practicing spiritual disciplines.

Our spiritual makeover takes much, much longer than a mere external one. It takes our entire lifetime. Our transformation won't be complete until Christ returns for his church. At that time, whether we are dead or alive, we will receive a new, immortal body that will never die. Even our environment will be made over. Our spirit will be completely free from the effects, the power, and even the presence of sin. A makeover can't get more extreme than that.

December 13

* * *

By His doing you are in Christ Jesus.
1 Corinthians 1:30, NASB

I n December 1993, the U.S. Secretary of Defense announced that the Global Positioning System had twenty-four GPS satellites operating in their assigned orbits and available for civil usage. The Department of Defense developed GPS and continues to operate it. The system was originally used to provide all-weather, round-the-clock navigation capabilities for military ground, sea, and air forces.

Today, thousands of civil users own receivers that are able to locate four or more of the solar-powered satellites orbiting the earth, figure out the distance to each one, and use the information to pinpoint an exact location. Besides navigation and location determination, GPS is used for making maps, establishing precise timing, and tracking the movement of people, animals, and vehicles.

The Bible is "God's Positioning System." It lets us know where we are in our journey toward Christlikeness and helps us track our spiritual growth. It's tempting to compare ourself with other Christians, but that's not an effective way to monitor our progress. There will always be some who are less mature and others who are ahead of us. The Scriptures show us in what direction we should be moving.

The Bible also reminds us of our position in Christ. According to Scripture, believers are coheirs with Christ of God's glory (Romans 8:17), God's dwelling place (1 Corinthians 3:16), "God's masterpiece" (Ephesians 2:10), his dearly loved children (Ephesians 5:1), "citizens of heaven" (Philippians 3:20), and God's "chosen people" (1 Peter 2:9). We are forgiven, reborn, sealed with God's Spirit, and freed from any condemnation. Satan tries to make us forget our identity in Christ so we'll be vulnerable to his attacks. We need to keep using our "GPS" to remind us that we are in the perfect location—in Christ.

December 14

* * *

*Our lives are a Christ-like fragrance rising up to God. But this fragrance is
perceived differently by those who are being saved and by those who are perishing.*

2 CORINTHIANS 2:15

F irst, movies were silent; then they were "talkies"; then movies appeared as "smellies." The first film that attempted to incorporate scent into a movie premiered in December 1959, with the tagline: "You must breathe it to believe it!" The documentary about China entitled *Behind the Great Wall* used a process called AromaRama to pipe thirty-one "Oriental scents" through the theater's air-conditioning system.

In February 1960, Smell-O-Vision released *Scent of Mystery*, with special guest star Elizabeth Taylor. Viewers received clues to the murderer's identity through scents piped to each individual seat, such as a trace of pipe smoke at the crime scene. The idea never caught on, possibly because the smells didn't seem realistic, they were strong enough to cause headaches, and they didn't always dissipate as quickly as the scene required.

In 2 Corinthians 2:14-16, Paul uses the image of a Roman triumphal pro-cession that honored conquering generals and forced captives to march through the streets. The parade included priests with pots of burning incense as an offering to their gods. To the victors, the fragrance of the incense seemed sweet and pleasant; to the condemned prisoners it represented slavery or execution. The two groups of people perceived the same scent very differently.

Now that we are captives of God, "he uses us to spread the knowledge of Christ everywhere, like a sweet perfume" (2 Corinthians 2:14). To those who reject the gospel, we are like the repulsive smell of death. But to those who believe and receive Christ, our message is like "a life-giving perfume" (2 Corinthians 2:16). When someone rejects our witnessing efforts, we can't take it personally. They're probably reacting to how they perceive the aroma of the gospel, not to us.

December 15

* * *

Correct me, LORD, but please be gentle.
JEREMIAH 10:24

One of Italy's most famous tourist attractions, the Leaning Tower of Pisa, reopened on this day in 2001, after almost twelve years and a twenty-five million dollar correction. Built as a bell tower in 1173, the builders noticed the tilt during construction, but they decided to complete the tower anyway. It's commonly believed the tilt is due to unstable soil in the sandy foundation.

In 1990, engineers determined that the white marble tower was so far out of perpendicular that it was in danger of toppling over. Officials closed the tower as an international committee devised a plan to remove part of the shifting foundations and add counterweights. Today, the tower looks the same as before to the naked eye, but the lean has been corrected by forty-five centimeters, or almost eighteen inches.

Even the most sincere Christian needs a correction from time to time. The world we live in and our old sinful nature constantly pull on us. In spite of our good intentions, we can end up leaning away from God. If we don't notice the shift in our devotion or if we refuse to face it, we'll be in danger of toppling over.

God loves us too much to leave us "leaning." He disciplines and corrects his children for our own benefit. Sometimes he uses circumstances; sometimes he uses other believers who care enough to lovingly confront us with the truth. Many times God uses his Word to correct our attitudes or actions. His Word is "sharper than the sharpest two-edged sword" and able to expose our innermost thoughts, motives, and desires (Hebrews 4:12). Even when we look straight to the naked eye, God's Word can reveal where we need to correct a lean in the wrong direction.

How is God trying to make a correction in your life?

December 16

* * *

The LORD Almighty has purposed, and who can thwart him? His hand is stretched out, and who can turn it back?

ISAIAH 14:27, NIV

I
n December 1997, Cuban president Fidel Castro announced that Christmas would once again be a national holiday for the first time since 1969. Castro intended the move as a gesture of goodwill in deference to Pope John Paul II's scheduled visit to the island in January. Castro said he wanted to do everything possible to ensure that the visit would be historic.

Cuba officially became an atheist country in 1962, but celebration of Christmas continued until Castro decided it was interfering with the sugar harvest. He dropped Christmas from the calendar of holidays in 1969, when the government pushed for a record sugar harvest. When he reinstated Christmas as a holiday in 1997, Castro explained that the previous decision "didn't have anything to do with our traditions, just our climate."

Outward celebration of Christmas can be suppressed, but nobody can stop Christmas, because it has already happened. The Messiah has already come and accomplished his purpose, in spite of Satan's efforts to thwart God's plan. King Herod ordered all the boys two years old or younger near or in Bethlehem to be killed, but God had already warned Joseph to escape to Egypt. Later, in the wilderness, Satan tried to sidetrack Jesus from his mission, but Jesus resisted him with Scripture. And again, Satan prompted Judas to betray Jesus to death, but his crucifixion was already a part of God's plan.

Each year the climate in our nation grows more hostile toward any expression of the true meaning of Christmas. Many places allow symbols of other religious or secular holidays but not Christmas. Governments may forbid outward expression of Christmas, but they can't remove the most important event in history. Even when Christmas isn't on the calendar, it's in each believer's heart.

December 17

* * *

When Jesus woke up, he rebuked the wind and the raging waves.
The storm stopped and all was calm!
Luke 8:24

H alcyon days are the seven days before and the seven days after the shortest day of the year, which falls around December 21. In sea tradition, this is a time of calm and tranquility. The title comes from the ancient Greek word for the kingfisher. According to Greek folklore, the halcyon built its nest on the ocean's surface. The bird quieted the winds and waves during the time that its eggs were hatching.

When the disciples were crossing the Sea of Galilee by boat and a fierce storm struck suddenly, the terrified men woke Jesus from his nap. Jesus displayed his power over nature by commanding the wind and waves. Instead of dying down gradually, the storm immediately stopped. Then Jesus rebuked his amazed disciples, "Where is your faith?" (Luke 8:25). The men's fear seemed like a natural human response, but Jesus obviously expected something more from his followers.

Tranquility may seem impossible during times of trouble, but it is available for God's children. David experienced a lot of turbulence in his life, but he also displayed calmness and trust in God. He explains his attitude in the three verses of Psalm 131. Instead of being haughty and concerning himself with matters too great or awesome for him to grasp, he calmed and quieted himself like "a weaned child who no longer cries for its mother's milk" (131:2). David had anchored his hope in God and was content with whatever God brought into his life. When we accept that God is in control, then no matter what's going on around us, we can trust Jesus to either calm the situation or calm our soul—even if our nest is in the middle of a raging storm.

December 18

* * *

Coming to the borders of Mysia, they headed north for the province of Bithynia,
but again the Spirit of Jesus did not allow them to go there.

ACTS 16:7

A small group of French physicians established Médecins Sans Frontières (MSF), or Doctors Without Borders, in December 1971 to aid victims of armed conflict, epidemics, and natural and man-made disasters. MSF also helps those who lack health care due to geographic remoteness, politics, or ethnicity. MSF believes that the needs of these people supersede respect for national borders.

MSF was the first nongovernmental organization to provide emergency assistance and focus media attention on injustices within the populations they serve. Every year, more than twenty-five hundred volunteer doctors, nurses, medical professionals, logistics experts, water and sanitation engineers, and administrators serve alongside fifteen thousand locally hired staff to offer medical aid in more than eighty countries.

Paul traveled extensively to spread the gospel, but on his second missionary journey, he found that God had specific borders in mind. First, the Holy Spirit prevented Paul from going south to preach, and then the Spirit stopped him from going north. Paul went west to the coast, where he had a vision of a man in Macedonia pleading for him to come. So Paul sailed across the Aegean Sea and took the gospel to Europe. God later used others to preach the gospel in the other areas according to his timetable.

Sometimes God leads us by closing a door to make us go in another direction. He may do it through circumstances, advice from a friend, or an unmistakable nudging from his Spirit. When he seems to be shutting the door on a plan, a ministry, or a relationship, we'd better look for a new direction. It's always wise to respect our God-given borders.

December 19

* * *

Train up a child in the way he should go, and when he is old he will not depart from it.

PROVERBS 22:6, NKJV

O n this day in 2001, a botanist from Sydney, Australia, announced that he had rediscovered a shrub thought to be extinct for more than 160 years. *Asterolasia buxifolia* is so rare that it was never assigned a common name. It grows about six-and-a-half feet tall and bears golden, starlike flowers.

Botanists originally found the plant in the Blue Mountains west of Sydney in 1830. It disappeared soon afterward, so many scientists believed it to be extinct. In 2001, Bob Makinson made the announcement that he had found a cluster of around fifty shrubs in the Blue Mountains. DNA analysis confirmed the identity of the plants.

Many adults who were exposed to the gospel as children reject it, either claiming to not believe in God at all or looking around for some other version of the "truth." But often one day, something triggers a hunger for God and they "rediscover" the gospel. Seeds planted during their childhood grow and bear fruit, leading them to accept Christ. Other people come to Christ at an early age, but then wander away from their faith as they grow older. At some point, God awakens their spirit to help them find a faith they thought was extinct.

Sometimes God leads us to a place where we rediscover an old dream that we once cherished. Just because we didn't go into missionary work as we once planned doesn't mean that it isn't in our future. Maybe we've given up on being a Christian counselor, but God may plan to use us in that way at some point. If we're committed to doing God's will, we never know what seemingly extinct desire, goal, or dream is waiting to be rediscovered—in his timing.

December 20

*** * ***

All of us who have had that veil removed can see and
reflect the glory of the Lord.

2 Corinthians 3:18

I n December 1934, workers in Corning, New York, poured the molten glass for the first two-hundred-inch-diameter telescope mirror. The Pyrex glass at 2,700 degrees Fahrenheit filled a ceramic mold that had taken several months to build. Over the next eleven months, workers lowered the temperature of the glass a degree or two per day. The manufacturers shipped the twenty-ton disk by train to the California Institute of Technology, where it underwent an eleven-year process of grinding and polishing to make it ready for use.

The giant mirror became a part of one of the world's largest and most powerful reflecting telescopes at Mount Palomar, in California. The namesake of the Hale telescope is American astronomer George Ellery Hale, who conceived and designed the project but died ten years before the dedication of the telescope in 1948.

God designed believers to be mirrors. In 2 Corinthians 3, Paul explained that when people heard the old covenant read, a veil covered their minds and kept them from understanding the truth. Only belief in Christ can remove this veil. Once we have the Spirit living in us, we can see the glory of God. We then reflect his glory as he "makes us more and more like him as we are changed into his glorious image" (v. 18).

Many people are hostile toward Christianity. They don't want to read the Bible or hear about our conversion. It's our job to reflect an image of Christ to them—a testimony they can't deny. God is continually polishing us so that we can reflect him better. People should be seeing less of us and more of God's image. Our goal is to be a mirror that reflects "the fairest of them all."

December 21

* * *

Thank God! The answer is in Jesus Christ our Lord.
ROMANS 7:25

The first known published crossword puzzle appeared in the *New York World* on this day in 1913. A journalist named Arthur Wynne, who had immigrated to America from England, created the word puzzle, called a "word-cross" at the time. His puzzle was diamond shaped and contained no internal black squares.

By the early 1920s, newspapers across the country picked up on the new pastime, and within ten years, almost all American newspapers featured crossword puzzles. During this time, crosswords began to develop into the familiar form known today as the most popular and widespread word game in the world.

Many people think of the Bible as a puzzle that can't be solved. Some verses and passages seem to contradict each other when they're isolated. Some passages seem to have no apparent reason to be included in Scripture. Others seem impossible to interpret. But when we dedicate ourselves to prayerfully study the Word and open up to the Holy Spirit's teaching, we can usually fill in the answers to what puzzled us before. We see that the whole Bible fits together perfectly. Passages that we thought contradicted each other actually complement each other. We see applications for our life from Scriptures that seemed irrelevant before.

The key that unlocks the Bible is Jesus Christ. He is Eve's promised off-spring who would crush the serpent's head. He's pictured in the scarlet thread Rahab tied in her window so her life would be spared (Joshua 2). He's represented in every object in the Temple. He became the perfect Passover lamb sacrificed for sin. Jesus is the fulfillment of three hundred prophecies about the promised Messiah. Seeing how the Old and New Testaments fit together is more exciting than solving a crossword puzzle because we come to see that there's a cross all through the Word.

December 22

* * *

The Temple of the LORD was restored to service.
2 CHRONICLES 29:35

Hanukkah, or Chanukah, is the Jewish Feast of Lights, or Feast of Dedication. The eight-day celebration starts on the eve of the twenty-fifth day of the Hebrew month of Kislev, usually falling in December. Hanukkah commemorates the Jews' victory after a three-year struggle against Antiochus IV Epiphanes, a Syrian king who had invaded Judea and desecrated the Temple. Under Judas Maccabeus's orders, the Temple was cleansed and rededicated on Kislev 25.

Hanukkah also celebrates a miracle described in the Talmud. After cleansing the Temple of Syrian idols, the Jews found only one small jar of oil that had not been defiled. The jar contained enough oil to burn for only one day, but it miraculously lasted eight days until new consecrated oil could be found.

When Hezekiah became king of Judah, he told the people that their ancestors had been unfaithful and had abandoned the Lord. He reopened the doors of the Temple and ordered them to be repaired. He instructed the Levites to first purify themselves and then to purify the Temple. They spent sixteen days cleansing and removing defiled things. When they were finished, the people held a rededication ceremony with praise, worship, and offerings. The people rejoiced because the Temple was restored to service.

Sometimes Christians need to do some rededicating. As time passes, our devotion to the cause of Christ can cool, our priorities can shift, or we can get involved in things that are against God's will. It might be time for an internal cleansing through extended prayer, self-examination, and repentance. We may even have to get rid of some defiled things in our life. Then we can again wholeheartedly enjoy praise and worship, dedicated anew to serving our Lord and rejoicing that, like the Temple, we are restored for service.

What areas of your life need a cleansing and rededication to God?

December 23

* * *

Deal well with me, O Sovereign LORD, for the sake of your own reputation!
PSALM 109:21

One of the most popular television game shows premiered in December 1963. Monty Hall hosted *Let's Make a Deal*, where contestants wearing outlandish costumes brought unusual odds and ends from home to trade. Each show, Hall picked about eight people to participate in three or four deals. Near the end of the show, Hall offered contestants the chance to keep what they had or trade it for a chance at the Big Deal hidden behind one of three doors. Prizes could be valuable or worthless ("zonks").

Many cable channels show reruns of the original episodes. Fans can see live productions of the show at locations throughout the country. Germany, Mexico, India, France, Poland, Spain, and Portugal have all recently produced their own versions of *Let's Make a Deal*.

Many people try to make a deal with God. When we are in serious trouble, it's tempting to promise God that we will change our ways or give up some bad habit if he will help us out. If someone we love is seriously ill, we may vow to serve him the rest of our life if he will heal our loved one. But God doesn't work that way. We can pray and make requests, but there is nothing we can trade in to gain his favor or get him to do what we want.

God doesn't make deals, but he does make us an offer. We can receive forgiveness and eternal life by becoming his children through faith in Jesus Christ. Or we can live our life without him and receive condemnation and eternal punishment after we die. Our choice is clear and straightforward. There are only two doors, and we already know what's behind both of them.

December 24

* * *

My soul, wait in silence for God only, for my hope is from Him.
Psalm 62:5, NASB

The familiar carol "Silent Night" was performed for the first time on this night in 1818. Joseph Mohr, a young priest in Austria, wrote the original six stanzas for the song in German. On Christmas Eve, he took the words to his friend, musician and schoolteacher Franz Gruber, and asked him to write a melody and guitar accompaniment.

That night at Midnight Mass at St. Nicholas Church in Oberndorf, the two men sang "Stille Nacht! Heilige Nacht!" backed by the small choir repeating the last two lines in harmony. Later, an organ repairman took a copy of the composition home with him, and the carol began to circulate around the world. "Silent Night" has now been translated into hundreds of languages and is sung by millions every Christmas season.

We forget that God sometimes moves powerfully in quiet, humble settings. A Christmas carol that has touched the hearts of people around the world arose from a modest curate and a musician known only within their village. God stepped into our world through a baby born in a stable in an obscure village. This event, which would change the world forever, occurred in quietness and humility except for the host of angels praising God in the sky before the shepherds.

When Elijah needed a touch from God, God sent a mighty windstorm, an earthquake, and a fire. But the Lord was not in any of these. God's presence came in a gentle whisper (1 Kings 19:11-12). Our modern Christmas celebrations are often like a powerful windstorm or earthquake, and God is often lacking in them. What many of us need for Christmas is a silent night so we won't miss God's gentle whisper.

December 25

Jesus replied, "If you only knew the gift God has for you."
JOHN 4:10

Most countries around the world have Christmas customs involving gifts. This seems appropriate, since the Scriptures show that God loves to give gifts. The Bible begins with a description of God giving the gift of life to Adam and Eve and then presenting them with a perfect garden to live in—the ultimate handmade gift. The Bible ends with promises of gifts that God has in store for our future.

Unlike Santa Claus, God doesn't operate on a wish list, although we may try to give him one. Since he created us, he knows what will truly bring us joy. More importantly, he knows exactly what we need. Even spiritual gifts are chosen specifically for us by the Holy Spirit (1 Corinthians 12:11). When we receive a gift from God, we can be sure that it is just the right size and color for us.

God's greatest gift, which transcends all others, is the gift of salvation. Like Christmas presents, salvation is a free gift, not something we earn by being nice instead of naughty (Ephesians 2:8-9). However, this precious gift required that a holy God had to be born into a sinful world and die a horrible death on our behalf. We could never do anything to deserve such a gift, but we can accept it through faith in Jesus' sacrifice.

How can we respond to such a generous God? We would be hurt if a loved one put away our carefully chosen gift in a closet without opening or using it; God is also hurt when we don't respond appropriately to his lavish gifts. He wants us to use the gifts he gives. Paul wrote that God "richly gives us all we need for our enjoyment" (1 Timothy 6:17). God wants us to enjoy the blessings he bestows on us. Our spiritual gifts are to be used to help and build up the body of Christ. As for the gift of Jesus, that's one present God wants us to enthusiastically share with others.

December 26

* * *

"If only the LORD had killed us back in Egypt," they moaned. "There we sat around pots filled with meat and ate all the bread we wanted. But now you have brought us into this wilderness to starve us all to death."

EXODUS 16:3

The day after Christmas is National Whiner's Day. Rev. Kevin Zaborney founded the holiday on this day in 1986 to encourage people to be thankful for what they have rather than unhappy about what they don't have. Suggestions for celebrating National Whiner's Day include visiting a mall or store to watch people whine as they return or exchange unwanted gifts or inviting friends over for a "Whine and Geeze" party. Each year, the most famous whiner(s) is announced, from nominations accepted through December 15.

God has been listening to a lot of complaining since he created humanity. After he miraculously delivered the Israelites from slavery and led them through the Red Sea, they whined that he was trying to starve them. When God gave them manna, they whined for meat. He sent them quail, but also a severe plague. The Israelites' attitude revealed rebelliousness and a lack of trust in the God who had promised to take care of them and bring them safely into the Promised Land.

God is the One who decides the details of our life. He chooses what abilities, personality type, and spiritual gifts we possess. He assigns our ministry and places us in the environment where he wants to use us. When we express discontent with who we are or whine about our circumstances, we are complaining about his provision. God wants us to demonstrate trust that he knows what is best for us and will work things out for good. We are better off using our mouth for prayer and praise instead of whining.

What situations tempt you to whine and complain?

December 27

* * *

The waves of death overwhelmed me; floods of destruction swept over me.
2 SAMUEL 22:5

I n late December 2004, the most powerful earthquake in over forty years struck deep under the Indian Ocean off the northwestern coast of the island of Sumatra. The magnitude 9.0 earthquake triggered massive tsunamis that hit the coasts of fourteen countries from Southeast Asia to northeastern Africa.

The disaster obliterated cities, villages, and holiday resorts. As of February 16, 2005, the death toll from the catastrophe totaled close to 288,000. Nearly two-thirds of the deaths occurred in Indonesia, with high death tolls also reported in India, Sri Lanka, and Thailand.

Our life can change in an instant. Catastrophe can suddenly strike and take away everything we have. God called Job "blameless" and "a man of complete integrity" (Job 1:8), yet through a series of disasters, Job lost his children, his wealth, and his health overnight. Even in his grief, Job did not blame God, although he questioned why these things happened. When his questioning turned into complaining, God revealed his power and majesty to Job in a new way. Job acknowledged God's sovereignty, and God restored him to greater things than before.

When we're reeling from sudden disaster, it's hard to think about anything except to wonder why. It seems impossible to focus on God's goodness at times like that, but that's what he wants us to do. It helps to remember that our life can also change for the good in an instant. He is working in all things and will bring healing and restoration in his timing. As believers, we can recall that time when his forgiveness and grace swept over us and brought redemption and eternal life. Even if we lose everything, including our life, we will still have the most important thing.

December 28

* * *

[Elijah said,] "I am the only one left, and now they are trying to kill me, too."
1 KINGS 19:14

P resident Richard Nixon signed the Endangered Species Act into law on this day in 1973. Legislators designed the act to ensure the preservation of plant and animal life within the United States. Before a species qualifies for protection under the ESA, it must be placed on the Federal List of Endangered and Threatened Wildlife and Plants. An "endangered" species is defined as one in danger of extinction throughout all or a major portion of its range.

Any individual or organization can petition to have a species considered for the list. If the petition is accepted, officials conduct a status review of the species, including a public solicitation of relevant information. Once a species makes the list, officials develop a recovery plan that identifies conservation measures to help the species recover.

When Jezebel threatened Elijah's life, he felt like an endangered species. He told God that Israel had broken its covenant and killed all of God's prophets. Elijah felt as though he was the only person left alive who was faithful to God. But God assured Elijah that he had preserved seven thousand others who had never bowed to Baal, and he instructed Elijah to get back to carrying out his work (1 Kings 19:15-18).

Sometimes we may feel as though we're the only ones left who are faithful to God. This sense will only increase as the end times approach and many who seemed to be believers turn away from God. We can be assured that God will always preserve a remnant of true believers for himself. There are others all around us quietly serving him, even if Christians seem to be in danger of extinction.

December 29

* * *

*Christ has been raised from the dead, the first fruits
of those who are asleep.*

1 CORINTHIANS 15:20, NASB

K wanzaa, or Kwanza, is an adaptation of a traditional African festival of the harvest of the first crops and is celebrated from December 26 to January 1. Maulana Karenga, a professor at California State University in Long Beach, created the holiday in 1966. *Kwanzaa* is part of a phrase that means "firstfruits" in Swahili.

Each day of the celebration focuses on one of the seven principles of black culture developed by Karenga: unity, self-determination, collective responsibility, cooperative economics, purpose, creativity, and faith. In the evenings, the family gathers to light a candle and discuss the principle for that day. Near the end of the holiday, families join in a community feast called the "karamu."

The Jewish people celebrated a festival of firstfruits. God instructed them to bring the first bundle of grain from their harvest as an offering to him. They were not allowed to sell or eat their grain until after they had made their offering of firstfruits. The firstfruits offering represented the promise of a harvest to come.

The Jewish festival pictured the resurrection of Jesus Christ, who later became the firstfruits of believers who had died. Although Jesus had raised Lazarus and others from the dead, he was the first to be raised with a permanent body, never to die again. Jesus is the promise of a harvest to come—a resurrection of all those who have believed in him. Because of his resurrection, we will gain an immortal body someday too. Our assurance of this is what Paul referred to as the "first fruits of the Spirit" within believers (Romans 8:23, NASB). The Spirit is a foretaste of the blessings and glory we will enjoy someday—a promise of the harvest to come.

December 30

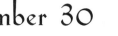

* * *

Don't be drunk with wine, because that will ruin your life.
Instead, be filled with the Holy Spirit.
EPHESIANS 5:18

n late December 1938, the first successful machine for testing blood alcohol content by breath analysis was officially introduced in Indianapolis. Dr. Rolla N. Harger of Indiana University invented the "Drunkometer." A person blew into a balloon, the air was released into a chemical solution, and the solution changed color according to the level of alcohol.

In 1948, IU faculty began offering one-week courses on breath alcohol testing. Robert Borkenstein, one of the instructors, later developed the Breathalyzer, a more practical and portable instrument. Although the use of breath analyzers remains controversial, since individuals react differently to alcohol, many versions are used around the world.

The Bible gives many warnings about the dangers of excessive consumption of alcohol. In Ephesians 5:18, Paul gives two instructions: Don't get drunk on wine and "instead, be filled with the Holy Spirit." God does not want us to be controlled by alcohol but by his Spirit. The Holy Spirit indwells us, seals us, and baptizes us at the moment of our conversion. But we need to be filled regularly for renewed strength and power. We get this filling by asking God for it while living an obedient life.

Ephesians 5:19-21 describes how people controlled by the Holy Spirit act. They sing psalms, hymns, and spiritual songs among themselves. They communicate with God by making music to him in their hearts. They are thankful to God for everything and they submit to one another, out of reverence for Christ. Being drunk offers only a temporary high; being filled with the Spirit gives lasting joy. Alcohol clouds our judgment, but the Spirit bestows wisdom and discernment. God wants us to be intoxicated only with him.

December 31

* * *

If anyone is in Christ, he is a new creation; old things have passed away;
behold, all things have become new.

2 CORINTHIANS 5:17, NKJV

The midnight Ball Drop at Times Square in New York City, one of the world's most famous New Year's Eve traditions, dates back to 1906. The ball is a six-foot-thick geodesic sphere covered with 504 Waterford crystal triangles bolted to 168 translucent Lexan panels. The ball is illuminated by 168 exterior crystal bulbs, 432 interior colored bulbs, 96 high-intensity strobe lights, and 90 rotating pyramid mirrors—all computer-controlled. The Ball Drop is a worldwide symbol of the turning of the year. In addition to the many people who fill Times Square each New Year's Eve, more than a billion people watch it by satellite.

Paul serves as a good example of how old things pass away when we become a new creation. In his old life as Saul the Pharisee, Paul persecuted Christians and had them stoned or sent to jail. He was proud of his heritage, education, and status. When he met Christ, he left his old life behind, including his old name. Like Paul, we become re-created when we accept Christ. We leave our old ways of thinking behind, along with our old sinful nature.

Some of us try to live our new life while hanging on to old sins, old wounds, or old failures accompanied by a load of regret and guilt. God doesn't want us dragging around baggage from our past that weighs us down and stifles the joy he longs to give us. Jesus' death on the cross was enough to save us from sin, and it's fully adequate to free us from things from our past that haunt us. Each year that passes away brings us closer to the time when "this world as we know it will soon pass away" (1 Corinthians 7:31). Time is too precious to waste it dragging around old things that we need to "drop."

What "old thing" in your life does God want you to release?

INDEX

377

Keep your
Devotional Time
fresh
with these
popular

devotionals.

For Youth

The One Year® Book of Devotions for Kids
ISBN 0-8423-5087-X

The One Year® Book of Devotions for Boys
ISBN 0-8423-3620-6

The One Year® Book of Devotions for Girls
ISBN 0-8423-3619-2

The One Year® Devos for Teens, by Susie Shellenberger
ISBN 0-8423-6202-9

For Family

For Couples

The One Year® Book of Family Devotions
ISBN 0-8423-2541-7

The One Year® Book of Josh McDowell's Family Devotions
ISBN 0-8423-4302-4

The One Year® Book of Devotions for Couples, by David and Teresa Ferguson
ISBN 1-4143-0170-7

General

The One Year® Great Songs of Faith
ISBN 1-4143-0699-7

One Year® through the Bible
ISBN 0-8423-3553-6

The One Year® Book of Praying through the Bible, by Cheri Fuller
ISBN 0-8423-6178-2

If You Need a
Quick Moment of
refreshment
during Your Big Day,
Try These

The ONE YEAR® MINI Gift Devotionals.

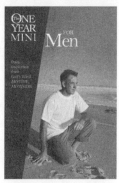

The One Year Mini for Women
helps women connect with God through
several Scripture verses and a devotional
thought. Perfect for use anytime and
anywhere between regular devotional
times. Hardcover

ISBN 1-4143-0617-2

The One Year Mini for Men
helps men connect with God anytime,
anywhere, between their regular
devotional times, through Scripture
quotations and a related devotional
thought. Hardcover

ISBN 1-4143-0618-0

Releasing April 2006

The One Year Mini for Students offers students from high school through
college a quick devotional connection with God anytime and anywhere. Stay
grounded through the ups and downs of a busy student lifestyle. Hardcover
ISBN 1-4143-0619-9

The One Year Mini for Moms provides moms with encouragement and
affirmation for those moments during a mom's busy day when she needs to be
reminded of the high value of her role. Hardcover
ISBN 1-4143-0884-1